REVA

REVA

A TALE OF LOVE, LITHIUM, AND LOSS

HOWARD PROSNITZ

Epigraph Books
Rhinebeck, New York

Reva: A Tale of Love, Lithium, and Loss © Copyright 2022 by Howard Prosnitz

All rights reserved. No part of this book may be used or reproduced in any manner without the consent of the author except in critical articles or reviews. Contact the publisher for information.

Hardcover ISBN 978-1-954744-87-5
Paperback ISBN 978-1-954744-88-2
eBook ISBN 978-1-954744-89-9

Library of Congress Control Number 2022913713

Book and cover design by Colin Rolfe

Epigraph Books
22 East Market Street, Suite 304
Rhinebeck, NY 12572
(845) 876-4861
epigraphps.com

MY HUSBAND, MY LOVE
by REVA E. PROSNITZ

Your hands are like a nest
Where I fit in comfortably.
Your arms are the shield
That protects me from the world.

Your smile is sweet and kind.
You mean so well for me.
I love you, you're mine.

WIFE
by HOWARD PROSNITZ

She was thirty-two, and I, forty-two, when we began dating. We married three years later. Her parents were refugees from Europe. My parents were born here. She is soft and I am strong. She is passive and I am aggressive. She has more love than anyone I have ever known, and she gave it all to me. I love and protect her. I am her crossing guard, her Columbia lion, her big lug. Nobody else has ever called me a big lug. We have developed each other and continue to develop each other. She asks for little. Her wages for living are kisses. Almost thirty years ago I went into her heart and her heart is deep. There is no way to extricate me. My heart is guarded by fortresses, but she got through them; moats, but she crossed them. "The soul selects her own society—then shuts the door."

CONTENTS

Preface   xi

1. Paterson   1
2. Fair Lawn   7
3. Spiritual Autobiography   16
4. Last Journal   19
5. From Concentration Camp to Christmas Tree   26
6. Beginnings   31
7. Summer   35
8. Insomnia   39
9. Wedding   43
10. Passaic   47
11. Elmwood Park   51
12. Jewish Wedding   56
13. Mania   59
14. Turquoise   62
15. Route 280   66
16. Rutherford   70
17. Up the Mountain   74
18. Graduation   78
19. Fordham Essay   82
20. NYU   86
21. Bone of my Bones   89
22. World Trade Center   92
23. Prospects   95
24. Dialysis   99
25. Intermezzo   102
26. Warning Rattle   106

27.	Bite	109
28.	Venom	112
29.	Rehab	115
30.	Warning the Public	118
31.	Steps and Stairs	122
32.	Aftermath	125
33.	Saved from the Slaughterhouse	128
34.	Teaneck	139
35.	Return to Work	142
36.	Good Friday	147
37.	Return to Philadelphia	151
38.	Plaza	154
39.	Hackensack Meridian Hackensack University Medical Center	159
40.	Art School	163
41.	Health Concerns	168
42.	The Lurking Presence	172
43.	S	175
44.	Into the Dark	178
45.	Sunday Morning	181
46.	Inferno	185
47.	Last Spring	189
48.	Mixed News	192
49.	Darkening Clouds	196
50.	Holy Name	201
51.	Lightning Bolt	204
52.	ICU	207
53.	Amputation	210
54.	Waking	214
55.	Intermediate Floor	218
56.	Planche Urea	221
57.	First Do No Harm	223
58.	LTACH	227
59.	God Save Me for I am Only a Woman	230
60.	Limbo	233
61.	Return and Return	239
62.	Dr. Death	244

63.	Transfer	248
64.	SELECT	252
65.	St. Joseph's	255
66.	Last Days	260
67.	Death	266
68.	. . .	271
69.	Work	276
70.	Cardinals	281

PREFACE

This is a book I wish I never had to write, but Reva would have wanted her story told, and parts of the book are in her own words. As a compassionate person and a social worker, she wanted to warn others of the dangers of psychiatry and psychiatric drugs.

I have no formal medical education. The opinions about medicine and psychiatry and my understanding of medical conditions and treatments expressed in this book are my own and are opinions. They are based on personal experience, observation, discussions with medical practitioners, and research.

Some names of persons and institutions have been changed. The names of the hospitals in which Reva was a patient have not been changed.

Most of this book was written during the long Covid-19 summer of 2021, and writing it was largely a solitary experience. I do, however, want to thank readers of the manuscript who provided prepublication comments: My former writing workshop teacher, Charles Salzberg, who promptly read each chapter as I sent it to him and replied with useful suggestions; Deacon Peter Emr of Our Lady of the Visitation Church; and Linda Poskanzer, LCSW. There are others who have helped me and continue to help me through their emotional support. The death of a beloved spouse is a crisis like no other.

I want to thank the University of California Press for permission to quote from *Psychiatry and Its Discontents* by Andrew Scull, (University of California Press, 2019).

CHAPTER ONE

PATERSON

Reva was born in Paterson, New Jersey, the same city in which she died sixty-six years later. She was born Reva Evelyn Brzezinski on November 2, 1952, to Isaac and Bronca Brzezinski in Barnert Hospital, which closed in 2008. She died on September 10, 2019, in the intensive care unit of St. Joseph's Hospital.

Her parents were refugees from Europe, Holocaust survivors who had lost their first spouses in concentration camps. Many members of Reva's family were killed by the Nazis. After the war, Bronca joined a group of Jewish female survivors who visited survivors recovering in hospitals. There, she met Isaac. They married, and Reva's brother Joseph was born in Fürth, Germany in 1947. In 1949, all three immigrated to Paterson, where Isaac had American relatives, Sid and Sylvia Zlotnick, who sponsored them for immigration. They settled in a Jewish immigrant section of Paterson. The Zlotnicks lived nearby. Reva used to call the neighborhood, "the ghetto." Isaac found work as a weaver in one of Paterson's silk mills, and Bronca worked as a seamstress and joined the International Ladies Garment Workers Union (ILGWU).

Paterson, once known as the Silk City, was the first planned industrial city in the United States. Its Great Falls, the largest waterfalls on the East Coast after Niagara, provided manufacturing power. In the 1950s, Paterson had a large Jewish population, and the silk mills along the Passaic River were still active. Isaac worked in the mills until he retired.

In 1954, when Reva was two, Bronca, Isaac, and Joseph became naturalized American citizens. In the process, they changed their name from Brzezinski to Brezin. For whatever reason, Isaac and Bronca did not include Reva in the name change. Reva was a US citizen from birth, and, perhaps, they reasoned they would save money by not doing a separate name change for Reva. Isaac had been informed by an acquaintance that Reva could use Brezin as the family name without legally changing it. So Isaac saved a few dollars, and Reva remained legally Reva Brzezinski.

From early childhood, however, she used the name Brezin. Her elementary school, high school, social security and tax records, and her driver's licenses all record her name as Brezin. Our marriage certificate shows that on January 29, 1988, I married Reva Brezin. But Reva Brezin never existed as a legal entity. Her name had never been legally changed. Her birth certificate from Barnert Hospital, which is in my possession, having been given to Reva and me by Joseph after the death of Isaac and Bronca, gives her name as Reva Evelyn Brzezinski, and until she married me that was the only legal name she had.

The name issue must have come up, since Reva told me the story on several occasions, both before and after our marriage. Perhaps school registration in Paterson and later in Fair Lawn, New Jersey, required her birth certificate. There were four in the family, three with the name Brezin and Reva with the name Brzezinski, although Reva used the name Brezin from an early age, as she was instructed to by her parents. One legal document builds on another, but she was never Reva Brezin. This casual separation from her family imposed by her parents, her namelessness, had an incalculable impact on her mental health. Next to our breath, our names are the most important part of us. She was isolated, made different by her parents. She had a first name, like a dog or a cat, "Fido" or "Minerva," but no surname.

One might attempt to excuse Isaac and Bronca as having lived in this country for a short time and being ignorant of its laws. But they knew enough of the law to seek naturalization for themselves and Joseph and to change their name. Furthermore, from what Reva told me, they made no effort to legally change her name to Brezin, which they could have done at any time years later, when Reva was a young child or teenager. One must conclude that Isaac did not want to spend the money. After all, what value is a girl? When she marries, she will take her husband's name, he may have reasoned. Why waste money? In the meantime, she can pretend she has a name. This sense of devaluation and separation undoubtedly affected Reva's mental health from an early age.

When Reva was in her twenties, she went to the Bergen County Courthouse, I believe with Isaac, and paid twenty-five dollars to fill out an application to change her name to Brezin. She believed she had changed her name, but she had only filed an application. She and Isaac received no documentation of a name change. Decades later, after 9/11, the US government required birth certificates or green cards for renewal of drivers' licenses. We needed the intervention of our state senator for Reva to renew her license. A notarized letter from Joseph, now a medical doctor, explaining what had happened fifty years earlier, was worthless. There was no legal connection showing that Reva Prosnitz, née Brzezinski, had ever been Reva Brezin. Isaac and Bronca had made her birth certificate invalid. Reva is dead now, but when Donald Trump was elected President, I became fearful that Reva could be swept up and deported. Where? She was born in the United States but was not able to prove it.

Bronca and Isaac were not well-educated and were new to this country, but their experience as Jews in Nazi-occupied Poland should have made them aware of the importance of having legal papers.

Reva told me that in her early twenties she saw a lawyer about changing her name, but he was unpleasant and did not help. I was never clear about what happened, but nothing was done.

Her parents were middle-class to lower middle-class. They both worked, and each received a monthly reparation check from Germany. Isaac invested in real estate in Paterson, which he did not sell until after Reva and I were married.

Isaac worked in the silk mill by day, and Bronca worked as a seamstress in the evenings—or it may have been the reverse. When Reva was a small child in Paterson and her brother was in school, there was about an hour every weekday when she was alone in the apartment. She was about four. She hid, as instructed by her parents, behind the couch until the parent who was home in the evening arrived. The family lived in a house that Isaac owned. He rented rooms to roomers. The property was one of his investments.

Reva was the only white child in her kindergarten class, but there was no racial animosity.

She recalled how she and other children were given mild corporal punishment by some of the teachers: rapped on the knuckles or hit on a shoulder with a ruler if they wrote the wrong answer on the blackboard. She remembered two teachers in particular who taught different grades in the elementary school.

I was surprised to learn that as late as the 1950s and early 1960s teachers in Paterson were allowed to hit children. In Longfellow School in Teaneck, which I attended from kindergarten through the sixth grade, and I presume in other Teaneck schools, no teacher ever hit a child, at least I never observed it, and had it occurred, it would have been a scandal. Corporal punishment in schools was and is illegal in New Jersey. A typical Longfellow School punishment was exile from the classroom: standing in the cloakroom or the disgrace of standing on one of the traffic circles in the hallway.

Although her classmates were mostly Black, her friends were children of the Jewish immigrant population of Paterson, second-generation survivors of the Holocaust. There was Marilyn, who later went to a yeshiva. Reva did not see her for many years after childhood until she and her husband Jerrold became acquainted with us after we married. Marilyn and Jerrold have since moved to Israel. They called often, and in September 2019, when Jerrold called, I informed him that Reva had died in St. Joseph's Hospital. I remember Jerrold's long, disappointed groan and a woman shrieking in the background. The phone in Israel may have been on speaker, and I presume the woman was Marilyn. They have never called since when I have been able to answer the phone. Their caller ID always said "restricted."

As a child, on the Jewish High Holidays in the fall, Reva would go *shteple* hopping, a Yiddish word that she told me means synagogue or shul. There were a lot of them in Paterson in the 1950s and early 1960s. She would go to various synagogues with friends. One of these friends was Allen G., like Reva, a child of Holocaust survivors.

Reva may have been seven or eight years old when on one Yom Kippur, playing with Allen, she jumped into a pile of leaves. Unknown to her, mud wasps had built their nest inside, and she was stung all over her body. She ran home. Her mother tried to whisk the wasps off her, but her brother, who may have been twelve or thirteen, convinced her parents to take her to the emergency room. Her body was swelling, and she was in the beginning of an allergic reaction which, had it continued, could have been fatal. At the ER, she was given shots. The experience of the wasp attack was traumatic. Later in life, when she underwent something very painful, she described it "like bring stung by dozens of wasps." Even at that young age, she was brave and, alas, sometimes reckless.

She recalled that as a child she inadvertently rented a room in her parents' house to an ex-con. She also remembered that the tenant in one room decorated it with replicas of Greek sculptures. She did not, at the time, recognize the association of Greek sculpture collected by adult men with homosexuality. But she told me of only two episodes of physical abuse (except for the Paterson school teachers) when she lived in Paterson. Once, her father slapped her, but I do not know the details, and this may have happened later, after the family moved to Fair Lawn. But it was in Paterson that her parents locked her in a closet on her birthday. This abuse appears to have been an attempt to control her excitement. She said she had broken a phonograph record, probably a 78 rpm. I don't know how long they kept her in the closet, but it was her birthday. Children never forget parental abuse.

In all, however, she seemed to have been happy in Paterson, surrounded by a close community of Jewish refugees, survivors of the Holocaust.

She was much loved. She recalled that adults would pinch her cheek.

Her father once came home from work with a naked doll for her. This may not have been her only childhood doll, but she didn't have many.

Her father taught her to ride a bicycle. I don't know what age Reva was then, but this is the story she told me.

They were on top of a long hill near Eastside Park in Paterson. It is a steep hill and runs for several blocks in traffic. Her father held the back of the seat. My father taught me to ride a two-wheeler the same way, but my father taught me on the level block where we lived.

I remember my father telling me the first time that I rode without him holding. As difficult as my father was, at that time, at the age of about seven, I could feel secure that he was behind me, holding the seat or ready to grab it if I began to lose my balance.

Isaac did the same, that is, he held the back of the seat while Reva was learning to ride a two-wheeler. But when she rode down that long hill, Isaac let go of the seat while she accelerated into city traffic. Was he trying to kill her? Or perhaps Isaac lost control of the seat because of the steepness of the hill, but if that were the case, he never explained or apologized to Reva. Somehow, she wasn't hit or killed. It was a stupid idea to hold the seat while going downhill, unless Isaac planned it that way. Reva believed, because Isaac never told her otherwise, that he deliberately let go, as if he wanted to kill her. After all, what use is a girl? First her parents left her nameless. Then why not do away with her? It would save a lot of money and future trouble.

CHAPTER TWO

FAIR LAWN

When Reva was eleven and Joe sixteen, the family moved to Fair Lawn, a leafy, middle-class, almost exclusively white town (then and now) just north of Paterson. Many Jews, escaping the growing crime rate and the increasing Black and Hispanic population of Paterson, moved to Fair Lawn, and Fair Lawn developed a thriving Jewish community.

The house they moved to, 13-01 Alexander Avenue, was a block from Fair Lawn High School and three blocks from the Fair Lawn Jewish Center, where Rabbi Simon Glustrom served as rabbi. Rabbi Glustrom, who presided at Reva's funeral, is in his nineties at this writing, retired but still active and a neighbor in the building where Reva and I lived together and where I now live alone.

The house was small but attractive, and I got to know it well after I met Reva. Joe had lived upstairs in a converted attic but left to attend Rutgers at seventeen and never returned except for visits and some summers. Reva had her own first-floor bedroom. There was a master bedroom, living room, dining room, and an enclosed porch that her parents had added. But Reva was not happy in Fair Lawn.

She had skipped half grades in Paterson schools and was two years younger than her classmates. (My father was in a similar position and graduated from West Side High School in Newark in 1930, a month after his sixteenth birthday. He had to repeat a half year. Otherwise, he would have graduated at fifteen.)

Reva was bullied by her classmates. She told me that on her first day of class in a Fair Lawn elementary school, a boy chased her waving a chicken's head. In junior high school and high school, she was bullied and taunted by girls, most of whom were two years older. At the

Fair Lawn municipal swimming pool, a girl with a German surname cornered her in deep water away from the lifeguard and, for a while, would not let her escape. But the girl eventually swam away.

It wasn't only students. She told me that she was eating an orange with her hands in the high school cafeteria when a male teacher passed by and said, "Is that how Jews eat oranges?" But Reva had a hypersensitivity to anti-Semitism inculcated by her parents, especially her mother, and I know from our life together that she sometimes misheard innocuous remarks and believed that they were anti-Semitic. I urged her to do reality checks, to ask people to repeat what they said when she believed that she heard someone say something anti-Semitic or otherwise hostile. Of course, this would not matter for blatant anti-Semitism, but I know from my own experience that the human ear plays tricks.

In high school, she was enrolled in an academic program, but a French teacher gave her the "evil eye." After that, she transferred to a business program.

Her home life was difficult. Every advantage seemed to go to her brother. After Rutgers, Joe went to Georgetown University School of Medicine and earned an MD degree. He became a doctor, the joy of every Jewish parent's heart. Reva graduated from Fair Lawn High School and, after a two-week tour of Europe with her mother, perhaps intended to compensate for not sending her to college, went to work as a clerk-typist, a job that she held at various Bergen County companies for the next fifteen years.

Reva longed for the normal freedom of a teenager and, later, of an adult. She was earning her own living, but even when she was in her twenties her parents demanded control over her life. She had a parakeet. Once, when she was either visiting her parents or living with them temporarily, she let it out the window. It flew away and never returned. The act was symbolic of the freedom that her parents would not allow her, even as an adult. She wasn't imprisoned in an attic or a basement, but her parents had psychologically imprisoned her.

Reva told me that she didn't even know she was legally an adult when she turned eighteen and that her parents had no legal power over her. Nobody told her this, certainly no one in her family. Every move—taking a job or renting a furnished room—was scrutinized by her parents. She told me how embarrassed she was when her father came into her workplace, apparently to check up on her. She was in her twenties at the time.

Yet she loved her parents, and in her spiritual autobiography in Chapter 3 of this memoir, describes them as "wonderful people."

Of course, Reva knew them better than I did, and I almost hesitate to write about these episodes because of her love for her parents. She had a loving nature, but her parents harmed her and, in subjecting her when she was a teenager to experimental psychiatric drugs, contributed to—indeed caused—her years of physical suffering and ultimately her premature death. I would be dishonest to myself if I did not write about her parents' abuse.

And Reva was and is my life. Her suffering and early death have affected me in ways for which there are no words. This account of Reva's life is self-prescribed therapy for my grief. A man and a woman are one flesh. When Reva died, part of me died. Therefore, her parents hurt me. I have become the victim of victims.

Her parents were difficult: "Difficult old people," as a psychologist who counseled Reva and me and who knew her parents, called them. I knew them in their old age. Her father appeared to have a limited emotional range. He seemed stolid and stoic, but the stiffness and rigidity of his personality may have been exacerbated by his Parkinson's disease, which worsened over the years.

Bronca was another story. A cousin of Reva's, who has studied psychology and who knew Bronca, has suggested that even without Hitler and the Holocaust, even in her native Poland, Bronca would have been considered mentally ill. In later years, after both her parents were dead and after Reva had earned her Master of Social Work degree from NYU, where she studied therapy and mental illness, she diagnosed her mother with Munchausen's syndrome by proxy (MSBP). Reva recalled that from her early childhood, Bronca took her to doctors, looking for something wrong with her, but Bronca never went to a doctor herself. When Reva was a young child in Paterson, one of those doctors subjected her to multiple full-body X-rays. Her mother was always taking her to doctors, even when she wasn't sick.

Bronca inculcated Reva with tales of the Holocaust and murdered Jews. Reva often told me that Bronca wanted her to replicate the suffering of Holocaust victims in her own life. I am sad to say that Bronca's wish came true: Bronca's work was effected.

I have found poems by Reva about Jewish children murdered, drained of their blood and their bodies thrown out of windows by Nazis. While other children, even those of Holocaust survivors, grew up with Goldilocks and Cinderella, the stories that Reva's mother told her were about blood, violence, and death. From an early age, Reva became terrified of anti-Semitism. She would sometimes hallucinate swastikas. Born in the United States, my American beauty with a huge smile, surrounded by roses, became Bronca's Holocaust victim, and I, losing my beloved wife to the insanity of her parents, have become their victim also.

The stories Reva told me about her childhood are disconnected, and it is hard to tell sometimes when the incidents occurred and which followed which. But the move to Fair Lawn and the bullying she faced at Fair Lawn middle school and high school seem to be a dividing point.

Many other "greenies," as Reva called them, moved from Paterson to Fair Lawn. She seemed to have spent her childhood in a close-knit community of Holocaust survivors in Paterson. Fair Lawn was a change.

She was also a teenager, and her parents would not allow her to grow. Her relationship with her mother, to this day, seems inscrutable. Yet when we were dating and I criticized something about her parents and asked how she could stand it, she replied simply, "They're my folks." Reva was habitually good-natured and compliant. The dark side of her personality she repressed, except when it came out in furious manic episodes, which were the door to her destruction. They limited her life and led to her early death. Bronca had taught her, coerced her, choked her into not expressing anger.

Blocked from normal expressions of anger, blocked from channeling her normal aggression constructively and creatively, blocked from becoming the American girl that she was born, the emotions in her early teens began to come out in dark and destructive forms. I often told Reva that I wish I had come into her life ten years earlier. But she was thirty-two when we met, and the damage had been done, the seeds of her destruction planted. She was put on lithium for what is termed "bipolar disorder" when she was fourteen and remained on it for the next eighteen years.

Long-term use of lithium can cause irreversible kidney damage. Surveillance of Reva's kidney functions was lax. Blood tests were infrequent. Psychiatrists, especially at public clinics where Reva was a patient in the 1970s and 1980s, were, and still are, loath to remove patients from psychiatric drugs. By the time she was taken off lithium, after swallowing the poison for eighteen years, her kidneys were permanently impaired: her creatinine was abnormally high and would not go down. She told me that the psychiatrist at the public clinic where her parents sent her—Isaac wasn't one to spend money on a private doctor for Reva. Even her nephrologist when we began dating worked out of a public clinic. I encouraged her to find a nephrologist in private practice, and she did-- told her that they had just caught the kidney damage in time, and Reva was switched from lithium to tegretol. But the damage had been done. It was not caught in time. She was taking tegretol, which can cause life-threatening anemia, when we started dating. She eventually showed signs of anemia and was switched to depekote, which causes liver damage. However, during the years that she took depekote, which was for most of our marriage, her nephrologist and primary care physician monitored her liver functions. Had Bronca allowed her to express her emotions in a normal way, had her parents allowed her to grow up as a normal teenager and young woman, she would not have had to take any medication/poison. But she was taught to repress her normal emotions. I have no idea what guidance Bronca gave her about her sexual development. Reva never discussed this with me.

It is noteworthy that Joseph, by this time a physician and nephrologist, seemed, from what Reva told me, passive and uninvolved throughout Reva's teenage and young adult years.

When I met her, she was already doomed: doomed by medicine, doomed by doctors and those demonic doctors called psychiatrists, and most of all, doomed by her parents.

Reva never hid her health problems from me. On our second date she told me about her kidney disease, which at that time had been diagnosed as nephrogenic diabetes insipidus. But Reva did not have diabetes and never used an antidiabetic drug. I was then working as a professional reference librarian at the Passaic Public Library, and she asked me if there was anything in the library about her kidney disease.

The next day (I remember this second date was on a Sunday, and we went to Manhattan to the Jewish Museum and the Museum of the City of New York), I found a few articles about this specific diagnosis, photocopied them, and gave them to her the next time I saw her.

Her only symptoms in those days, as I recall, were thirst and mild urinary frequency. The only treatment prescribed at this time was to limit her protein intake, a standard precaution for anyone with signs of kidney disease. She adhered to this regimen, methodically weighing the meat that she cooked on a scale in the kitchen of the residence where she lived. But the disease was progressive.

Reva was hospitalized in psychiatric hospitals for short periods at least twice during her high school years. At one time, she was hospitalized in Gracie Square Hospital on the Upper East Side of Manhattan.

At some point, her parents took her into Manhattan to see Dr. Nathan S. Kline, a psychiatrist who was experimenting with lithium on patients in Rockland State Hospital, and Reva was prescribed this toxin which, over a course of many years, destroyed her kidneys, put her into dialysis for sixteen years, and killed her.

Lithium is an element and a heavy metal. It is best known as a component in batteries. Cell phones use lithium batteries. Reva was swallowing lithium pills prescribed by various psychiatrists for eighteen years, from the time she was fourteen until just before we began dating, when she was thirty-two.

While in high school, she was hospitalized in the psychiatric ward of Bergen Pines County Hospital. The hospital still exists but has changed its name, and the Bergen County Freeholders have long since leased it to private management.

It was in her senior year of high school, after returning from a stay in Bergen Pines, that she took to her bed for several weeks with a severe depression. Nevertheless, she managed to go back to high school in time to take exams and graduate.

Reva told me that the depression began after a visit with her father to Mrs. Katz, her Fair Lawn High School guidance counselor.

Oy, Mrs. Katz.

I didn't know her but have known similar Mrs. Katz-type Jewish women, as Reva described her: Nervy, full of chutzpah, dominating. In the Jewish ghetto ethos, a shy woman is defective (in contrast to Oriental culture where diffidence in a woman is a virtue). This is a cultural remnant from the European ghettos, where Jewish men spent their days in the shul studying Torah, and the women were responsible for managing the often-large families. Reva was shy. She also had begun accruing the onus of the mental illness label.

According to Reva, Mrs. Katz told her father that Reva could go to college "but would have to work twice as hard as other students." Mrs. Katz never explained why Reva would have to work twice as hard, but it was what her father wanted to hear. "Then she is not college material," her father said, and Isaac ushered Reva out of Mrs. Katz's office. It was Joe who would go to college and later to medical school; Joe, who, according to Reva, his parents would supply with money for expensive clothing. According to emails from Joe, his parents did not pay his college tuition, and he subsidized his medical school education through loans, which he later re-paid. But tuition is only part of college expenses. Joe did not live at home. Rutgers is too far for commuting from Fair Lawn. Did his parents provide any money for his education? How am I supposed to know? I do know that they provided no money for Reva's education and would not allow Reva to attend college, although in her twenties she took an occasional course at Bergen Community College. But she became confused and had no guidance. In at least one course, she became fearful and did not take the final exam and failed the course.

How could there be anything left for Reva? Reva's fate was to work as a clerk-typist. Yet when I was dating her, and she had been a clerk-typist for seventeen years, the chief psychologist at Mill Pond Mental Health Center, who knew Reva and her parents and had access to Reva's testing and reports, told me that she was extremely intelligent. Although the psychologist did not know Joe, he said that Reva had the intelligence for as intellectually challenging an endeavor as medical school. She was her brother's equal in intelligence but not in opportunity.

It was probably the same summer after high school, when Reva took the two-week grand tour with her mother, that she went with her mother to Israel. Bronca left Reva on a kibbutz with relatives where Reva lived for the duration of the summer. This was the first time Reva had been alone, away from her parents' clutches, and she was ecstatic. In addition, she was off the lithium and did not have a problem. For Reva, it was a summer of joy. The year would have been approximately 1969. Reva described herself as so happy that she would sing in her sleep, which disturbed some of the other girls in the bunkhouse, and she had to sleep separately.

One incident that she related to me stands out. She left the kibbutz for the day and hitchhiked to Mount Tabor, the mountain of the Transfiguration in the New Testament (so ascribed by a third century pope. The mountain is not named in the Gospels) where the disciples had a vision of Jesus with Moses and Elijah. She hiked to the top of the mountain, where there is a Roman Catholic church and a nearby cemetery. Reva rested on the cemetery wall and, as she described it, fell off the wall and into the cemetery. She then heard a voice. I am not sure if it was audible or inside her head, but it said, "The first half of your life will go slowly; the second half, fast." She regained her footing and climbed out of the cemetery. She rang the church chimes and the priest invited her in. There was an American couple inside and Reva and the American couple had tea with the priest. Afterwards, she hiked down the mountain and several miles to the kibbutz.

Reva told me this story many times over the years, both before and after our marriage, and it is astonishing how prophetic the voice was, almost with precision. She lived sixty-six years. From the time she graduated high school until she met me when she was thirty-two, she worked as a clerk-typist and lived in her parents' home, in residences for psychiatric patients, or in furnished rooms. Then in the second half of her life, she was a wife, attended college and graduate school, earned a BA and MSW, and worked as a professional social worker.

Her health declined because of the damage done to her as a teenager and young adult, and her life ended early. Whether fast or slow, dull or vigorous, her life divides into two almost equal segments of time and action.

I have never been to Mount Tabor, but pictures on the Internet show the Church of the Transfiguration and a low stone wall lining each side of the road leading to it.

She swam in the Dead Sea and fell in love with an Israeli soldier. (I don't know much about the relationship, but I think it was platonic.) At the end of the summer, her mother came for her and took her home to Fair Lawn where she returned to lithium and began her career for the next seventeen years as a clerk-typist.

She lived at home but eventually moved out and lived in furnished rooms in Elmwood Park and Hackensack. But every room had to be approved by her father, even though Reva was working full-time, paying her own way, and over eighteen. She told me that she had found a nice room in a good part of Paterson, but her father disapproved and would not allow her to rent it. She was over twenty-one.

Reva told me that when she was in her early twenties, she had lost a job and moved back to her parents' house. She was in the car one day with Bronca, who was driving. As they approached the house, Bronca made her hide on the floor of the car so the neighbors wouldn't see her in the daytime and know she wasn't working.

She saw psychiatrists at a public mental health center, who continued to prescribe lithium and occasionally checked her blood. She also lived, at times, in residences run by the center. One residence was in Montvale, another in Elmwood Park. When we began dating, she was living in a residence in Saddle Brook. Unlike the other residents, she always worked.

She saw a nephrologist once a month at the clinic at Bergen Pines Hospital, the Bergen County public hospital.

I began dating Reva in February 1985. At that time, she had already been diagnosed with a progressive kidney disease.

CHAPTER THREE

SPIRITUAL AUTOBIOGRAPHY

In 2012, after we had been married for almost twenty-five years and I had converted from Judaism to Christianity and joined the Episcopal Church, Reva and I took the first year of Education for Ministry (EFM), a four-year program of the Episcopal Church sponsored by the Episcopal Seminary of the University of the South in Sewanee, Tennessee. The first year focuses on reading the complete *Hebrew Scriptures* (that is, the *Old Testament*). Part of the first year required writing and delivering orally a spiritual autobiography. Reva remained a committed Jew to the end of her life. She attended the synagogue when she could and lit Sabbath candles. She was buried in a Jewish ceremony. But she was broad-minded and open to new experiences and knowledge, as her spiritual autobiography demonstrates.

SPIRITUAL AUTOBIOGRAPHY
By REVA E. PROSNITZ

I was born in Paterson, New Jersey. My parents were Polish Jews who survived the Holocaust. My brother was born in Germany after the war and came to America with my parents when he was two years old. I am the only member of my immediate family born in the US.

My father was interned in a few different concentration camps, one of which was Dachau. My mother was in a work camp in Bergen-Belsen. My parents were married after the war, their first spouses having been killed in concentration camps. All but one of my mother's six siblings were murdered, as was her mother. Her father had died before the Nazi regime. Her father's sister was killed.

I attended public schools in Paterson until I was eleven when we moved to Fair Lawn. I was the only white child in my kindergarten class.

My parents were wonderful people. I was taught to be altruistic by my mother and to be a hard worker by my father. Both my parents worked in factories: my mother was a seamstress and my father, a weaver. When they had enough money, they bought a little real estate.

I graduated high school at age sixteen, but my father did not believe in higher education for girls. That affected me greatly, as I was a good student and aspired to go to college, like my older brother. So I did not go to college after high school. The only schooling that I received outside of public school was piano lessons and Sunday School at the YM-YWHA, where I learned to read Hebrew. I was confirmed at thirteen with seven other girls and I gave the valedictorian speech.

I worked full-time as a secretary and started to take courses at night at Bergen Community College, taking one course at a time for many years. When I married, Howard encouraged me to finish my education on a full-time basis. I graduated from Montclair State University and earned a master's degree in social work from NYU. I am a Licensed Social Worker.

Spiritually, I have never questioned the Jewish religion, in which I was instilled with a strong belief by my mother.

There are incredible stories about how my parents survived the war. I will cite two.

My mother was walking on a field to find some food for herself and her first husband. A German soldier ordered her to halt. My mother fell and prayed to G-d with all her being, and a German shepherd, she said, froze in the air. The soldier did not shoot and told her that he did not know why he had not shot her.

My father had a close friend in the concentration camp. There was supposed to be silence at night. The friend spoke and some German guards heard the voice. A guard asked who had spoken. My father said that he had. The soldier said that my father would be shot dead in the morning. However, for some reason, the Germans did not shoot him.

I struggle with the concept of the Messiah. Why did the Messiah not come to stop the Holocaust? Were Jews an erring folk? We all sin.

After high school, when I was eighteen, I visited Israel for the summer. I lived on a kibbutz near the Sea of Galilee. I would pick apples there with students from all over the world. I saw Mt. Tabor every day while picking apples, and I wanted to climb this mountain.

Mt. Tabor is the traditional site of the Transfiguration of Jesus. I did not know of its history at the time.

One morning I hitched a ride on a tractor to the base of the mountain and found a paved road of little stones that encircled the mountain to the top.

I hiked up the path and near the summit came to a low cobblestone wall. I tried to climb over it but I fell face-first into a cemetery on the other side. I felt as if I had died. Slowly, I realized I was alive and got up and sat on the wall.

I then had what might be called a mystical experience. I heard a voice inside my head say that the first half of my life would go slowly but the second half would go very fast. This has proven to be prophetic.

I saw the church at the summit and I climbed some stairs and pulled the rope that rang the bell that I would often hear on the kibbutz. I had tea with the priest and some visitors from Paramus. In the church I saw beautiful paintings of Moses, Elijah and Jesus. I was unable to get a ride back to the base from these people from Paramus, so I walked down the mountain and walked back to the kibbutz.

I think about time a lot. My parents' conception of time was as if it did not exist. My mother could look out a window for hours. I believe that this lack of the sense of time came from their incarceration in the camps.

Today, I attend the Episcopal Church. I attend the synagogue when I can which, because of my schedule, is only a few times a year. I find no real conflict here. I consider myself a Jew who has an open mind. I find attending the Episcopal Church an education.

It has been an incredible journey.

CHAPTER FOUR

LAST JOURNAL

Reva kept journals throughout her life. The following are the final entries of her last journal before she entered Holy Name Hospital on June 18, 2019, for a procedure. She never returned home. After transfers to two other hospitals, she died in the fall.

***

April 28, 2019

I feel very good and confident.

I am grateful that I woke up as a whole person who can accept her feelings no matter what they are without acting impulsively on them.

Howie, my husband of 31 years, feels better today. He still has aches and pains. He is recovering from a mild form of RA.

I am recovering from a cold and wondering about becoming high, as I called Susan Behar and Lynn Kloch and Peggy Dressel.

Howie doesn't bother people. He always asks if this is a good time to talk.

ANGELS
by R.E. PROSNITZ

Angles spinning
On a pin
Quiet and dizzy
Not a sin.

Loving every
One of us
Singing bells
So we can trust.

Protection is
Their very game
Happiness
Helping all
Is forever flame.

April 28, 2019, continued

    I must write all my recollections for Sylvia Z and my descendants, Laura and Amy. My therapist, Marla, did not call.

    Marla called about being at a conference. H said she was apologetic. Well, she said she would call but did not!

    I will forgive Marla, Harriet, Howard, Dixon, Dr. Weizman, Joey, Susan, Irving, Bronca, Marie, Susan, Dr. Waldinger, Dr. Zaide (etc.), Dr. Nathan S. Kline, Macon, Robert, bad children, bad teachers, Dr. Ellison, Aunt Jean, Helen the history reviser and Usher, Katherine, Linda's landlady, the Jewish Federation, my Sunday school teacher.

May 1, 2019

    Right now Howie is on a telephone call interview for a position at Ramapo College. I hope he gets it. It will do wonders for his self-esteem [illegible word].

    The first thing I remember is going to school in Paterson. In an all black neighborhood, we were afraid to go out at night except mom went to work early till 2 and pop left for work at 2:30. Marilyn lived a block away. Joe was a crossing guard. We moved from 220 Graham Ave. to 316 Hamilton Ave. near the railroad. Miss Patterson lived next door. Butch and Kenny lived next to them. Lila Waldman, an only child, lived somewhere on the other side. Mr. and Mrs. Erder lived around the corner near the candy store. There was a park and still is on Broadway where now stands a statue of Costello. Joe broke his arm riding a bicycle, and I was in the mountains or seashore every summer.

When I was eighteen I spent two weeks touring Israel with mom. I spent the rest of the summer on Kuryot David in Jishel Valley. I had so much fun. I was off lithium and survived. I travelled to Tel Aviv by bus.

May 2, 2019

Life has changed since I am in a wheelchair. I wish we went to the city more, especially the Metropolitan Opera. I would have liked to have seen the ballet in person. However, we are planning to see the Bolshoi Ballet in person May 19, 2019. An easy day to remember, as Howie and I got married May 19, 1988, in a temple in Fair Lawn by Rabbi Yudin. I can't forget the other wedding at City Hall. A police woman who worked in Fair Lawn got killed. My parents witnessed the wedding. We went to the Ramada Inn for dinner/dance and went home to Elmwood Park. We went to Canada for our honeymoon.

We did a lot of sight-seeing in Quebec and Montreal and Schenectady, New York. We even went to the fabulous insect museum in Montreal. I drove part of the way home. I fell asleep at the wheel but continued driving. On the Isle d'Orleans we saw a man who had a suitcase and was seemingly stranded there and no one picked him up. He was on a piece of grass between roads. Metaphor for humanity. No one really cares. There are seven billion of us here now. The shadow has been cast. The image is askew.

Hot day. 90 degrees. [illegible] Bad at dialysis. [illegible]

TO PAINT
by R PROSNITZ

I am
Paint
My drawing
Ain't

Dot by dot
I'll hit
The spot

Green
Vermillion
Red
Rose

Next
I'll paint
A
Huge bouquet

SURGERY
by R E PROSNITZ

Dialyses for the young
Sinful sorrowful one
Get a kidney as they say
In good time and lucky day.

When you're old
and grey
Operations
Risky they

Save me
Save my life
G-d and the doctor
G-d in his mercy
The doctor
With her knife

May 5, 2019

Is my life over at 66? H better get a job teaching. He is getting on my nerves. I enjoyed watching Rachel Ray and also the documentary about Blacks on Saturday.

I went to church today. We are together too much. I am stopping at Sears definitely tomorrow. My therapist says I am strong. I say it to myself too.

I
Am
Strong

It is very sobering to talk to Bev. (She is going for heavier chemo.) I cried. I hope she couldn't tell. I told her practical things that I use (tools to cope). We are sending help and prayers. It's sad about Bev having cancer.

Tired of ERs
Dream
[illegible]

5-13-19

Day of the Mom

Anyway
I'm memorizing
-Morse
L
U
V
K
Y
Z
A—By Stephen C. Phillips
B
C
D
E
F

G
H
I
J
K
L
M
N
O
P
Q
R
S

I spoke to Mr. Fitzgibbons and asked about process and
Slept
Slept
Slept
Holy sleep
Case over

Worried Road
Oh it's good to sleep.

June 7 D Day 75 years.

Bad day at dialysis. I had to wait long for taping up (as usual). I was in pain. I could not put legs down. I cursed the nurse. I told H and therapist. I'll see Marla Mon. at 9 a.m.

I woke up [illegible].

Jesus is so good but cannot be imitated literally today.

June 14, 2019

This is Flag Day, which I will always confuse with flagellation or Independence day in France. France=Freedom. *Enfants allons de la patria. Je tu regarde et arrive. Contre nous de la tyrannie contre nous.*

Oh Say can you see

LAST JOURNAL

By the Dawn's Early Light
On the Ramparts we Hold
At the Twilight's Last Gleaming
And the Rockets Red Flared...
Exercise Prayer Opera

....

This is the last entry in Reva's last journal. Thereafter follow eighty blank pages.

CHAPTER FIVE

FROM CONCENTRATION CAMP TO CHRISTMAS TREE

Many girls born to Holocaust survivors, including some of Reva's friends, were not denied the opportunity for a college education. The bias of Reva's parents, especially her father's, against a college education for Reva, probably had less to do with their sufferings under the Holocaust than working class prejudice and the devaluation of women. Isaac was also penurious: He didn't want to spend money on Reva's education.

As perverse as was the behavior of Bronca and Isaac to Reva, I do not minimize their sufferings under the Nazi regime. According to Reva, Isaac was interned in several concentration camps, including Dachau. He was shot in the leg and developed typhus after hiding in a ditch filled with polluted water. Reva told me that he and other inmates or former inmates ate a horse. I do not know when these episodes occurred and which came first. I do not know if he was shot in the leg after being discovered in the ditch and whether eating the horse was before he was interned or after his liberation. He never spoke about his internment to me, except once when he told me that he had been whipped by the SS. But Reva said that he recorded his experiences in the camps for a government project and that the recording is on file in the Library of Congress or the Holocaust Museum in Washington. In any case, he survived physically intact. Neither he nor Bronca was sterilized by the Nazis, as was, according to Joseph, Bronca's sister, Jean.

Aunt Jean lived in Lakewood, New Jersey, and came to our wedding. Reva fondly remembered her first husband, Uncle Willie. After Uncle Willie's death, Jean remarried. Her second husband was an importer of pottery and gemstones. She was, of course, childless. Both husbands were dead by the time I met Reva.

Both before and after our marriage, Reva and I would sometimes drive on a Sunday to visit Aunt Jean in her apartment, where we were always served a good lunch and generally had an enjoyable afternoon. Although Lakewood today has a large Orthodox Jewish population, Jean was not Orthodox. When she was younger, she owned a chicken farm in Lakewood or neighboring Lakehurst. She also had been a waitress in Lakewood hotels. During the three years that Reva and I dated, she reminded me more than once that she wanted to dance at Reva's wedding. She did, indeed, dance at our wedding, but because Reva and I chose to marry at an Orthodox synagogue (several months following our civil marriage by the Fair Lawn municipal judge), she had to dance with other women, as Orthodox Jews do not dance with the opposite sex. The reasons for our choice of an Orthodox wedding will be explained later. We enjoyed the visits to Jean, and we usually stopped at the shore on the drive home. Lakewood is more rural than northern New Jersey, and there was a sheepfold near Jean's apartment. Reva and I would leave the car and observe the sheep.

Bronca had six siblings. Her mother was killed by the Nazis, as were four of the siblings. Bronca and Jean survived the camps. According to a cousin of Reva's, one sibling died in infancy.

Bronca's father, Reva's grandfather, died before the German invasion of Poland that began World War II. He was an educated man, a chemist by profession, a musician, and a devout Jew. But his income was the sole support of his family, and after his death his wife and children were left on their own. They knew hardship. The children went to work or were boarded with members of the extended family. Bronca, who had little formal education, began working at an early age.

She had married before the war. Unlike Isaac, she would speak about her experiences. Indeed, she spoke about them to me as if they had happened, not fifty years ago, but yesterday. She brought up her children with tales of the Holocaust, which affected Reva far more than Joe, who was able to escape home to Rutgers at seventeen. The following story I heard from both Reva and Bronca.

Bronca was rounded up by the Germans and sent by train to a concentration camp. I do not know which one. There she stood in a line of women to be examined by a Mengele type SS officer, perhaps Mengele himself, who determined where the inmate was to go: to the death chamber or to a work camp. Waiting in the line, Bronca said a prayer in Yiddish, which, according to Reva, translates as, "God save me for I am only a woman." Reva said this same Yiddish prayer when she was in the ICU at Holy Name Hospital in Teaneck, which she entered in June 2019.

Immediately after saying the prayer, Bronca heard a voice, whether inside or outside her head, telling her to throw away her wedding ring. She tore the ring from her finger and tossed it into the brush. When she reached the SS officer, he sent her to the work camp line. Bronca believed that if she had presented herself as a married woman, she would have gone to her death.

Bronca was farmed out with other girls to a work camp supervised by a German whom she described as a decent man, "a human being," to use Bronca's words. The girls were not harshly treated. Bronca said there were days off when they went on picnics. The girls were well fed but not Bronca, but this was her own choosing. She would not eat non-kosher food and survived the war largely on potatoes. Neither she nor Isaac was tattooed with a number. Jean, I recall, was.

Bronca's personality was arbitrary and impulsive. In her later years, before she was admitted to the nursing home where she died from complications of Alzheimer's disease, she was briefly hospitalized in Bergen Pines psychiatric ward.

On Yom Kippur Eve, Bronca would light candles for the Jews who had perished in the Holocaust. "God strike me dead if I do not," I remember her saying.

Joseph, or Joey, as his parents called him, was so grateful to them for their encouragement and emotional support through college and medical school that he rewarded them in a way they could not have anticipated. While studying at Georgetown, or perhaps after he graduated and had begun his medical practice, he became engaged to a young gentile woman, a school teacher named Susan Cauffman, who was not only a Christian but also of German ancestry. The effect of this relationship on Bronca, as Reva described it, was cataclysmic. Both Bronca and Isaac were ready to disown Joseph unless Susan converted to Judaism. She did, and she and Joseph were married in a Jewish ceremony, although I never learned any details about it. The marriage, which took place years before I met Reva, has apparently been successful, as they have been married more than forty years and have two grown daughters. But the relationship between Susan and Bronca was always distant, and Susan's conversion apparently didn't take. Joseph and Susan attended a Unitarian church for a while and then, apparently, dropped regular religious worship entirely. Even in her later years, Bronca would sometimes refer to Susan as "the *shiksa*," a derogatory Yiddish word for a gentile woman.

In the thirty-five years that I knew Reva—from 1985, when we started dating—to 1988, when we married—to 2019, when Reva died—I met Susan on no more than a dozen occasions, and two of those were after the death of Bronca and Isaac. Joseph and Susan lived in an affluent Philadelphia suburb, and Joseph practiced medicine in Philadelphia. The drive from Philadelphia to Fair Lawn takes less than two hours. Joseph visited his parents, perhaps four or five times a year, never staying overnight and almost always coming alone. Bronca and Isaac rarely saw their grandchildren.

Reva told me about an ill-fated visit to Joseph and Susan's home that occurred soon after their marriage. Reva was then in her early twenties.

Bronca, Isaac, Reva, and Jean were invited to visit. It was December. The visit lasted less than five minutes. The visitors never got beyond the front porch.

It glittered: horrible, loathsome, taunting, menacing, at least to Bronca, to whom it might as well have been a swastika. Although Susan had converted to Judaism, a fully trimmed Christmas tree stood on the front porch. Bronca turned around. She refused to enter the house. The others dutifully followed her, although Reva told me she wanted to stay. But Bronca would have none of this. All four went back to the car and returned to New Jersey.

Perhaps Reva's memory of this episode is why, after I converted to Christianity in 2013 (Reva remained Jewish but often accompanied me to church), Reva urged me to buy a Christmas tree. I bought a small artificial tree with a cord of electric trimming, and Reva delighted in setting it up in our apartment. Vivian, our home health aide at the time, helped with the wiring. We had a *mezuzah* on the door frame outside and a Christmas tree inside. I remember Reva's pleasure in the tree and how she urged me each succeeding December to set it up, which I did.

I recall one of Joseph's visits to his parents after he had moved to a house costing a million dollars in an even more affluent Philadelphia suburb. As usual, he came alone. Reva and I and her parents were sitting with him at the dining room table in the Fair Lawn house, and Isaac kept saying incredulously, "A million dollars, Joey, a million dollars." It was more than Isaac could comprehend.

And we visited the million-dollar house: Isaac, Bronca, Reva, and I—the only visit that Bronca and Isaac paid to their son's home during the time that I knew Reva. We drove there on a Sunday. It was a big house with spacious grounds. There was a full-sized outdoor swimming pool and a living room large enough to double as a dance hall. Beyond this, I don't remember much about the house. There was coolness between Bronca and Susan but no flare-up of hostility. We were served cold cuts for lunch, which Susan pointed out were kosher. The two girls, Amy, the oldest, and Laura, were both in elementary or middle school. They never attended public schools but expensive private schools. We stayed a few hours and then drove back to New Jersey.

There are three other occasions I remember seeing Susan. In the 1990s she and Joe, in a rare gesture, came to Fair Lawn with the two girls. It was in the spring or summer, and Reva and I joined them, and we all spent some time at the Glen Rock Duck Pond. The other occasions were both after the death of Bronca and Isaac: Laura's wedding in Philadelphia in 2012 and a visit to our Hackensack apartment with Joe around 2016, just after he retired but before he and Susan moved to San Clemente, California, where they live at this writing.

CHAPTER SIX

BEGINNINGS

I first met Reva in the early summer of 1980 when she was twenty-eight and I was thirty-eight, but I didn't get to know her until the spring of 1984, and we didn't begin dating until February 1985. From that time forward, our lives were intertwined and her story cannot be told separately from mine.

Like Reva, I came from a toxic home, but the poison was different. Both my parents were born in the United States, as was my father's father. His mother was born in Germany but came to New York City at a very young age with her two sisters and mother following her father's death. This was in the late nineteenth century. My mother's parents were born in Russia but came to the US separately as teenagers in the early twentieth century. My mother was born in 1915 in Elizabeth, New Jersey; my father, in 1913 in the Bronx, New York. Thus, my family had no direct experience of the Holocaust. Four of my uncles fought in the US Army or Navy during World War II, and a cousin of my mother's was killed in the Battle of the Bulge.

As a result of the violent and abusive home in which I grew up, and the complications ensuing from it, none of which is relevant to this memoir of Reva, I did not begin college until I was twenty-seven. I earned a BA degree with honors in English from the School of General Studies at Columbia University in 1975. I applied to two graduate programs at Columbia, the PhD program in English and the Master of Science program in library science. I was accepted into both.

I had applied to the library school, not because I wanted a career as a librarian—a useful but passive and poorly paid profession and one unsuited to my temperament—but because I had accepted financial aid as an undergraduate with the stipulation that I pursue a career as a librarian. The details are complicated and irrelevant to this memoir. The grant also covered my tuition and expenses in library school. Financial necessity compelled me to accept it and attend the library school, but it is a decision that I have regretted for many years.

However, I would not pass up the opportunity to study in one of the world's most prestigious graduate English departments. I requested that the Graduate School of Arts and Sciences hold my admission for a year, which it did. I earned the MLS degree in 1976. I then earned an MA in English, but I did not continue toward the PhD because of the pressure to find work as a librarian. Having nowhere else to go when I finished both masters, I returned to my mother's house in Westwood, New Jersey (my father died in 1961), and began the frustrating search for a job as a professional librarian.

From 1977 to 1980 I went on more than a hundred interviews, yet none of the old women—male or female, chronologically young or old—would hire me. The library profession is essentially feminine, and I don't think I was feminine enough for those employers. I am not a woman and I am not gay. I also have an assertive and independent streak, a legacy, perhaps, from my father and my two grandfathers, all independent small-business owners.

My job search took me from the Bronx to Long Island, through Manhattan, seven New Jersey counties, and Rockland and Westchester counties in New York. It was a depressing experience that ultimately caused a mental breakdown. After two sleepless nights in December 1979, I signed myself into 4 West, the psychiatric unit of Valley Hospital in Ridgewood, New Jersey. This unit no longer exits. It was, in effect, closed by the insurance companies. It was entirely voluntary and open-door, with a community, homey atmosphere. It was short-term—two weeks or less. If a patient wanted to leave the unit for a few hours, the patient needed only permission from his or her doctor. Insurance companies did not like to pay for unlocked psychiatric units. Their reasoning seemed to be that if a patient is well enough to walk out at will, or leave on a day pass, the patient did not need a hospital.

But in 1979, Blue Cross still paid for hospitalization in open psychiatric units. While in 4 West, I took advantage of the services. My outlook was that I would use the hospital; it would not use me.

One of the services was the social worker who informed me about the CETA (Comprehensive Employment and Training Act) program. After my discharge, just before Christmas of 1979, I registered with the CETA office in Hackensack. Several days later, I received a letter inviting me to come in for an interview. I was offered the opportunity to join a two-week, six-hour a day workshop in job hunting skills. There were many such programs. What made the CETA program special was that participants were given financial encouragement. They were paid the minimum hourly wage to attend the two-week workshop. Such a program would be unthinkable in today's political climate, and CETA no longer exists. It was a signed into law by President Nixon, lasted through the Carter administration and was killed during the Reagan administration. But CETA worked. There was a paid facilitator and a dozen clients in the workshop, which met in a Bergen County administrative building. We spent the days in mock interviews, job skill exercises, reading want ads in newspapers, calling and responding to the ads, and going on actual interviews. At the end of the two weeks, half of the group, myself included, had found jobs—not CETA-created jobs but jobs in the private or public sector.

I began my first library job as a cataloger in the Hoboken Public Library, a job for which I was hired while attending the CETA program.

But I was let go after four months. The job, although categorized as a professional librarian position, consisted of typing catalog cards, and I am not a professional typist. The other cataloger, who worked at the desk across from mine, was a clerical worker who was attending college part-time.

So I resumed my job search and, because of stress, began psychotherapy with a counselor at a nearby mental health out-patient facility, Mill Pond Mental Health Center.

On a warm day in May 1980, I kept my appointment with the therapist and afterward walked to the bus stop at a nearby mall for the bus home to Westwood. I did not have a car at this time. As I waited for the bus, I felt a rush of panic and thought I was about to die. I ran back to Mill Pond and asked to enter the day hospital program. It was midafternoon. After a short conference of administrators, I was assigned to the day program immediately.

The clients were engaged in several workshops, for which they earned small sums of money. In one workshop, clients prepared packets of test tubes for later use by phlebotomists to draw blood. I was introduced to a young woman who showed me how to put the test tube kits together.

She was the gentle rain from heaven. I had come in from a storm, and this beautiful, soft-voiced woman carefully and caringly showed me how to assemble the kits. I became calm. I remember thinking that I had never met anyone so gentle.

This was my introduction to Reva.

CHAPTER SEVEN

SUMMER

I attended the Mill Pond program through the summer of 1980, but I also continued my job search. I went on several interviews that summer, including one for a librarian at the New York Academy of Medicine in Manhattan. I spent a sleepless night, for reasons I do not remember, but I kept the interview regardless, traveling by bus and subway. I was not hired.

In the Mill Pond day program, there were trips to Lake Sebago in Rockland County, picnics in Van Saun Park, and other activities. I refused to participate in the menial workshop jobs, but I agreed to work one day a week in the kitchen, assisting in the preparation of lunch for the clients and staff. When I arrived home in Westwood in the late afternoon, I rode my bicycle. Mill Pond charged me only five dollars a week to attend. It was a restful summer.

I had limited contact with Reva that summer. She was one of several attractive young women who attended the program. On one occasion, the clients were driven to a nearby YMCA where we played volleyball. Reva was on the other side of the net. When it was my turn to serve, I served the ball directly to her. I didn't do this purposefully; it just went her way. But Reva was not an athlete. She made a valiant attempt to return the serve, but could not. My next two serves also went to her. Again, I did not direct them to her. They just went her way.

Every morning the program began with a group meeting attended by all clients and staff. I was seated next to Reva when she announced to the group that she was leaving the program and returning to work. Then she read a poem she had written that concluded that her heart was filled with love. I remember thinking to myself, "She's a nice girl. I will never see her again."

Reva left the program, and in late August 1980, I left it. I had three interviews over a two-week period: at Glen Rock High School, Franklin Lakes Public Library, and Elmwood Park Public Library.

The Elmwood Park Library Director, Virginia Colburn, was a generous and kind woman who lived in Passaic with her middle-school son. Her husband was a scientist who lived and worked in Indiana but returned to New Jersey periodically. She was a devout Methodist and Sunday school teacher. The library board of trustees had recently cut the hours of the second professional, the job I applied for, to thirty hours a week. But this was still considered full-time and qualified me for medical benefits. Virginia Colburn hired me.

I worked at the Elmwood Park Public Library from September 1980 until September 1982, when I took a job at a higher salary at the Passaic Public Library. I never took a day off in Elmwood Park, and in August, when I gave notice, I was required to take time off to compensate for unused personal and vacation days. I was the reference librarian, cataloger, and children's librarian (the last, for a year, until the library hired a former elementary school teacher as children's librarian. I organized and supervised the summer reading program in the summer of 1981). I was also the acquisitions librarian for the reference department, and I supervised the library staff in the absence of the director. Elmwood Park is a small working-class town. I was well liked and did an effective job. The other employees were library assistants, all very nice local ladies. The only other male employee, when I began, was the part-time custodian. Later the library hired a male library assistant.

I saw Reva twice in those two years in Elmwood Park. Once I saw her from my car. She was standing near a bank on the town's main street. The other time she came into the library looking for books on mathematics. I think she was considering entering a practical nursing program at Bergen Pines Hospital. I showed her the shelves containing the math books. Neither she nor I gave any sign of recognition. It would have been inappropriate in a work environment. She seemed shy when she was in the library. Our interaction lasted less than five minutes.

The Passaic Public Library, where I began working the day after Labor Day in 1982, was a larger library than Elmwood Park, with a main library, where I was assigned, and three branches. There were eight professional librarians and more than twenty library assistants. I joined the reference staff and was also in charge of periodicals. Following the illness and retirement of another librarian, I took over her duties as local history librarian. I worked in the Passaic Public Library from 1982 to 1988, eventually attaining the civil service title of Senior Reference and Adult Services Librarian.

In the spring of 1984, I took a week of my vacation time and traveled to Rhode Island, where my mother had moved to be near my brother; his then wife, Carol; and their two young children, Sandra, the oldest, and Brian.

The reason for the visit was Sandra's *bat mitzvah*. All went well for several days until the Friday night service. The actual *bat mitzvah* was on Saturday. Many relatives had already arrived. I was staying at my mother's apartment.

At this time in my life, in fact for most of my life, I suffered from severe insomnia. In the 1980s, a doctor prescribed Benadryl. He might as well have prescribed water. Eventually a doctor at Mill Pond prescribed Dalmane, a popular sleeping drug at the time, and that worked. I took 30 mg and some nights I had to take 60 mg.

As Dalmane has a half-life of several days, I found I usually didn't need it more than two or three nights a week.

However, I had discontinued Dalmane at the time of the Rhode Island visit following what I thought was an adverse reaction. I had eaten grapefruit just before taking it one night, and the effect was almost to knock me out. Instead of gradual, gentle sleepiness, the sleep came on with a powerful force that overwhelmed me. I barely made it to my bed before I lost consciousness. I was fine in the morning, but I decided that Dalmane was dangerous. I didn't know then about the interaction between grapefruit and grapefruit juice with certain medicines, including benzodiazepines, of which Dalmane is one.

After the Friday night service, my mother and the relatives socialized in the lobby of the hotel where the relatives were staying. I knew from past experience that if I did not go to bed by eleven, I would not be able to sleep. I urged my mother to drive me back to her apartment or leave early, but she would not. Finally, probably after midnight, we got back there. My sister, then unmarried, was also staying at my mother's apartment, sleeping in the living room. I had the guest bedroom.

True to my prediction, I spent a totally sleepless night. When I realized I couldn't sleep, I turned on the radio and listened to an all-night program of Ella Fitzgerald recordings. In the morning, I attended the synagogue service. The lunch, precooked (they were observing the Sabbath) was served in the synagogue social hall. There was no dancing. Then the guests converged on my mother's apartment. I was exhausted, and I knew people would be in the apartment until late evening. Fortunately, an aunt and uncle from New Jersey were leaving Saturday afternoon, and they drove me back to my Hackensack apartment, where I fell asleep watching an old movie on television.

A month later, the Saturday night before Mother's Day 1984, I experienced another sleepless night. I eventually went back on Dalmane after learning about the adverse grapefruit interaction, but I do not remember if I had returned to it by this time. I decided to seek therapy for insomnia. Having been in individual therapy on and off previously with limited success, I decided to try group therapy and called Mill Pond to find out if group therapy was available there. I was given an appointment with Robert T., the director of Mill Pond.

Two sleepless nights in the spring of 1984 and my decision to deal with them through group therapy changed my life.

Those sleepless nights led to greater joy than I could have ever imagined and, later, to deepest sorrow.

CHAPTER EIGHT

INSOMNIA

For the insomniac, there is no more dreadful sound than that of birds beginning to sing in the early morning while the sky is still dark. As nature awakes, the insomniac has lain sleepless through the night.

I have heard that sound many times over the years and have suffered from insomnia at least since my early teens. I used Dalmane in the 1980s, but in earlier years I used such drugs as chloral hydrate and barbiturates. These days, I take Valium for sleep but only for sleep.

And there have been periods of months when I did not need any sleeping drug, but that was many years ago.

At my interview with Robert T. at Mill Pond, I learned that there was a group for former day hospital patients. (I was a day hospital patient in the summer of 1980.) The group met one evening a week. Some, but not all the members, worked. I decided to join.

There were about eight members of the group, which was led by Robert T., a psychologist. The members spoke about a variety of problems they were trying to cope with. One member smoked a lot of marijuana, and when high on weed, believed a machine was controlling his brain. It never seemed to have occurred to him to stop smoking marijuana. There was Janet, a divorced woman with two young daughters. Her ex-husband had custody of the children. Janet had gotten a bad deal from the divorce settlement. She spoke about her difficulties managing her life and her desire to have more time with her children. I spoke about my insomnia. And there was Reva, a member of the group. Reva spoke about problems with her social life and with her parents. She was dating a guy named Bob, with whom she would go dancing. (She loved to dance.) But she said in the group, "I have Bob, but Bob isn't enough." I could see longing in her. She was thirty-two and I was forty-two.

Reva was always well-dressed in business attire. She would come to the group from work, as I did. She was living, at this time, in a Mill Pond residence in Saddle Brook with three other women, but Reva was the only one of the four who worked. She worked in an office. From the time she finished high school until she began college full-time after we married, she worked in offices as a clerk-typist.

During the summer of 1984, Reva was out from the group for a couple of sessions. She had been hospitalized for one of the breakdowns or manic episodes from which she had suffered since high school. "Bipolar disorder" they call it, but I fail to see what it has to do with the Arctic or Antarctica. In fact, I fail to see what it has to do with anything. I don't believe it exists as a disease and, to put it bluntly, I believe that psychiatry is a fraud, and worse, a form of social control that has harmed many people and killed some, including Reva. I remember a dermatologist telling me how he and other specialists see patients whose bodies have been ravaged by psychiatric drugs.

Psychiatry isn't medicine. It is quackery and worse. It is crime and should be banned. As this memoir unfolds, the reader will see how psychiatry ultimately killed Reva.

This is not to say that heightened excitement, despondency, and erratic behavior are not real. But there are ways of channeling exuberant energy instead of drugging potentially creative human life into oblivion. But Reva was never taught those ways when she was young. Indeed, few sufferers are. They turn, or are turned by benighted parents who are unable to see the flaws in their own behavior and to change it, to psychiatry.

Reva and I found each other. Our first date was to see the movie *1984* with Richard Burton. This was in February 1985. We were always a little late.

After the movie we went for ice cream. Then I drove Reva home, and she invited me in for tea.

I noticed a scale on her kitchen table, and she explained that she had to weigh the amount of meat she consumed each day because of her kidney disease. I made some offhand remark about the quality of the meat, thinking that people in the residence bought low-quality or McDonalds. But Reva said that she bought her meat from Harold's Kosher Butcher, a popular and expensive kosher butcher and delicatessen in Paramus. At first, I thought she was joking. Then I knew she wasn't. Reva wasn't ordinary.

Before I left, we agreed to go to Manhattan the next day, Sunday.

Reva called me at about eight in the morning to say she was ready. I was still in bed, but I rose, showered, dressed, and drove over to her house. We went into the city and Reva seemed deeply content. We visited the Jewish Museum and the Museum of the City of New York and had lunch.

On the ride home, as I noted earlier, Reva asked me if there was anything in the Passaic Library about her kidney disease, which was, at that time, diagnosed as nephrogenic diabetes insipidus (NDI). I said I would look it up, and when I returned to work, I photocopied some pages from the *Merck Manual* and gave them to her.

NDI is a kidney disease and is unrelated to the diabetes caused by insulin deficiency. Reva did not have, nor ever have, type A or type B diabetes. When she died thirty-five years later, she had multiple ailments but not diabetes, which afflicts many hemodialysis patients. At her death, she had been in hemodialysis for sixteen years.

Reva's NDI was a direct result of toxicity from lithium, which she had taken for eighteen years, but was no longer taking by the time we began dating. About 20 percent of long-term lithium users develop NDI, which is a progressive disease that can cause end-stage renal disease, where the short-term option is dialysis or death. The long-term option is dialysis and death unless the patient has a successful kidney transplant.

If Reva had not been kept on lithium by psychiatrists for almost two decades, barring the unforeseen, she would be alive today.

Reva was an excellent pianist, having begun piano lessons when she was a child in Paterson. Piano lessons were the one advantage her parents gave her. And this was because of Reva's initiative. She had heard a friend play and wanted to learn. Her parents yielded.

My father did not. In my early teens, I wanted to study piano, but my father would not allow it. (In my late teens, I did have some piano lessons, but that is irrelevant to this memoir. I studied piano again as an adult after Reva and I married.) I heard Reva play at Mill Pond and in her parents' home in Fair Lawn.

The first time I visited her parents' home, I met her mother. (Her father wasn't home.) My impression of Bronca was that she was a controlling woman. She was a Polish Jew and a Holocaust survivor. I learned that Reva's brother, five years older, was a physician, a nephrologist practicing in Philadelphia.

There was something about Reva that called for protection, especially as I observed her mother, and later, her father. She seemed to need protection from them and from much else. And I could see her yearning and her determination to do something more with her life than work as a clerk-typist.

Reva was beautiful, with black hair and huge eyes. She was refined and, as I have written earlier, very gentle.

We were destined for each other. For me, and I believe for her, the years before were preliminary to our coming together. They led us to this place in our lives.

The years that remain to me following her death in 2019 are an aftermath of my life.

CHAPTER NINE

WEDDING

Reva wanted to marry me within two months of our first date, but I wasn't ready. I wouldn't be ready for almost three years, but I sometimes wonder how life would have changed for both of us if we had married earlier, perhaps in May 1985 instead of January 1988. I was employed by the Passaic Public Library until the spring of 1988 and had medical and dental insurance. I earned a modest salary, and I was living in a studio apartment in Hackensack where my rent was less than $600 a month. I drove a second-hand Ford Mustang that gave me no end of trouble until I bought a new Toyota Corolla, which my mother paid for. I did not have money for a new car and had just enough to live on from paycheck to paycheck. I had bought an annuity, and I was also paying double into the state pension plan because, for some unknown reason, no pension deductions had been taken from my salary at Elmwood Park. The pension and annuity deductions further reduced my biweekly paychecks. In addition, I was paying off my student loans.

But I have thought that if I had married Reva early in our relationship, as she wanted me to, we might have had a child. When I did marry her, I was working in the Jersey City Public Library and earning less than I earned in Passaic.

But was it a realistic idea to have a child? Reva wanted one, as almost all women do, but I did not. However, after we married, she saw things my way. She was already thirty-two when we began dating and had a progressive kidney disease brought on by lithium. Although we hoped that the disease would not ultimately lead to dialysis, we knew it could. And she had periodic manic episodes for which she was hospitalized on the average of once every two years while we were married and more often before I knew her.

Some of the manic episodes were frightening, especially those that she told me about that occurred before we met. She had manic episodes throughout our marriage, throughout her life—the last one, just weeks before her final illness and hospitalization in June 2019. I believe they could have been controlled without the poisonous drugs she was prescribed through enlightened counseling and creative and athletic outlets. But this approach should begin early. People need to learn to respond to stress without cracking just as a smoker needs to learn not to turn to cigarettes. Reva was certainly not too young for this learning process at fourteen when she was put on lithium, but her parents were ignorant and cruel, and the blind worship of medical or quasi-medical authority is too strong for most people to resist, especially if it is not they who are the victims—but their children.

However, even late in Reva's life, I was able to abort psychotic episodes by encouraging her to channel her energy in progressive directions. I will say more about this in a later chapter.

I was already forty-two when we began dating. The thought of fatherhood did not appeal to me. We both needed to develop ourselves. I can say with some certainty that had Reva become a mother, she would never have gone to college, let alone graduate school. Bringing a new life into the world is an enormous responsibility. On the whole, I think we made the right choice.

Reva was in love with me. My love for her grew more slowly. Within the first few months of our dating, she bought a wedding outfit for herself—not a white gown, but a very nice beige top and skirt. When we married almost three years later, she did not wear it.

Reva told me when we first began dating that she feared she would never marry and was destined to care for her parents in their old age, a prospect that she dreaded.

The thought of marriage was awesome to me. In fact, up to the time Reva entered Holy Name Hospital in June 2019 for a procedure on her left leg, went into cardiac arrest before the procedure could begin, and never left hospitals until she died three months later, I would periodically be amazed that I was a married man and, even after more than thirty years of marriage, would say to her, "I can't believe I have a wife." Her reply was usually, "You sure do."

For three years we were inseparable. We lived apart but spent weekends together. We had fun. We saw plays and movies and went to concerts. We went dancing and dining and did a hundred other things that couples do. And we broke up seven times, every breakup initiated by me and none lasting more than a week.

One breakup stands out in my memory. It was late spring or early summer. We were in my apartment on a Friday evening. I had called her and asked her to come over. She anticipated what I was going to say, "Don't break my heart," she said. But I told her I needed to be away from her for a while. She left the apartment immediately without saying a word.

A few days later I received a letter from her in which she said she was in a "tizzy," an old-fashioned word, and Reva was an old-fashioned girl. She wrote, in effect, that's life and that she has to go on from the experience.

A week went by. I went to work, and life seemed to proceed normally. Then I had a sleepless Saturday night. I called Reva Sunday morning and said I wanted to talk to her. She was no longer living in a residence but had moved with Janet to the second floor of a two-family house in Garfield. Reva would not talk on the phone. She said she wanted to see my face. We agreed to meet in the early evening in Saddle Brook Park. I did not sleep during the day. Then, as now, it is almost impossible for me to nap, even when I have been up all night.

In the afternoon, a light rain began. When I drove to the park to meet Reva at six, as we had arranged, it was deserted, except for Reva. She was wearing a blue zipper jacket and sitting on a swing. She watched me as I parked my car and got out. I walked toward her. We didn't say a word. We embraced.

There was no blame, no recrimination. This was love. We were together again. Ours is a love built on a rock.

In the spring of 1987, I moved from my Clarendon Place studio in Hackensack to the first floor of a two-family house in Elmwood Park. The landlord and landlady, a Polish refugee couple, lived on the second floor. One reason for the move was that Reva and I were planning to marry in June. But now it was Reva's turn to hold back. She said she had developed doubts. They had crept into her mind. We continued to date, but I moved in alone and spent a hot summer without air-conditioning, my relief coming from a window fan. But one evening in September, Reva called me. She was staying with her parents after a disastrous rental in the winter of a room in a private house in Teaneck, a room she didn't know was unheated. (She and Janet had moved from Garfield and gone their separate ways.) The Teaneck landlady was psychotic and attempted to choke Reva when she moved out. She had become sick from the lack of heat and had moved back to her parents' house to recover.

The evening she called me her parents were out. She asked me to come and take her, and I did. We later moved in some of her clothes and her rocking chair. Her piano came later. Reva had overcome her doubts.

On January 29, 1988, we were wed in holy lawful matrimony.

It was actually a civil ceremony in Fair Lawn Municipal Court, just before court began. We had a Jewish wedding in May. Reva died on Sept 10, 2019, after thirty-one years and eight months of marriage.

The courtroom was almost empty when Judge Jonathan Harris, the Fair Lawn Municipal Judge, married us. The traffic violators, disorderlies, and drunks would come later. Reva's parents were the only guests. We had a camera, and our wedding photographs were taken by Fair Lawn's only female police officer at the time, who was standing by for court and volunteered to take the pictures. Mary Ann Collura, the police officer, came to a tragic end in 2003 when she was shot dead in the line of duty.

CHAPTER TEN

PASSAIC

After the wedding, which took place late on a Friday afternoon, Reva and I went for dinner and dancing at the Ramada Inn in Saddle Brook, where we had often dated. Then we returned home to Elmwood Park.

Reva was working at this time as a clerk-typist for a company located in one of the many offices carved out of the former 140-acre Curtiss-Wright Plant in Woodridge. The plant had been a major manufacturer of aircraft engines during World War II.

But a local newspaper reported that toxic waste had been found in soil near the site, and a child who had played in the soil developed leukemia. Although Reva did not drink the tap water in her office, she washed her hands and may have drunk coffee brewed with it. I urged Reva to quit for the sake of her health, and she did. She soon found another office job. In the interim, she worked part-time as a checkout clerk at the A&P near our new home.

Some weeks before our marriage, I was suspended with pay from my job as reference librarian at the Passaic Public Library, a job I had held for five and a half years. The circumstances of my suspension are enveloped in the chicanery and corruption of the City of Passaic. In March 1988, the library board of trustees met to accept my resignation. I had retained a lawyer and demanded a full year's salary as a condition of resigning. The board complied, or at a least I agreed they had. I received a few thousand dollars, and they counted the salary they paid me while I was suspended. They also paid me for more than thirty unused sick days. The total was the equivalent of about a year's salary. As an example of the duplicity of the board and the falsity of their charges against me, one of those charges was excessive absenteeism. Yet I was paid for more than thirty unused sick days.

Joseph Lipari, who was mayor of Passaic at the time, was later sent to federal prison on corruption charges. Lipari had appointed a man whom I will call Ben Gold as director of the library board of trustees. Ben Gold had a particular vendetta against the library director, Thomas Schear. The source and circumstances of the vendetta are irrelevant to this memoir and, frankly, are only partially known to me, except that they were evident before Gold joined the board of trustees.

Ben Gold was also president of his Passaic synagogue and of the local B'nai B'rith chapter. He was a pugnacious, aggressive, short-tempered, and loudmouthed man whom I would hear shouting at Schear from behind the closed door of Schear's office off the library's reference department. Gold soon brought other members of his synagogue onto the board of trustees, including the rabbi's wife. They, with other board members, pressured Schear, who had hired me and who had been library director for twenty-five years, into resigning.

I recall the morning that Schear gathered the professional librarians in a corner of the main reading room to inform us of his resignation. There had been a board meeting the previous evening at which the angry and abusive Gold had accused Schear of malfeasance.

I was a competent and hardworking reference librarian, who was also in charge of local history and periodicals. At a staff meeting, Schear once called me the "iron man" because I could be counted on to work a twelve-hour shift or to come in on my day off if a librarian called in sick or went home sick.

After Schear was gone, the board turned on me, perhaps because I was earning a higher salary than any of the other nonsupervisory librarians. My salary had grown over the years as a result of longevity, my promotion to senior librarian, and my two master's degrees. The library had a salary differential for librarians with a second master's degree.

Because I had the civil service classification as Senior Reference and Adult Services Librarian Permanent, the board, led by Gold, trumped up a series of charges against me. They couldn't fire me outright because of civil service regulations.

I will never forget the humiliation of coming with my lawyer to the hearing in March when five members of the board, a quorum, including the three from the synagogue, voted to accept my resignation.

Tom Schear had been a role model for me in a profession that I entered reluctantly. He was a World War II veteran and was married and had five children. He lived in a large house surrounded by tall hedges not far from the library. He would walk home for lunch. He had to because his wife worked and took the family car. Schear was a disabled veteran, but the nature of his disability was not apparent, and he never spoke about it. I have speculated that he may have suffered from what today is called PTSD but was then known as shellshock. Perhaps he chose the library profession because of its popular reputation as a low-stress job.

Schear was always well-dressed and took some pride as a connoisseur of fine food and wine. When I applied for the job in the summer of 1982, I spent less than twenty minutes with Schear in his office. He then invited me to lunch. The librarian who was head of the reference department joined us. The real interview was over lunch, but it wasn't grilling and questions. That had taken place in Shear's office. The lunch, rather, was for Schear to evaluate how well I integrated with the library staff, as represented by him and the head of reference. This was Schear's style. He didn't hire me on the spot. He couldn't, as hiring had to be approved by the board of trustees, which at that time included a retired school superintendent, Passaic school teachers, and other respected members of the community but did not include Ben Gold or his synagogue colleagues. In fact, Joseph Lipari was not mayor then but was on the city council. He later defeated the incumbent mayor in a recall election. In August 1982, Schear telephoned me to give me the news that the board had approved my hiring. I was to start the Tuesday after Labor Day.

Schear was not only a role model to me but a type of father figure. He could infuriate me, such as when he delayed my promotion to senior librarian, but at the same time, I looked up to him.

He went. And then I went. Schear's adversary, the library's assistant director, was appointed director. The board accepted my resignation at the beginning of his administration.

After I resigned, I did not go on unemployment. I had responded to an advertisement in the *New York Times* from the Jersey City Public Library for librarians and was hired as children's librarian at the Five Corners Branch in the Journal Square neighborhood, the busiest branch of the multibranch Jersey City system. In Elmwood Park, I had done everything: reference, cataloging, programming, and children's work. I suppose the head of children's services in the Jersey City system thought it would be a novelty to hire a male children's librarian.

Most of the children who participated in the Five Corners summer program at the Jersey City Public Library, and, indeed, most of the children who used the Five Corners Branch, were Indian. This was a time of tension between some white residents of the city and the recently arrived Asian residents, and there had been acts of violence. The Journal Square neighborhood was home to many Indian families.

I worked as children's librarian at the Five Corners Branch through the summer of 1988, and in September was transferred, at my request, to the reference department of the main library on Jersey Avenue. I was more at home doing reference work, but I am grateful for the education I received in children's literature and for my experience with children and their parents from my work as a children's librarian, both in Elmwood Park and Jersey City.

CHAPTER ELEVEN

ELMWOOD PARK

After I was hired by Jersey City, I telephoned Isaac with the news. He was relieved. He did, after all, want his daughter's husband to earn a living.

There was no laundry room in the two-family house in Elmwood Park, and once a week I drove Reva and our laundry to a local laundromat and picked her up when the laundry was done.

Mr. and Mrs. Wynosky were our landlords. In fairness to them, they were an elderly couple whose previous tenant had been a woman who lived quietly alone. We were younger, recently married, and we played the piano. I think Mrs. Wynosky regretted renting to us almost as soon as we moved in. She had the legal right to evict us at will with a thirty-day notice, as it was an owner-occupied, two-family house. But when she decided to evict us three years later following her husband's death, she did so through a lawyer.

In the summer, I would sometimes do grocery shopping late at night at the 24-hour A&P. When I returned and brought my purchases from my car into the house, Mrs. Wynosky would yell from her second-floor window, waking up the whole block. Yet she also spoke to us of the persecutions she and her family suffered under the Nazis, at least she did so once to me.

One early spring morning during the period when I was suspended with pay from the Passaic Public Library and before I was hired by Jersey City, Reva was at work and I was in the kitchen putting on *tefillin*, the phylacteries that observant Jewish men put on every day except the Jewish Sabbath. At that time, I had been studying with the Lubavitch Hasidim and was trying to become a more religious Jew. I was, as I put it years later to a coworker, trying to get God on my side.

The Wynosky's had a vegetable garden in back of their house, and our kitchen window faced the garden, although the window was high, so I was not visible from the garden. On this lovely morning, Mrs. Wynosky was in the garden talking to a neighbor. I, not being allowed to go to work and facing unemployment, began putting on the tefillin, as I had been doing daily for a year or so. I heard the voices of the two women in the garden. I heard the birds singing and felt the warm breeze coming through the window. Then I thought, "Why am I doing this? Why am I binding myself this way? Why am I putting on handcuffs? For Ben Gold? For the rabbi's wife? For those Jews and the way they treated me?" I tore the tefillin off and did not put them on again for more than thirty years. I put them on in the summer of 2019 when Reva was in the ICU of Holy Name Hospital. A Lubavitch rabbi came at my request to pray for her. I explained to him that I was a convert to Christianity, but he said I had a Jewish soul. He showed me how to put them on, and I recited the prayers in Hebrew after him. Reva, who was in a hopeful state of improvement at the time and was conscious, recited the prayers too. She was seemingly recovering, although her left leg had been amputated.

One summer evening when we were still dating, Reva and I were walking near my studio apartment on Clarendon Place. Reva was passionate to marry me, but I kept putting marriage off, although I had bought her an engagement ring with a small diamond. That evening Reva described herself as having such a "yearning" to marry me. "I will be a good Jewish wife," she assured me. Jewish, to Reva, did not mean observances and attendance at the synagogue, although it included some of this too. For Reva, it meant goodness. Godliness. Early in our relationship, I asked Reva what being Jewish meant to her. "Being alive," she replied.

After Reva's death, the social worker who had been Reva's therapist and is mine at this writing, said that Reva was too good. She checked herself from saying, "Too good for this world," but I think that is what she meant.

After Reva became disabled in 2004, she sometimes would say to me that a lot of guys would have abandoned her or put her in a nursing home.

I would never do either, I assured her. I needed her as much as she needed me.

Once, after we had been dating for a while, she told me that she felt I was a snowman who would melt away. Over the years, I recalled this. "I didn't melt away," I said. "No, you didn't," Reva replied.

We had been married for perhaps two years when Reva confessed to me that she had always wanted to call me Howie. She had been calling me by the more formal, Howard. Thereafter, I was Howie to her to the end.

Our marriage, especially its early years, had its ups and downs. If marriage did not, it wouldn't be marriage. Marriage is a roller coaster, but although we had wide swoops and swings, we always stayed in the same cart, screamed together, and always, deeply, loved each other.

I recall that after one argument we had in Elmwood Park Reva left and went home to her parents. Mrs. Wynosky, concerned about her rent, said to me bluntly, "Your wife left you." I don't recall the rest. But the parting was brief, perhaps a day or two. Reva called. She came back. We could not live without each other.

The Passaic Public Library subscribed to *New Jersey Audubon* magazine, which I read on my breaks. I had always liked the outdoors, and Reva and I took up bird watching, although we never got beyond the novice stage. We bought binoculars at the New Jersey Audubon Society in Franklin Lakes. We bought only one pair to share, but they were a good pair and expensive. I forget the magnification, and I no longer have them, but I wanted an even stronger pair. With the stronger pair, I was able to read the numbers on the metal plate on a telephone pole across the street from the sanctuary. But Reva found this pair too heavy, so we bought the lighter-weight binoculars, and they worked out well.

One our favorite places for bird watching was the Celery Farm in Allendale, a preserved wetland that had long years before been a celery farm. The trail circled a pond. In the early spring, we heard spring peepers and in midsummer, bull frogs. A huge snapping turtle lumbered across the trail. There were barn swallows in an old barn adjacent to the sanctuary, where a horse was tethered.

Along with the binoculars, we carried *Peterson's Field Guide to*

North American Birds. Besides the barn swallows, I remember pileated woodpeckers, red-wing blackbirds and finches. And there were certainly other birds I do not remember. Reva loved those trips to the sanctuary. She told me that she had always thought woodpeckers were a myth until she saw and heard them. We usually would circle the pond three times.

She had her mood swings. Unfortunately, she had never mastered techniques for channeling her emotions.

One Sunday morning, we took a ride into Ringwood, a heavily wooded borough in upper Passaic County. We quarreled in the car on the ride home. When we arrived back to Elmwood Park, I went into my study to allow our emotions to cool. The apartment had two bedrooms, and I had set up one as a study. Reva then dramatically started to cut her wrist, but I don't think she drew any blood. I think she called 911 herself.

The police came, including a detective. I remember him speaking on his radio about hesitation marks on Reva's wrist. An ambulance was called, and Reva was transported to Hackensack Hospital, as it was then known. It was not yet Hackensack Meridian Hackensack University Medical Center.

I followed the ambulance in my car.

We spent most of Sunday afternoon in the ER. A psychiatrist on call interviewed Reva and cleared her for discharge. She was not admitted to the psych facility at the hospital. We were lucky that time.

Reva loved to cook and read cookbooks like some people read anthologies of poetry. She introduced me to such delicacies as stuffed artichoke leaves, and she would prepare a dish of yogurt, vegetables, and sardines. She baked chicken, but only after boiling the chicken to clean it.

Reva's piano came with us from Alexander Avenue. I called a teacher in Teaneck, and we began taking lessons together. We shared a lesson each week. Reva, of course, was on an advanced level and I was a beginner, although I had studied piano for a short time when I was sixteen.

Donna E., our piano teacher, also taught violin and played it professionally. Her husband, Mario, was an opera singer and taught voice. The studio was in their home.

Donna was a good teacher. Sadly, her husband, only in his early sixties, developed acute leukemia and was hospitalized in Mt. Sinai Hospital. I drove into Manhattan to donate platelets, but the nurse would not let me because I had a cold. I had not known that someone with a cold cannot donate blood.

Mario died a few weeks after his admission to the hospital. Donna was devastated. They had no children.

She did not give lessons for a while but then resumed, and we came back as pupils. Reva and I played in one of the annual student recitals that piano teachers present. But our funds were short, and we had to discontinue lessons. We studied with Donna for about three years.

Reva continued to work as a clerk-typist. I worked for the Jersey City Public Library for a year but left after my car had been stolen a second time from the streets of Jersey City. It was recovered both times but with damage. The second time it was recovered in Brooklyn, oddly, with a spool of piano wire on the back seat. It was time to leave Jersey City.

CHAPTER TWELVE

JEWISH WEDDING

In Elmwood Park, we made the acquaintance of Mr. Barringer, a ninety-year-old World War I veteran. He was hitchhiking home from the A&P carrying groceries, and I picked him up. You don't often see a wiry ninety-year-old with a long white beard stick out his thumb. Reva and I invited him for dinner, and he dined with us several times. We also sometimes took him out to a diner.

He lived in a duplex a few blocks from us. His daughter occupied the other half of the house, but we never met her. His wife was dead. He had been a physical education instructor in the Marine Corps, but I don't remember his civilian occupation. He seemed to be in excellent condition for a man his age. He attributed his good health to diet, especially avoiding meat which, he said, was tainted with chemicals and antibiotics.

He was a parishioner at St. Leo's Roman Catholic Church in Elmwood Park, but he stopped attending, he said, when some parishioners complained that he sang too loudly.

I took him to the Celery Farm, hoping the contact with nature would raise his spirits, which were low. But the walk to the trail was too much for him. I ran errands for him and brought food to him. When I was in his home, he would speak vaguely about his sins, but he did not elaborate. He seemed at times despondent. He would say that the misery of his present life was punishment for his past sins. I made the grievous mistake, which I have regretted ever since, of telephoning the priest at St. Leo's. My intention was, I think, benign, even good. I wanted to know if the church could send an occasional visitor to speak with him and keep him company. I thought this was one of the things churches do. But I did not know the Roman Catholic

Church or foresee its authoritarianism. When I gave the priest my name, an obviously Jewish one, there was a mutter of surprise. I stated my request. I said that Mr. Barringer would feel psychologically better if the church could send an occasional visitor. How naïve I was.

The next thing I knew, Mr. Barringer had been moved to a nursing home in Rochelle Park. It was probably not the priest who locked him up, but the priest most likely contacted his daughter, who may have decided that he was annoying the neighbors and put him away while he was still physically and mentally able.

Reva and I visited him at the nursing home once, and he was angry at us. But I never thought that my effort to be a good neighbor would end with his incarceration. I thought Christian churches took interest in people and sought to guide and comfort them. Many years later, when I made the decision to convert from Judaism and join a church, it was certainly not a Roman Catholic church. In fact, my decision to convert was many years in the making, and during the period when I was most actively seeking, having found Judaism unfulfilling and having encountered a number of unpleasant Jewish people, I interviewed clergy of several Protestant denominations, but I did not speak to a Roman Catholic priest. Reva and I both enjoyed Mr. Barringer's company while it lasted.

Reva continued to work as a clerk-typist, and together we did shopping, visited friends, and worked on the foundation of our marriage.

In May 1988, Reva and I had a Jewish wedding at Congregation Shomrei Torah, an Orthodox synagogue in Fair Lawn. Reva and I were not Orthodox Jews, but at this time, I was seeking a religion and a religious community to give stability and purpose to my life. I began with the religion of my birth.

Our wedding was on a weekday evening after we had both returned home from work. We were, after all, already married. Rabbi Benjamin Yudin, who was then rabbi at Shomrei Torah, said that Jewish law required that we have a separate ring for the ceremony: we could not use the rings from our civil ceremony. So Reva went into a five and ten and bought an inexpensive costume jewelry ring. My gold ring, which is on my finger as I type these words, and Reva's gold ring, which she was buried with, were purchased from a jeweler for the civil ceremony. Reva later gave the ring we used in the Jewish ceremony to her mother. (There was only one ring. Orthodox Judaism apparently does not condone, or at least does not encourage, a man to wear a wedding ring.) I don't know why she did this. Her mother asked for it, and she gave it to her. Although it was an inexpensive ring that we kept in a drawer, one that was bought for a specific ceremony, it was still a wedding ring. I was disappointed that she gave it to her mother. I never saw it again.

The intricacies of Jewish law determined the date of our wedding. Orthodox Jews observe a period in the spring when no weddings are permitted, but there is one day during this period, which lasts approximately five weeks, when the ban is lifted, and it was on that day in May that we married in a Jewish ceremony.

Most of the people that evening were strangers, members of the congregation. We had a few friends and relatives among the guests, including Reva's parents, my aunt and uncle from Metuchen, and another aunt and a cousin from Bergen County. My mother, who suffered from severe rheumatoid arthritis, was unable to make the trip from Rhode Island.

A certificate in Hebrew, a language I do not understand but can sound phonetically, was presented to us at the ceremony. It is called a *ketubah* and it is the marriage contract. The ketubah had an English translation. A few years later in a fit of rage after Reva had gone home to her parents following an argument (she returned a day or two later), I ripped it up. Our marriage survived.

There were sandwiches and dancing (same sex) after the ceremony. Then we went home. So throughout our married life, we celebrated two wedding anniversaries, but for me the civil ceremony with gold rings and traditional vows was the primary anniversary. After all, how many times can a person marry the same partner without an intervening divorce? But for Reva, the Jewish ceremony overshadowed the civil marriage. She told me later that she was in ecstasy at the Jewish ceremony. To stand under the *chuppah*, the wedding canopy, fulfilled her greatest dream. Yet photos from that ceremony show her parents with dubious, quizzical expressions on their faces.

CHAPTER THIRTEEN

MANIA

In the spring of 1985, after we had been dating a few months, Reva organized a surprise anniversary party for her parents in the basement of their Alexander Avenue home. Her parents found out about the plans and, in typical fashion for them, took over the organization themselves. The party, however, was a success. There were about thirty people gathered in the basement, and I met Reva's brother, Joseph, for the first time. He came alone, unaccompanied by his wife or daughters.

Almost all the guests were "greenies," as Reva always called them: Holocaust survivors who had settled in Paterson and among whom Reva grew up. Most had moved by then from Paterson to Fair Lawn or other nearby communities. Sylvia and Sid Zlotnick, the American couple who sponsored Isaac and Bronca for immigration, were also at the party. Sylvia was a relative of Isaac's.

Reva was bursting with enthusiasm and love. She gave a toast to her parents, calling them "two of the most wonderful people on earth." From behind me, I overheard a woman say to another guest, "I've known her all her life. She would never hurt a fly."

That was Reva—the most gentle, self-effacing, and compassionate person I have ever known. Her care and love for others, as well as her instinctive tact in dealing with them, seem today to me almost supernatural. Divine would be the better word. As a convert to Christianity, I can grasp through Reva the concept that Jesus was fully human and fully divine. Reva was fully human yet divinity was in her. "A light shined from her," as a friend and neighbor expressed it after her death.

In later years, I would sometimes ask Reva how she acquired so much love. She would joke that she had been given love shots as a child.

Perhaps it was not altogether a joke. Of course she didn't receive injections or potions. Our love was not a *Tristan und Isolde* derivative, except that all love has a magic love potion element. How else to explain it? But the Paterson Jewish community of Holocaust survivors and their children, in which Reva grew up, was close-knit and caring, from the stories Reva told me. And having a brother five years older gave Reva a sense of subordination, but admiring and loving subordination. Reva had no sense of entitlement. Throughout my life, I have known many self-important people, at Columba University and elsewhere. But Reva was not like them at all. I once suggested to her that she Google herself. This was after she had earned her MSW and was working as a social worker. She looked at the floor. "I'm nobody," she said in a low voice.

That close-knit community of Holocaust survivors also had horrific stories, too horrific to tell to a child. Reva heard them from her mother. Reva never knew her grandparents. Her maternal grandfather died of natural causes before the war. The others were killed by the Nazis. Reva liked the fact that I had a large, extended family.

She was people-oriented. Her stimulus for living was her contact with others. I asked her once why she first wanted to take piano lessons as a child. She smiled, remembering something lovely and long ago, and told me that (a girl in Paterson whose name I forget) had a piano in her home and that she (Reva) always liked it. In Reva's case, a person, not hearing music, was mentioned first.

She was a gentle, sweet, compassionate, and caring woman. But there was a dark side.

A rabbi who knew Reva told me when we were dating that Reva had tremendous love that she had saved up. I was the lucky recipient of that love. She gave me her whole heart. But Reva also saved up anger. She had been conditioned from childhood not to express negative emotions. Reading her journals after her death, I find many entries about events that I wished she had discussed with me. I would have had a deeper understanding of her and more guidance on how to respond to her sometimes erratic states.

The manic, often angry, episodes began when she was in high school. Some of the most dangerous ones she told me about. They occurred before I met her.

There was the time she abandoned her car in traffic on the West Side Highway. She began walking toward Midtown Manhattan and some guy offered her a ride and she got into his car. She was sane enough to realize she had made a mistake, and she jumped out of the moving car in the middle of traffic. It may have been on this occasion that she tried to walk the catwalk through the Lincoln Tunnel to New Jersey. She was lucky. A man she said was a detective picked her up and drove her home to the residence in New Jersey where she was then living. The psychiatrist promptly put her in a psych ward.

Once, following one of our seven breakups before marriage, she tore down the partitions in the office where she was working. The psych ward again.

In a manic state, while we were living in Rutherford, she was almost hit by a car in the early morning. Her glasses came off in the street. We spent much of the later morning looking for them but could not find them.

After she had earned her MSW, she worked three days a week for Liberty Healthcare in Jersey City. She took our car to work, as her job involved setting up social services for clients throughout Hudson County. But one morning, she drove into Jersey City at about 4:00 a.m. while I was sleeping, parked on a side street and waited for her office to open at 9:00. She told me that she was observed by some rough looking men who began moving toward the car. Again, she was sane enough to become scared and drive away.

Some of her manic episodes were accompanied by angry, verbal attacks on me. Unfortunately, her parents, especially her mother, had trained her not to express anger. As a result, it smoldered inside her until it exploded. She never learned from her parents how to release negative emotions in small increments and into creative channels.

These manic episodes occurred less often after we married. They usually lasted two or three days. We discussed what triggered them and determined that they often followed prolonged lack of sleep. The Westside Highway episode, she said, occurred in the summer when she had drunk a large amount of iced tea and slept little the night before. Therefore, I always tried to ensure that she had the conditions for sufficient sleep.

CHAPTER FOURTEEN

TURQUOISE

After I left the Jersey City Public Library in March 1989, I worked at a variety of jobs, some full-time and some part-time. I worked for several months for a library temp agency that sent me to the South Plainfield Public Library, an hour's drive each way on the Garden State Parkway. I had not yet begun to suffer from the agoraphobia that made it impossible for me to drive on the Parkway alone. I worked as a substitute public school teacher and as a telemarketer, but only business-to-business telemarketing. I didn't call people at their homes except for a few weeks when I worked for the *New York Times*, whose telemarketing department was located in Hackensack. I did fund raising and sold subscriptions for the New Jersey Symphony out of the old Robert Treat Hotel in downtown Newark, and I worked as a telemarketer for the publisher Prentice Hall in Englewood Cliffs. Reva worked as a clerk-typist for companies in Saddle Brook and Fort Lee.

In the late summer of 1990, while I was working for Prentice Hall, a coworker informed me that with a master's degree in English I could teach as an adjunct professor. I had not known this. I called William Paterson College (today, William Paterson University) and Kean College (today, Kean University), went for interviews, and was hired by both schools for the fall 1990 semester. At William Paterson, I was assigned a section of introduction to literature and a section of freshman writing, both morning classes. Two afternoons a week I drove down the Parkway to Kean College in Union, New Jersey, where I taught one section of freshman remedial writing.

Reva was working at this time as a customer service representative at a camping and outdoor store on Route 17. Her job was to take orders for merchandise on the phone. This was before the Internet was widespread, and customers throughout the country would call in orders to the business, which distributed its catalog nationwide.

Reva enjoyed talking to people from all regions of the country. She would invariably start the conversation by asking about the weather. But the business had a diverse group of employees, and Reva occasionally heard anti-Semitic remarks. One day, one of the other customer service reps said to her, "We're gonna get you." The next day when I picked her up from work, she was crying. The employees brought in their own coffee cups. The cups were kept in a common area with the employee's name on his or her cup. When Reva took her coffee break and began to drink the coffee, she smelled feces. Someone or several of these riff-raffs had apparently contaminated her cup. We went straight to the Paramus Police Department and reported the incident to a muscular, young detective, who, I remember, kept knotting his fists while we told the story, as if he wanted to punch someone. But we had no proof nor did we know who was responsible. The detective said that one of the Paramus police officers worked part-time on the floor of the store and would keep his ears open. And there we had to leave it. Reva quit the job. More importantly, she did not get sick.

I taught my courses at William Paterson and Kean. I had never taught before in a university, and I had some rude and disrespectful students at William Paterson, particularly in the introduction to literature class. The students were freshmen who had not adequately transitioned from high school to college. They seemed to have the attitude that, having paid tuition, they deserved an A. I have been teaching as an adjunct professor on and off now for more than thirty years and can say that students today are more respectful, or maybe I have become a better teacher. But I had some nasty and obnoxious students at William Paterson in the fall of 1990.

I teach at William Paterson at this writing, in 2021, and although I live in Hackensack and in 1990 lived in Elmwood Park, I take the same route to get to the school. As I approach the campus from Haledon Avenue, I pass Camp Veritans, a wooded tract that was once a day camp serving the Paterson YM-YWHA. As a child, Reva attended Camp Veritans. As I would drive past this tract in 1990 on my way to teach the rude, disrespectful students whose behavior was on a junior high school level, if that advanced, I would think of gentle, sweet Reva who hungered for a college education but was denied one by her parents, and I would become deeply sad. I would think of the words from a sixties rock song, "We want the world and we want it now." They typified, I thought, the attitude of some of the students I taught at William Paterson in the fall of 1990, young people with a grand sense of entitlement, surprising for students in a state college. Reva, by contrast, had no sense of entitlement. I am comforted today in my grief knowing that Reva ultimately received an excellent education and began a professional career, cut short, alas, because of the poison implanted in her by her parents and the demonic doctors who kept her on lithium for eighteen years, enabling Bronca to realize her ambition that Reva replicate the suffering of Holocaust victims.

When Reva was attending Camp Veritans as a child, a live rattlesnake was found in a bunkhouse. A counselor killed the snake, smashing its head with a shovel. The turquoise-colored poison spilled from the snake's fangs onto the floor of the bunkhouse. The experience created a dislike and even fear in Reva for the rest of her life of the color turquoise.

Neither William Paterson nor Kean rehired me. From 1990 to 1995, I worked at many jobs and I can only approximate the chronological order. I worked in the classical music department of a new Tower Records store on Route 17. I worked as an adjunct professor and as a public-school substitute teacher, and I worked for my uncle and cousin, owners of Prozys Army and Navy in Hackensack. The business was founded by my grandfather in the 1920s and remained a family business for more than eighty years, into the third generation of ownership, until it closed in 2004, when Milton, my uncle, and Ted, his son, sold the property. My grandfather and his three sons, Milton, Henry and Sanford, my father, co-owned the business. But my father died in 1961 at age forty-nine, and at his death his share of ownership passed to the surviving partners. According to my mother, she and her three children received nothing.

The store was a Main Street Hackensack fixture from the time when Main Street was the business hub of Bergen County. When it closed, the *New York Times* ran an article about it in its business section. Over the years, when I couldn't find other work, or during the summers when I was in college, I worked as a salesman in the business, which had expanded to several stores. Although I had no share in ownership, I got free apparel, and the rugged, warm clothing and footwear from Prozys got me through many cold winters. I worked there for several months as a salesman in the early 1990s at seven dollars an hour with no benefits.

Reva and I had by then moved from Elmwood Park. Mrs. Wynosky, who legally could have simply given us thirty days' notice, hired a lawyer to evict us. We found another two-family house in Fair Lawn, but the deal fell through at the last minute. When moving day came, we had nowhere to go, so we temporarily moved into Reva's parents' house, storing our belongings in their basement.

To her parents' credit, they accepted the inconvenience uncomplainingly. At the time, her father was becoming increasingly disabled from Parkinson's disease.

We remained in her parents' home for only a few weeks. We then found an apartment in Rutherford at 130 Orient Way, Apartment 3L.

The rent was $850 a month. It was a two-bedroom apartment; the second bedroom became my office.

We lived in that apartment for sixteen years, and they were the most productive and fulfilling years of our marriage, indeed, of our lives. But they were also the years that marked the beginning of the decline of Reva's health.

CHAPTER FIFTEEN

ROUTE 280

The thought of Reva and the possibility that I might never see her again saved my life in the early years of our marriage.

In 1992, when we had been married four years, I was hired to teach two courses for the fall semester at Seton Hall University in South Orange, New Jersey and one course at what was then Jersey City State College. (It is now New Jersey City University.) The Seton Hall courses met back-to-back four mornings a week from 8:00 to 10:00; the Jersey City State course, two afternoons a week beginning at noon.

The drive from Rutherford to South Orange takes about a half hour on the Garden State Parkway. But my agoraphobia had set in and precluded me from taking the Parkway or any road where there were no people, stores, gas stations, or phone booths on the roadside. So I took an alternate route, driving through Belleville, Newark, and East Orange. This drive took about an hour.

Nevertheless, my plan was to take Route 280 from South Orange to Jersey City on the days I taught at Jersey City State. Route 280 is a busy, multilane highway that runs from the Oranges through Newark and the industrialized swamp known as the Hackensack Meadowlands. For reasons I cannot explain, my agoraphobia allowed the highway spurt from South Orange to Jersey City.

There are at least two other routes from the Oranges to Jersey City. I could have driven though city traffic to Newark and taken the Pulaski Skyway, immortalized by Philip Roth in *Portnoy's Complaint*. Another route was to drive to Newark and then north to the Bergen/Hudson County border and take the Belleville Turnpike, a largely unpaved road though the Hackensack Meadowlands to Jersey City.

On a very hot morning in early September, I taught my first classes at Seton Hall. By ten, when I had finished, the temperature was already close to 90. I pulled out of the Seton Hall parking lot and onto Route 280 and headed east to Jersey City. I had a brand-new Toyota Corolla, which Isaac and Bronca bought for Reva and me as a gift so I could continue to work, my old car having died. If all went well, I would be in Jersey City in twenty minutes.

All did not go well.

As I drove, I realized I had no drinking water in the car, so I pulled off 280 in downtown Newark to buy a bottle of water. But I could not locate a grocery store, so I drove over a bridge across the Passaic River to East Newark, a small industrial town with the reputation of having a bar on every street corner.

I went into one and bought a quart of off-brand cold cola, returned to my car, drove back to Newark, and pulled onto the ramp to Route 280.

Some of my phobias had a physical basis. I had a fear of chemical fumes. However, I had been overexposed to chlorine in the 1980s. The details are unimportant for this memoir, but for months afterward I could not be near chlorine in bleach or any other form. In fact, I could not even walk down a supermarket aisle containing cleaning products without becoming faint. This was not a phobia but a toxicity, and my doctors assured me that if I stayed away from chlorine products, the toxicity would gradually leave my body.

But in the 1990s the physical reaction to a specific toxin, chlorine, had exfoliated into phobias involving other chemicals. Even today, if I smell an unfamiliar odor, I become anxious.

I drove up the ramp with the cold cola and back onto Route 280 East when, about half a mile ahead, I saw a mountain of compacted garbage on the side of the highway. Hundreds of cars sped past it without their drivers giving it heed, but as I approached it, I began to feel faint. I knew that methane gas was being harvested from the Meadowlands. Methane is an odorless, invisible, deadly gas, similar in its effects on the body to carbon monoxide. I was hypersensitive to chemicals. I could not approach that mountain.

I was not far from the ramp and backed my car onto the shoulder.

My plan was to back off 280 using the shoulder and take the Belleville Turnpike to Jersey City. But to my horror I saw that the shoulder narrowed and ended. Cars and trucks traveling at high speeds were racing from the ramp onto the highway where they joined two lanes of traffic already on the highway. I was trapped. I could not back off, and I could not go forward.

I was safe as long as I stayed within the white line boundary of the shoulder. I got out of the car and smelled the air. It was vile, but I did not feel faint. The car was fine. I was in trouble

It is important to note that in the early 1990s cell phones were in their infancy. Few people had them. I did not.

I got back in the car. It was very hot and there was no shade on the open highway, which was elevated above the Meadowlands. Periodically, I turned on the car's air conditioner but never left it on long, as I did not want the car to overheat. If I had not stopped for the cola, which I now sipped slowly, I might have fainted from dehydration. I watched the traffic, hoping to see a police car, but none came.

Hundreds of cars sped past me but none stopped. I didn't know if I would die on that ramp. The thought that I could was real, that this morning, in the hot sun on Route 280, was the last morning of my life. And it almost was.

I noticed that many tow trucks were traveling east toward Jersey City. I got out of my car and hailed one. It stopped on the shoulder in front of my car. There was no room for it to stop behind me. I was backed almost to the end of the shoulder.

A large, bulky man got out of the truck followed by a younger man. I explained my predicament. The large man said the younger man, his son, would drive my car past the mountain to the U-turn and return on the other side of the highway, where he would pick me up. He said that I could dash across 280 to the other side, and he would go with me as far as the concrete divider and then dash back to his truck.

I could tell he was nervous. Three lanes of traffic roared by and three lanes roared in the opposite direction on the other side of the concrete divider, where I would wait for a gap in the traffic, that is, if I made it to the divider.

I remembered years before traveling on a bus when traffic was stalled on a highway because a teenager had tried to dash across and was killed.

But I seemed to have no choice. I had to get out of the trap. I got ready and crouched in a sprinter's position, as did the bulky man, who looked too heavy to run fast, and watched for an opening in the traffic.

Then I seemed to see Reva's sweet face in the sky, and I knew I might never see her again.

I rose from the sprinter's position. "No," I said to the bulky man. "Go on. When you reach Jersey City, call the police and tell them I'm stranded."

I returned to my car and waited for a police car, but none came. I hailed another tow truck. Again, two men emerged. This time I got in the truck and asked the driver to turn on the air conditioning full blast, which he did. We drove past the garbage mountain to the U-turn and back to Newark. The other man followed in my car. Fortunately, I had enough cash to pay them. I was safe and I had my car. Never before or since have I felt like kissing the pavement of Newark, the city of my birth.

But hours had gone by, and I had missed my first class at Jersey City State. I called the college from a phone booth and explained that I'd had car trouble. "Oh" said the receptionist. "Classes don't begin until next week."

I taught the semester at both colleges but always took the Belleville Turnpike to Jersey City.

I had been desperate enough to have almost attempted a mad dash across six lanes of speeding traffic. The vision of Reva saved me.

CHAPTER SIXTEEN

RUTHERFORD

Rutherford and the two Bergen County towns south of Rutherford, Lyndhurst and North Arlington, do not form a peninsula, unless one imagines Kearny, just south of North Arlington and the beginning of Hudson County, as a body of water. It isn't.

But this sliver of towns in the far southwestern corner of Bergen County, bordered to the west by the Passaic River and the east by the Hackensack Meadowlands and the Hackensack River, was, for Reva and me, our own strip of land to grow in. Ridge Road, which begins in Rutherford and ends at the Kearny border, forms the spine of the imagined peninsula, which is detached geographically and, in our case, psychologically, from the rest of Bergen County and the poisonous homes in which we both grew up.

In Rutherford, our marriage deepened and our achievements enlarged. We lived in Rutherford for half of our thirty-two-year marriage.

Rutherford is a town permeated by poetry owing to the spirit of William Carlos Williams, who was born and raised in Rutherford and practiced medicine and wrote the poems and short stories in the big house at 9 Ridge Road that established him as one of the major American writers of the twentieth century.

I first read Williams's poems and his autobiography when I was fifteen. When we first moved to Rutherford, I would occasionally see Williams's son on the street, but I never approached him. He was an elderly doctor who still practiced medicine in the office attached to the house. After his death, however, Reva and I visited the house and met the son's widow, who was the poet's daughter-in-law.

My plan to visit the house involved a bit of subterfuge that proved unnecessary.

After the son's death, the house was put up for sale. I called the realtor intending to pose as a prospective buyer. But during the call, I confessed to being an English teacher who just wanted to go inside. The realtor conferred with Mrs. Williams, who gave permission. There had been many visitors over the years since the poet's death, Mrs. Williams told Reva and me, but we may well be the last. In fact, the house was sold shortly after our visit.

We got a tour from the realtor, who showed us the attic room where the poet wrote many of his poems and stories. There were numerous carved duck decoys stored in the attic. I know nothing about their history.

During Williams's life, many literary luminaries visited the house. Ezra Pound stayed there after his release from St. Elizabeth's State Hospital until he relocated to Italy, where he spent the rest of his life. Conrad Aiken was married in the living room, and Williams recounts in his autobiography how Maxwell Bodenheim faked a broken leg to escape New York City and rest awhile in Rutherford.

There were several modern paintings in the living room, including a reproduction of the famous *I Saw the Figure 5 in Gold* by Charles Demuth based on Williams's poem "The Great Figure."

Poetry seemed to be in the air of Rutherford when we first moved there, at least to me. Even the names of the streets seemed poetic: *Highland Cross. Summit Cross.*

Soon after we moved to Rutherford, Reva began taking courses in earnest at Bergen Community College. She had taken a few courses before I met her and received credit for some. But now she went on a regular basis, taking two courses per semester in the evening, and courses in the summer. She received her Associate of Arts degree in 1995. While she was attending Bergen, she worked full-time by day in an office in Fort Lee.

One incident stands out that demonstrates Reva's resilience, courage, and determination.

We had one car at the time, which we shared. It was midwinter, and

Reva drove to Bergen for an evening class. While she was at school, it began snowing.

Following a previous snowfall, I had attempted to push off an accumulation of snow from the front windshield using the windshield wipers. The snow was heavy and the attempt broke the wipers' motor. So our car had no functioning windshield wipers. It wasn't the wiper blades that needed to be replaced, but the wiper motor, and I couldn't afford to replace it.

Cell phones were still in their infancy and neither of us had one. By the time Reva's class let out, it was snowing heavily. I worried and waited for her in the apartment, fearing that I would get a call from the police that she had been in an accident.

But about a half hour after the time she would usually return home, she arrived safely. She had driven from the college to Rutherford, a distance of about twelve miles, in the snow without windshield wipers. She stopped periodically to brush off snow from the front windshield.

Her abilities and strengths were given no recognition by her family, nor her doctors, nor her guidance counselor at high school, and she was hardly aware of them herself. Yet by her actions, I know that she believed in herself.

During our early years in Rutherford, from approximately 1991 to 1997, I continued working at a variety of jobs. I returned briefly to the library profession, working as a reference librarian in the West New York Public Library. I was a public-school substitute teacher in several districts. I worked for a tutoring agency and tutored two young Japanese brothers in Demarest and a Korean boy in Palisades Park. In 1995, I began teaching in both the English and the Communication departments of Fairleigh Dickenson University in Teaneck, a job I held, with an interruption of a few years, for ten years. I also taught as an adjunct in the Communication and English departments at other colleges and universities, including Hudson County College, Essex County College, Bergen Community College, and Montclair State University. However, I held some of these positions in the late 1990s and 2000s.

In 1995 I was hired to work in the membership department of the Commerce and Industry Association of New Jersey, a regional chamber of commerce located in Paramus. It was a part- time job, four hours a day, for which I was paid a base salary and commission. My job was to make cold phone calls to various North Jersey businesses to try to arrange a meeting with me or, more often, one of the other reps, to interest the company in joining the association. The Commerce and Industry Association published the magazine *Commerce*, to which I later contributed some articles. I worked for the association for about two years, and the job led to a major change in my life.

CHAPTER SEVENTEEN

UP THE MOUNTAIN

Commerce and Industry used cold-call telemarketing to recruit potential members, but the association was legitimate. Local town chambers of commerce were members, as were many large-and-medium-sized businesses and not-for-profits, including universities and hospitals. The association promoted the businesses of its members and, in general, promoted free enterprise.

My supervisor, the director of the membership department, Daphne Bonita, was a former nurse and teacher of special needs children. She told me that one of her pupils had murdered his mother.

The association held meet-and-greets on and off location. Daphne did not object when I did a little personal networking during my phone calls.

One of the business owners I tried to recruit was William Cohen, publisher of the *Bergen News* and *Sun Bulletin*, weekly newspapers that covered the eastern edge of Bergen County.

Cohen was not interested in joining, but he seemed to be a friendly though reserved man. He was in his seventies and a lawyer turned publisher. I became bold and asked him how I could get a job as a stringer, a part-time newspaper reporter paid per story. "Come here," he said.

Cohen and his editor, Eleanor Marra, interviewed me at the newspaper's office in the town of Palisades Park. They asked me to report on a Rutherford Council meeting. Rutherford was not one of the towns their newspapers covered, and the assignment was not for publication but to see how well I reported. I did not get paid for it.

I was lucky the night of the council meeting. A group of neighbors were protesting a rooming house in town and the men who lived there. I had something substantial to write about.

I wrote my story and was hired to cover Teaneck Council meetings. The council met on alternate Tuesday evenings, and a meeting could easily end after 11:00. My deadline was Wednesday at noon, so I learned early on to write fast. I was too tired to write the story when I returned home to Rutherford, but wrote it the following morning, often at Commerce and Industry before my four-hour shift began at noon. I would then fax it to the newspaper. Before long, I added Leonia and Bogota council meetings to my coverage.

I can recall only a few occasions in my life when I have cried tears of joy. One of those was when I picked up my Columbia BA diploma with Honors in English printed on it. (I picked it up at the registrar's office. Nobody I knew was interested in attending my commencement, so I did not attend it myself.) Another occasion was when I saw my first story with byline on the front page of the *Sun Bulletin*. The *Sun Bulletin* was a "legal" newspaper, that is, it published legal notices, which were a major source of its revenue. A legal newspaper in New Jersey has to have a subscription and newsstand price. The *Sun Bulletin* cost fifty cents, and I picked up my first copy at a grocery store in Ridgefield Park, one of the towns the paper covered.

So at this time in our lives, approximately 1995, I was working for the Commerce and Industry Association part-time and as a stringer for the *Sun Bulletin*.

Reva, having earned her AA, was accepted by Montclair State University to continue the last two years for her BA.

Instead of taking several years to earn her BA as a part-time student, she decided to attend Montclair full-time. She got a partial tuition scholarship and borrowed money from student loan programs. The loans also covered our living expenses and, for a while, we had financial stability. Reva left her full-time job at the Fort Lee office but took a part-time evening job as a saleswoman in the bra department of Sears in the Paramus Park Mall. That mall was within walking distance of the office building in Paramus where Commerce and Industry was located, so we continued to manage with one car. Reva would often visit me at work before she began her shift at Sears, and she got to know Daphne and other people in the office.

She was a zealous student. Earning her BA, going to school

full-time, was the realization of a dream long deferred. I can still see her sitting on the couch in our living room studying for hours at a time, her mind thoroughly engaged. She was so high on learning, in fact, that for the first time since she was eighteen and spent a summer in Israel, she was able to go off all psychiatric medications. School supplied the real-world stabilization, stimulus, and purpose. She was off medication for about six months. At that time, she was a patient of Dr. Gerald Appel, a nephrologist at Columbia Presbyterian Hospital in Manhattan, whom Joe Brezin had recommended, and I would drive her in for her appointments. Dr. Appel was happy that she was off psychiatric drugs. Even though her kidneys had been permanently damaged by lithium, we had hope that she would never need dialysis.

However, during a period of stress, she had an emotional breakdown. I recall this was after the semester ended. She was put back on depekote.

She was a psychology major. However, she took an acting class and a singing class for non-music majors, and she sang in the Montclair State Chorus.

Montclair State has a reputation for its performing arts programs, and almost all the other students in the chorus, which was a graded credit course, were music majors. I once suggested to Reva that she might consider dropping the chorus and instead taking an additional psychology course. "That would rob me of my soul," she said.

She continued to sing in the chorus, which performed both on and off campus. She sang in Handel's *Messiah* and Carl Orff's *Carmina Burana*, among other works.

I remember listening to her rehearse a speech she had chosen for her acting class. This was from the last act of *A Doll House* by Ibsen. She read Nora's words to Torvald with anger and fury. There are other ways to approach this speech, but Reva emptied her anger into it.

While she was a student at Montclair, I applied for an adjunct position in the English Department. My interview for the fall semester was in the late summer, and Reva drove me to it, as she was familiar with the campus, which is located on a mountain and sprawls through parts of two counties and three towns.

As she drove up the mountain, she sang exuberantly, "She'll be

Coming Round the Mountain When She Comes." I gathered that she sang this often as she drove to school. It was her expression of joy at being a student, that finally, after years of being thwarted by her family and psychiatrists, she was able to use her God-given gifts and have a normal life.

Then she turned to me and said in her sweet, gentle voice, "It's my mountain, but I'll share it with you."

CHAPTER EIGHTEEN

GRADUATION

I was hired by the Montclair State College (now University) English Department to teach a section of introduction to literature and a section of freshman writing. This was not the first time I taught in a college where Reva was a student. I had done so at Bergen. Of course, she was never in any of my classes.

I was not rehired by the English Department for the spring semester, but I was also teaching public speaking at Fairleigh Dickinson University and was hired by the Montclair State Speech Communication Department, where I taught for four years, including three years after Reva graduated.

Although Reva was a psychology major, she took a broad liberal arts program. She had studied French in high school and at Bergen. At Montclair she took German. She did well and found the language easy, she said, because of its similarity to Yiddish, which is a Germanic dialect. She also took courses in philosophy, history, and, as I mentioned, the performing arts.

One of her most difficult courses was statistics, which she took at three different schools: Bergen; Montclair, for her psychology major; and NYU, for her MSW. I am thankful that I, as a humanities major, was spared statistics. Some of my friends from years back described to me their struggles with this subject.

Reva's professor for statistics was Katherine Ellison, who also taught a course in human sexuality, which Reva took.

Reva described how, on the first day of class, Dr. Ellison had all the students, most of whom were women, shout out, "penis." I wondered why they weren't also required to shout out, "vagina." Perhaps they were.

Reva developed a close relationship with Dr. Ellison after she graduated, which continued until Reva's death. In addition to being a full professor of psychology, Dr. Ellison was an ordained Presbyterian minister and pastor at a small church in Woodridge. She lived in neighboring Hasbrouck Heights.

Reva seemed to have a need for a nurturing older woman. Her mother had been incapable of nurturing.

I have never forgotten a question asked me by the Mill Pond psychologist, Robert T., when I was dating Reva and we were contemplating marriage. He asked it in an almost off-hand manner, "Can you nurture?" I was taken aback at the time. I associated nurturing with women, but I never forgot that question.

After our marriage, Reva saw LCSWs for psychotherapy. But until we were married, her only "mental health" treatments had been medication/poison. I think she may have also had ECT (electric convulsive therapy or, conventionally, electric shock treatment) in her teens or early twenties. As far as I know, she had no counseling until we married.

In choosing a psychotherapist, Reva sought what she called a "wise woman." She formed friendships with older women like Dr. Ellison and Laura B., her supervisor on her last job as a social worker. This, I believe, was an attempt to compensate for her mother's deficient parenting.

I, too, suffered from the lack of same sex-parental guidance. My father was a violent and abusive man, a tyrant demanding absolute, often irrational, control. He was unfit for fatherhood, and I left home to escape him at seventeen without finishing high school. I did not return to live in that house until after his death.

Long after Reva had completed her degree, after she had earned her MSW, she and I and Dr. Ellison, who was divorced, sometimes went out for dinner. On occasion, we were joined by Rev. Donald Pitches, now retired, but the long-time pastor of the First Presbyterian Church of Carlstadt. Dr. Ellison had trained for the ministry under Rev. Pitches.

I had gotten to know Rev. Pitches on my own as I continued my journalism career. In 1997, I left the *Sun Bulletin* to join the *South*

Bergenite, a weekly published by North Jersey Newspapers, publisher of the daily *Herald News* and many weeklies throughout Bergen and Passaic counties. (In 1998 North Jersey Newspapers was acquired by North Jersey Media Group, publisher of the *Record*, the Bergen County daily.)

I covered Carlstadt for the *South Bergenite* from 1998 to 2005. Pitches was active in the town and had served at various times on the board of education, the library board of trustees, and the volunteer fire department. He sometimes referred to himself, not as the pastor of the First Presbyterian Church, but as the pastor of Carlstadt. Reva and I formed a friendship with Pitches, who sometimes visited us in our Rutherford apartment. Long before I was baptized, Pitches anointed us both in our home using olive oil. He made the sign of the cross on my forehead, knowing my sympathies, and may have done the same on Reva's, but he anointed me in the name of Jesus. He said verses from the 23rd Psalm when he anointed Reva.

Some years before this occasion, when Reva was in the University of Pennsylvania Hospital following an unsuccessful kidney transplant that had disastrous consequences, she was deeply moved by a phone call from Rev. Pitches and a prayer he said for her.

The story of Reva's unsuccessful transplant will be told subsequently.

Reva graduated *cum laude* from Montclair in May 1998. Her brother came up alone from Pennsylvania for the commencement ceremony, which was held in the Meadowlands Arena, then home of the New Jersey Nets and New Jersey Devils. He and I were Reva's only guests.

After the ceremony, as we walked across the parking lot crowded with graduates and their families, Reva, in her cap and gown, demonstrated a rare moment of pride, flipping the colored tassel, which designated her as an honors graduate and which had fallen behind her cap, to the front.

She had withstood the assault on her life by her parents and psychiatrists and graduated college at the age of forty-six.

Reva continued to work at Sears through the summer and had begun the process of applying to graduate schools of social work in the spring. She was accepted by NYU, Fordham, Rutgers, and Kean.

She chose NYU, largely because of its reputation for training future therapists. Reva aspired to become an LCSW, a social worker licensed to practice psychotherapy.

She resigned from her job at Sears and, in the late summer, I accompanied her on the subway to show her how to get to NYU.

When Reva graduated from Montclair in May 1998, I was working as a stringer for the *South Bergenite*, which was headquartered in Rutherford and covered five towns in southern Bergen County, as well as Kearny in Hudson County.

I was assigned East Rutherford as my beat but was not limited to council meetings, so I often had several bylines each week. I was also permitted to write features outside of East Rutherford.

After a few months, the editor of the *South Bergenite* left and the managing editor became editor. I was then promoted to a steady part-time position for twenty hours a week at a straight salary but without benefits. My beat now included both East Rutherford and Carlstadt. So I covered news and features of two municipalities, three boards of education (East Rutherford and Carlstadt both have K–8 districts and send their high school students to Becton Regional High School), and two police blotters. The only work I didn't do, which kept my job part-time, was editing and layout. Those came later when I became full-time in 2002.

I was also teaching at Fairleigh Dickinson, and I had begun writing articles for the trade magazine *ANSOM* (an acronym for Army and Navy Store and Outdoor Merchandiser). I wrote two articles a month for *ANSOM* from 1997 until 2012, when it ceased publication.

By such means, with Reva's student loans, including those she received while at NYU, we managed financially.

CHAPTER NINETEEN

FORDHAM ESSAY

Below, in Reva's own words, is an essay she wrote as part of her application to the Fordham University School of Social Work. The essay required responses to specific questions.

* * *

Q. How did you become interested in social work? What experiences—personal, educational or professional—caused or confirmed your interest in social work? If you considered or were involved in another field before choosing social work, what were your reasons for such a change?

A. My interest in social work originates from my satisfaction helping people. I worked in three nursing homes in New Jersey as a recreation aid, a job that included playing the piano. Whenever I played and saw that people were enjoying themselves and sometimes sang along, I felt very good because their lives were brightened a little. I also worked for the Health and Welfare Council of Bergen County and for a while answered the crisis line. I have also volunteered for the Jewish Family Service and helped a new Russian immigrant family to get around Bergen County, New Jersey.

    The study of psychology has helped me to understand human nature better. Increasing this knowledge and applying it to the field of social work would give me the background to help people, a background for dealing with many types of people.

    For over twenty years, I worked full-time as an office worker. Although the employment enabled me to attend college part-time, it did not provide much personal satisfaction. I decided to complete my education by going to school full-time and working part-time. I would like to pursue a career in which I can use my educational background and my skills in working with people. Social work will permit me to fulfill these goals.

Q. How have your family experiences and relationships contributed to your interest in Social Work?

A. My mother is an altruistic person. She taught my brother and me to help others whenever possible. My brother is a medical doctor today. My mother understood much about other people and how to help them. She once nursed an elderly neighbor back to health. Her charity to people in need has given me a beautiful role model. My parents emigrated from Europe after World War II and settled in Paterson, New Jersey. I grew up in this city, which had a large minority and working-class population. Exposure and contact with many different types of people from an early age have given me a background for dealing with many types of people.

Q. What are your reasons for deciding to pursue graduate Social Work studies at this time? What expectations do you have for graduate education? What areas of difficulty do you anticipate, if any?

A. I will be graduating Montclair State University this May, and I would like to continue my education this September without any delay in order to have more time at working as a professional social worker.

I expect to learn more about therapy and how to help people in all kinds of life situations, such as substance abuse, poverty, mental illness and homelessness. I would like to learn to help people take control of their lives and help themselves. I would like to learn how to refer people to the proper agencies to expedite their receiving aid.

I've learned over the years that I've been working that there are sometimes a few difficult people to work with. This may also happen with difficult clients. I'm sure my education will prepare me to handle certain difficult people and situations.

Q. Discuss those personal qualities and abilities you feel will be helpful to you in the social service profession.

A. I am an empathetic person and a good listener. I have a strong interest in helping people help themselves.

Q. Discuss your career interests and goals. Which area of social work practice do you intend to pursue? As a graduate to social work, how would you contribute to achieving the goals of the social work profession?

A. I would like to learn about all of the options open to me in the field of social work before I decide to pursue a particular path. However, I am very interested in abnormal psychology and child psychology. I would like to learn about the needs in communities and about the various places social workers work before I decide. As a graduate, I would love to get a job that would enrich and help heal other people.

Q. Discuss briefly a current social issue that is relevant to the practice of social work.

A. An issue that concerns social workers today is detecting child abuse and determining what kind of intervention need be taken. Social workers, after investigating a case of child abuse or neglect, can first educate the parents or caretakers. For example, social workers can help them find appropriate day-care so children wouldn't be left alone. Education of parents about day-care or other services may be all that is needed to correct the situation. If severe child abuse has been substantiated, the removal of the child from the home is necessary to protect the child.

* * *

Reva describes her parents as wonderful people, but she always had trouble articulating her anger at her parents. Her former therapist told me that whenever Reva began to express criticism of her family, she (Reva) would quickly veer to another topic.

But she knew in her heart how much her family had hurt her. She told me on a number of occasions that her mother had choked her, and for a long time I believed she was describing a physical incident. But then Reva explained that it was a metaphor. Her mother had never laid hands on her throat but had emotionally choked self-expression out of her. Reva, as a child, teenager, and young adult, was never allowed to verbalize anger. This forced repression accounted for so much of her difficulties.

In Reva's journal from 2014, there is in an entry on her mother's birthday (her mother died in 1999), in which Reva wrote that her mother is watching over her. But in an entry a week later, she writes of giving her parents the middle finger in the next world.

CHAPTER TWENTY

NYU

Reva began NYU full-time in the fall of 1998. We continued to live in the Rutherford apartment. I worked at three part-time jobs: I covered East Rutherford and Carlstadt for the *South Bergenite* and was paid for a twenty-hour work week; I taught in the English and Communication departments at Fairleigh Dickinson University and the Communication Department at Montclair State University; and I wrote two articles a month for the trade magazine *ANSOM*. The two teaching jobs alone were equivalent to a full-time job. I was constantly working. The *South Bergenite* office was located across from a park opposite the Rutherford Municipal Building, but I did most of my work from home, which was three blocks away, although sometimes I worked in the office. I usually put the stories on floppy disks and brought them to the office on Friday mornings. Friday was deadline and layout day, but as a part-timer, I was not involved in layout.

Those months seem a blur. For me, work. For Reva, school. Hardly anything else.

At NYU, social work students, beginning with the second semester, worked as interns two days a week and took classes the other three. Reva was assigned an internship at the SERV Center, a mental health residency program based in Secaucus, New Jersey. The internship and her first year at NYU seemed to have been successful, although I have discovered a note written in my journal for that year saying that Reva seemed lonely and unhappy. I think her unhappiness arose from her loneliness. Reva was an older student, and she was a sociable person. I have often wondered why she chose to marry a loner like me. Occasionally, she swam in the NYU pool. Reva loved to swim. If she had one athletic outlet, it was swimming. She loved water. Years later, after she became disabled, she looked forward to aquatic therapy, although it exhausted her. This wasn't swimming, but at least it allowed her to get into the water.

I taught at Fairleigh Dickinson during the summer of 1999, and Reva studied Spanish there. She didn't have to pay tuition, as I was on the faculty. She also was hired as a full-time summer employee at the SERV Center, but she didn't like the conduct of some of the employees at staff meetings and resigned after a few weeks.

Her Spanish course at FDU was in the evening, as was one of the classes I taught. One evening, she was sitting on the steps outside a classroom building waiting for me to finish when she observed that a raccoon had approached her and was inches away. She screamed and the raccoon fled. Had the raccoon attacked her, or even licked her, she would have required rabies shots.

Soon after the beginning of the fall 1999 semester at NYU, Reva experienced severe menstrual pain and saw her gynecologist. An ultrasound revealed a mass. Surgery was necessary. Based on the ultrasound, the gynecologist suspected cancer. Reva took a leave of absence from NYU, dropping her fall courses. The gynecologist also ordered a CT scan which, he said, looked less suspicious for cancer. She had surgery at Valley Hospital in Ridgewood. The mass, which turned out to be benign, was removed, and after recovery from the surgery, she resumed her classes in the spring semester.

Her second internship in the spring 2001 was a disaster. She was assigned to a hospital for substance abusers in downtown Newark. She commuted to Newark from Rutherford by bus.

But the experience was traumatic because of poor supervision and a patient population that was incompatible with Reva's personality.

Her social work supervisor, whom I will call Josephine, bragged to Reva that when younger she had "mooned" a cop. I suppose recovering substance abusers may benefit from a tough love social worker. However, Reva had a poor relationship with Josephine, who gave her little supervision.

Reva's soft personality was more suited to caring for children, the elderly, and disabled patients. Still, she did not have a problem with the substance abuse patients. She conducted relaxation groups with them and arranged for out-patient placements. But the supervisor made her nervous and gave inadequate supervision. The issue is complicated and the details are unnecessary to go into here. But she did not get credit for the internship and was allowed to do another internship at Nutley Family Service in the summer of 2001, where she had better supervision and worked with clients on a one-on-one basis. She was allowed to participate in the graduation ceremonies in Washington Square Park in May, but her diploma was sent in the mail and the date of her graduation is September 2001, after she had completed the Nutley internship. I remember how happy she was when she received the diploma. She cried briefly from joy, but she quickly recovered from her tears. I don't know why she felt she could not express more joy and pride in her accomplishment. Perhaps she felt it would be disloyal to her mother. The last thing her parents ever expected of her was that she would earn a master's degree. Her mother, after all, had spent years grooming her to replicate the experience of Holocaust victims. I am looking at her master's degree now, which is framed and laminated and hanging with other degrees and certificates earned by both of us on a wall of the apartment where I now live alone. Let that degree give her parents the middle finger, wherever they are.

I was Reva's only guest at the graduation ceremony. I earned three degrees from Columbia University but never went to any of my graduations. The NYU graduation was a huge event, taking up the whole of Washington Square Park with trumpeters on the arch. Reva deserved nothing less. Afterward, I took some photos of Reva in cap and gown near the social work school. I was facing south when I photographed her. In the background of the photographs are the World Trade Center Towers. They would be gone in four months.

CHAPTER TWENTY-ONE

BONE OF MY BONES

If this memoir gives an incomplete description of Reva's personality, as it must, it is because for almost thirty-two years we were truly one flesh. She was part of me and I part of her. Her loss is a loss of myself. I can no more describe or define Reva than I can describe or define my inmost being. We became part of each other. But if there was one quality in her personality that best characterized her, it was her quiet presence.

She was always there to help me and to help others, but mostly to help me, sometimes by saying little or nothing—just by being there when I needed her.

Here is one incident among many:

I had been awake all night and all the following day, less from insomnia than from a terrible postnasal drip that prevented me from sleeping. I had a bad cold, but instead of a runny nose, the phlegm dripped back down my throat, making sleep impossible.

At about 10:00 p.m., after being awake for almost forty hours, I called my doctor to see if I should go to the emergency room, although I knew that what I needed most was a night's sleep, and for that the emergency room is the last place to go. Reva was lying in bed at the time, and I used our bedroom phone. My doctor called me back. She said that if I felt shortness of breath, I had a legitimate reason to go to the emergency room.

I didn't have shortness of breath. I didn't want to take Valium for sleep because I was afraid I might fall into a deep sleep and drown in my phlegm, and because Valium would have no effect on the production of phlegm. I was exhausted. I didn't know what to do. I decided to lie back in bed and think for a while. I put my head on the pillow. The next thing I knew it was six in the morning.

And there sleeping beside me was Reva. I knew that whatever I had to go through, she would always be there for me, although this time, it was simply her presence next to me in bed that calmed me so that I slept through the night. I had often said to her that she would walk on the ceiling to help me. Her love was, and is, the light that sustains me. If I didn't have that light, I would end my life.

Even before she became disabled, she would call me her carapace. I was the hard shell that protected her. She had been much hurt by the world. But in the end, my shell was too thin to save her.

I have never known anyone with more empathy for others than Reva. She told me about an incident that occurred when she was attending Fair Lawn High School. It was during the ten days between Rosh Hashanah and Yom Kippur, when Jews are supposed to seek forgiveness of anyone they have offended and to forgive those who have offended them. She knocked on the door of the home of one of the girls who had been bullying her, wanting to forgive her. The girl was alone in the house, vacuuming. To Reva's surprise, the girl was friendly to her, but before Reva left, the girl let Reva know that at school, she would continue to act toward her as she had before, as her friends did. As Reva described the bullying, it was verbal rather than physical: ridicule and taunts.

Reva took to heart the Jewish (and Christian and universal) teaching to forgive others. And so, she forgave people before her death, as is evident on the pages of her last journal written before she entered Holy Name Hospital in 2019, part of which is transcribed in Chapter 4. She seemed to have a sense of her impending death.

Reva loved me but there are two things that she especially enjoyed about me. One was my sense of humor. "How did you get to be so funny?" she would often ask. Reva loved to laugh. She also loved to hear me sing and sometimes accompanied me on the piano.

Reva also admired my physical strength, such as it is. I was her man. "My Hercules, Tarzan, and Ulysses all in one," she would say. I was so to her.

And I loved and love Reva and always will, as long as I am alive and, God willing, after I have parted from my body. I cannot think of love without Reva.

Early in our marriage, when we were still living in Elmwood Park, I asked Reva why she stuck with me, given my problems earning a living and my other problems. She replied, "Because man is man and woman is a rib."

In her heart, she realized her own growth potential, but she had no sense of vaunting or pride. She was a creative person and she knew it, but she had had no encouragement growing up except piano lessons.

In Rutherford, just before an episode that landed her in the psych ward, she said, "I can make things grow." This was before she began Montclair. It was as if she were seeing something from a distance and knew it was there but for so many years had been prevented from even beginning her journey that she didn't know how to reach it.

She died with her potential only partially fulfilled, but at least she was able to break away from some of the invidious pieces of her past. She died, ultimately, from the poison put into her for so many years before I met her by the collusion of her family and psychiatrists. I could not neutralize the physical poisoning. It took her life and the spirit from mine.

Reva began social work school at NYU in fall of 1998. The school's headquarters were located in one of the historic mansions on Washington Square North. She would sometimes eat her lunch in Washington Square Park. Other times she would go into one of the small restaurants nearby. She watched the annual Halloween parade in the Village and traveled to and from NYU by the A train and the 190 bus, which ran from the midtown Port Authority building to Paterson and stopped directly in front of our apartment building.

CHAPTER TWENTY-TWO

WORLD TRADE CENTER

In late August 2001, Reva and I drove into Manhattan to see a performance of an off-off Broadway show *Stage Struck*. The music was by our friend Ralph Carbone, a composer, arranger, and church organist who lived in Lyndhurst with his wife, Linda Heimall, an internationally renowned opera singer.

The theater was on 14th Street, and we attended a performance on a Sunday afternoon. After the show, Reva and I drove into lower Manhattan. We passed the façade of an immense building, and I asked Reva what it was. "It's the World Trade Center," she said.

I had never seen the World Trade Center except the towers from afar, but I knew lower Manhattan from my youth before the World Trade Center was built. In the late 1950s and early 1960s, the Battery, where the World Trade Center was located, was a remote area of Manhattan, notable mainly for Bowling Green, the oldest park in the city, and for the Staten Island Ferry. The Battery was one of my favorite places in Manhattan. I remember the window of a seamen's supply store on Maiden Lane, although I never went inside the store.

In my early twenties, I once walked from the uptown Port Authority on 181st Street to the southern tip of Manhattan. I hadn't intended to walk that far. I had taken a bus from New Jersey over the George Washington Bridge on a gentle September Saturday and began walking and just continued. I stopped for lunch on Canal Street. I reached the Battery in the late afternoon and rested on a bench. The World Trade Center was under construction behind me. I then walked back as far as Canal Street before taking a subway uptown.

That was many years ago: before Columba University, before my initial career as a librarian, before I worked as a teacher and a journalist, and long before I met Reva.

Changes had come to the *South Bergenite*. In 2000, it had gone from a tabloid format to a broadsheet. The editor who hired me was reassigned elsewhere in the company and a new editor, Chris O., was appointed. Chris had been a reporter for the New York tabloids and commuted from Manhattan.

I was still working part-time for the *South Bergenite*, but I was also working for the *Secaucus Home News*, an old weekly that covered the town of Secaucus in Hudson County. North Jersey Media Group didn't cover Hudson County, and Chris allowed me to work for the *Home News* as long as my work there didn't interfere with my reporting for the *South Bergenite*.

I began working for the *Home News* in the early summer of 2001. I had taken a hiatus from teaching.

It's a short trip from Rutherford to Secaucus, and I was the sole reporter for the *Home News*. I had three or four bylines a week. Reva often accompanied me to meetings, not because she necessarily wanted to (although I don't think she minded), but because of my agoraphobia. There is an open stretch of Route 3 between Rutherford and Secaucus. When Reva could not accompany me, I took the 190 bus.

Reva now had her MSW, but before she could look for a social work job, she had to be licensed by the State of New Jersey. This required passing a test. The testing center was in Paramus and candidates took the test on a computer with results available immediately. Reva didn't pass the first time but passed the second time, about a month later. She was now an LSW, a licensed social worker.

She had also obtained her substitute teacher's license in the summer of 2001, and in the fall, while looking for her first social work job, she substituted in the Rutherford, East Rutherford, Carlstadt, and North Arlington districts.

She also worked a few days a week with preschool-age children at the Ridgewood YMCA, a job she enjoyed, although she was concerned about the hygiene of some of the children, who blew their noses openly.

The job of substitute teacher is hard. I've done it. I once read about a substitute teacher who was arrested for threatening to burn down her students' homes. I hope the judge in her case had worked as a substitute teacher.

Reva had been substituting a class of second or third graders in a prefabricated temporary classroom in East Rutherford, which had been set up while a new school building was under construction. I drove to pick her up at the end of the school day. The children ran out of the classroom laughing and giggling, and one boy ran to my car and gleefully told me, "My teacher just told us to get the hell out of here."

The teacher was Reva. She told me later that the classroom was terribly hot, which contributed to her aggravation, and the children were obstreperous.

Chris used to arrive early in the Rutherford office so he could leave early in the afternoon and beat the rush hour traffic back to Manhattan. On September 11, 2001, both Reva and I were sleeping when the phone rang. It was Chris. "A plane just crashed into the World Trade Center," he said. We switched on the television and watched the live coverage and saw the second plane hit. Then we and everyone else knew that the hits were not accidents.

We watched the coverage for a while and then went to a Dunkin Donuts in Wallington for takeout coffee. The mood in the restaurant was somber. Everywhere, people looked grim. Returning to Rutherford, we observed soldiers at the railroad station.

CHAPTER TWENTY-THREE

PROSPECTS

September 2001 to the summer of 2002 was a significant period for Reva, for me, and for the nation.

The *South Bergenite* went to press on Mondays, so it was too late to include a World Trade Center story on Monday, September 11. Chris, who lived near the South Street Seaport, spent the night with a friend in Hoboken. On Tuesday, September 12, the staff became fully engaged in covering 9/11 from a local angle for the next edition. That edition, on September 18, identified all victims of the World Trade Center and Pentagon attacks who had lived in the towns that the *South Bergenite* covered. The six days following 9/11 were hectic and almost nonstop work. I also wrote stories about the World Trade Center attack for the *Secaucus Home News*. Work had the advantage of keeping me focused and my mind off anxiety, which at the time included the anthrax scare. The result was that on September 18, the *South Bergenite* published an edition that had profiles of all known local victims and interviews with relatives of most.

But Chris had problems with the company management and left the paper a few months later.

I will call the new editor Mona Bleak. She was a divorced woman who lived in Rutherford with her two young children. My relationship with her ultimately became contentious, but when she first became editor, she was helpful. In March, she promoted me to full-time, which increased my salary and provided medical and dental benefits.

As a full-timer, I now was involved in layout on Fridays, and I was appointed editor of the business and real estate section and of the obituary and religion section. The latter was usually a single page and I wrote all obituaries. But the former was a six-to-eight-page section that I had to fill every week. I established contacts with the Meadowlands Chamber of Commerce and used as many local sources as I could. I was also assigned Rutherford, the largest of the Meadowlands towns, in place of East Rutherford, which was assigned to another reporter.

I remained a full-time reporter with North Jersey Media Group for the next ten years. I was with the company from 1997 to 2012.

Through the fall of 2001 and winter of 2002, Reva continued substitute teaching, working for the Ridgewood YMCA, and searching for a social work job. In the spring, her efforts were rewarded, and she was hired as a full-time social worker at Prospect Heights Care Center, a recently opened rehabilitation center in Hackensack. She was one of four social workers hired by the facility. Her duties included discharge planning, referrals, and counseling patients and their families.

With both of us working full-time (I had to give up the *Secaucus Home News* job when I became full-time at the *South Bergenite*, but I continued to write articles for *ANSOM*), we enjoyed a relatively good income for a while.

Soon after Reva began working at Prospect Heights, her monthly blood tests came back indicating what we had sought so long to avoid. Dr. Alexander Ackad, her nephrologist, said that it was time for her to begin dialysis. Dr. Ackad later told me that he knew that she would need dialysis eventually but was surprised that the time came so soon. He thought she would be older when she began. She was now fifty.

I have speculated that, had Reva done little, had she treated herself as a semi-invalid, never had gone to college, never traveled to Manhattan to graduate school, never pursued a career, she might have been able to delay dialysis a few years. However, she would not have wanted such a life, nor would I, for her.

A physically more specific cause for her earlier-than-expected entry into dialysis might have been her internship at the detox hospital in Newark. Not only was the environment stressful, but after the internship, when she applied for her substitute teacher license, she tested positive on a PPD tuberculosis skin test. A chest X-ray showed her lungs were clear. She did not have tuberculosis, but the test indicated that she had been exposed to the disease.

Dr. Ackad put her on a six-month course of an antibiotic, and she was permitted to teach. The most likely place of her exposure to tuberculosis was the detox hospital where she worked with recovering addicts from the streets of Newark. Perhaps, had Reva been given another placement from the start, like the internship at Nutley Family Services instead of the detox hospital, dialysis might have been delayed. But the potential for exposure to tuberculosis and the effect on her health by the placement was something we had never considered. Reva went with whatever internship she was assigned by NYU. Either in her first or second year, she had been sent for an internship interview with the Jewish Family Services in Teaneck, a much safer and more convenient placement, but that agency rejected her.

There is nothing new under the sun.

I remember walking up a street in Rutherford to meet her when she had gotten off the bus from Newark after work in the detox hospital. She was smiling happily, but I noticed then how puffy she looked. She was retaining fluids.

Reva was reluctant to go into dialysis. "I don't want to depend on a machine for my life," she said. Hemodialysis is done three days a week, three to four hours a session, and it causes serious disruptions to a person's life. Reva's hope was for a successful transplant. She took some sick days from her job, and Dr. Ackad admitted her to Hackensack University Medical Center to try to delay dialysis. After a few days in the hospital, with medicines and intravenous fluids, her creatinine dropped low enough for her to be discharged without dialysis. But Dr. Ackad warned us of signs to be aware of, such as nausea and hiccoughs. "You're playing with fire," he told us.

About a month later, Reva developed nausea and other symptoms. Her creatinine was up, and she had to begin dialysis.

For a permanent access site in hemodialysis, a vascular surgeon fuses a vein and an artery in the nondominant arm to create a fistula. But a fistula takes weeks to heal before it can be used. In the interim, temporary access is gained from an opening made just below the neckline where a tube is inserted. The tube isn't visible above a blouse or T-shirt, and the opening closes without leaving a scar once the tube is removed. The surgery was performed and Reva underwent her initial dialysis immediately afterward. Thereafter, she would undergo dialysis at Hackensack Hospital outpatient dialysis unit on Tuesday, Thursday, and Saturday evenings.

After her first dialysis, Reva informed her supervising social worker about her medical condition. Her supervisor was angry because she had told Reva about her impending divorce and Reva had concealed her kidney disease from her—as if a divorce were equivalent to a medical treatment on which life depends. Now that she was in dialysis, Reva's diagnosis was end-stage renal disease (ESRD), which means that without dialysis or a transplant, the patient will die.

She continued to work at Prospect Heights until October, when she was fired, ostensibly because the floor was too hectic for her. Two of the other social workers who were hired at same the time as Reva had already been fired. Only the supervisor remained.

CHAPTER TWENTY-FOUR

DIALYSIS

The final fifteen years of Reva's life were years of pain, frustration, and disappointment but also years of courage, determination, hope, and some measure of triumph. But there can be no denying the pain—physical and emotional—that was caused by the ignorance and madness of her parents and the malign collusion of psychiatry that kept her on lithium for eighteen years, from age fourteen to thirty-two, permanently damaging her kidneys.

The following is an excerpt from Reva's journal. The entry is undated but was probably written in 2005. The events she describes will be narrated subsequently in this memoir.

How can I explain the visceral pain that goes along with my life now? My last operation, the kidney transplant, was a failure and not only that I am back on dialysis. . . . I came home with two contractures. That means my knee is in a locked position and so is my ankle. This is my driving leg. My right leg. I can't do the kind of social work I did. I want to work but there are other obstacles.

Right now I want to write the epoch of my life so far. I was born to a poor immigrant family that survived WWII in concentration camps. My brother was born in Germany after the war. He, a male, was much honored in my family. When my parents immigrated to the U.S., they changed his (and their) name from Brzezinski to Brezin when they became citizens, but they did not change mine. I would marry, they said, and would not need to change my name.

When Reva was in Holy Name Hospital in July 2019 and daily moving closer to death, her brother said, during a phone call I made to him at his home in California, that he felt badly because he was likely to lose the last member of his family from Europe.

Family from Europe, indeed! He was born in Germany but came to the US as a child with his Polish-born parents. Reva was born in Paterson, New Jersey. She was one-hundred percent American from the hour of her birth. How dare he refer to her as a member of his family from Europe. I was born in Newark, New Jersey. Reva was as American as I. But Reva's parents would not even give her an identity. It would cost too much money. They had money to buy real estate but not to change her name. Why didn't they use some of the reparation money that they each received from Germany every month? I will never know.

I return to the narrative.

Reva was now in dialysis three evenings a week. She had a working fistula in her left arm and no longer needed the emergency access below the neckline. The hole that was created for it closed without surgery.

There are two types of dialysis: peritoneal, which is performed by the patient at home, usually every night during sleep; and hemodialysis, in which all the blood in the patient's body is removed and cleansed three times a week. Reva's nephrologists, as well as her brother, recommended hemodialysis for her. It is an awesome process.

She had been advised by her brother about a year before she began dialysis to register for a cadaver kidney transplant. She did so at Hackensack Hospital, Columbia Presbyterian, Yale-New Haven, and the University of Pennsylvania. I could not donate one of my kidneys because my blood type did not match hers. That is the first requirement for a transplant. Then there is tissue typing, which is a complex process that I do not understand. Suffice to say that, even when blood types match, not every kidney is suitable for transplant to a particular patient.

Dialysis takes a lot out of a person. Although Reva underwent her dialysis in the evenings, she no longer had the energy for full-time work. So her dream of becoming an LCSW, the training for which requires full-time employment under supervision of an LCSW, was dashed. But in April 2003, she was hired as a part-time social worker by Liberty Health Care in Jersey City.

The job required three full days a week: Tuesday Thursday, and

Friday, and consisted of visiting clients in their homes throughout Hudson County and setting up services for them. Reva spent part of the day on the road and part working on charts in Liberty's office.

She loved the job, although it was tiring. She enjoyed the adventure and excitement of traveling to different locations in this densely populated urban county, and the work brought out her natural ability to empathize with people and to help them.

Reva used our one car for work. I didn't need it during the day, as I worked locally and could walk, get a ride, or take a bus to most events and interviews I needed to cover, and most meetings were in the evening. Reva visited clients in Jersey City, Bayonne, Hoboken—in fact in almost every municipality in Hudson County. She went into some bad neighborhoods and visited clients in the projects. When she went into the projects, Liberty provided her with a bodyguard. Reva called him a private detective, which he probably was. Liberty required its female health care workers in the field to wear a dark blue skirt and a white blouse and to prominently display their IDs for their own protection in the rough neighborhoods where they sometimes worked.

She told me about some of her clients, but Reva was highly ethical and never identified them by name. One man lived alone in a squalid basement apartment in Hoboken and suffered from ALS. Reva arranged what services she could for him. Another man was a depressed veteran. Reva told me how she persuaded him to accept services by pointing to the military awards displayed on his living room wall, praising his service to the nation, and convincing him of the continued value of his life.

On dialysis days, she would return home at about 6:00 p.m. and eat some dinner. I would then drive her from Rutherford to Hackensack Hospital. She would call me when she was finished, and I would pick her up, usually at about 10:00 p.m. She didn't drive herself to dialysis because the treatments lower blood pressure and could make driving home unsafe. Once home, she would eat a large meal (dialysis makes patients hungry) and go to sleep. She would sleep late on Wednesday and Saturday mornings, but as her schedule required her to work both Thursday and Friday, she would be up early on Friday to go to work. She was still strong.

CHAPTER TWENTY-FIVE

INTERMEZZO

In this chapter I will attempt to give a fuller description of who Reva is: her personality, interests, and hobbies. I use the present tense deliberately for, to me, although her earthly body is buried, she is alive and always will be.

Reva was a beautiful woman and a wonderful wife. No man could hope for a more loving, devoted, and supportive wife.

She had studied the piano, both as a child in Paterson and in Fair Lawn, and we took lessons together after our marriage. But Reva was on a much more advanced level than I. She played a variety of music: classical, show, pop, and jazz. She also studied alone later. Her last teacher, from whom she took lessons in the two years before her final hospitalization, was teaching her jazz piano.

She was an old-fashioned girl who loved to sing and accompany herself. When she took a course in singing for non-music majors at Montclair, she chose the song from the musical *Guys and Dolls*, "I'll Know When My Love Comes to Me," as her final exam piece, which she both sang and played.

She loved to dance and was an excellent dancer. We went dancing often when we were dating but much less so after we married. That, I am told, is not unusual. Even after she became disabled, when we would go to a wedding or some other celebration, she would dance with her hands.

She was a creative person and she knew it, and had she been able to channel her creativity before her parents and their hired fraudulent, sadistic, authoritarian, unscientific, bottom-of-the-barrel doctors called psychiatrists destroyed her, she would be walking, singing, and dancing today. She often said to me that her mother choked her, that her mother stifled self-expression out of her. Reading her journals now, after her death, I see how much she suppressed. She was coerced from an early age not to express herself.

In the four years before her death, she took art lessons every Monday at the Art Center of Northern New Jersey in New Milford, developing a talent she always had. During the summer of 2019, two months before her death, while she lay in the first of the three hospitals from which she never returned home, two of her pastels were accepted for a county-wide exhibit.

I remember telling her this news on Bastille Day, July 14, during a period when she was on a regular medical floor and seemed to be improving.

"I'm so proud of myself," she said. This was before her second cardiac arrest, after which she never spoke again. The two pastels hang above the piano in my apartment today.

She wrote poetry and kept journals throughout her life.

She enjoyed reading. We often would lie in bed together reading. The couple that reads together stays together. Her favorite authors included Margaret Atwood, Joyce Carl Oates, Ruth Rendell, and James Michener. But her favorite genre was historical fiction. She also enjoyed Dickens.

We liked watching old movies together. I would order the videos, later DVDs, from the library.

I introduced her to opera, a passion of mine, which she also came to love.

The first opera we saw together was a concert version of *Turandot* performed in Central Park in Manhattan. I had not been to the Metropolitan Opera in many years, and Reva urged me to take her. The first opera we saw together at the Met was *Madama Butterfly*. We were in the orchestra standing room. She loved the opera and cried at the end, but she hated standing. Thereafter, we bought family circle seats.

The second opera we saw at the Met was the *Dialogues of the Carmelites*. I told Reva the story first and she commented, "Who wants to see an opera about nuns who get beheaded?" But at the end of the performance, she spontaneously gave it a standing ovation.

We attended the Met many times and also the New York City Opera and performances of smaller opera companies. After she became disabled, when it was expensive and impractical to go the opera house, we would go to the cinema telecasts. In the winter of 2019, before she was admitted to Holy Name Hospital, we saw telecasts of *Die Walküre* and *Adriana Lecouvreur*.

She wanted to go to the ballet, but we never went.

Reva was a compassionate, people-oriented person. She had a deeper soul than most people. She had no malice in her heart, but her parents, especially her mother, had squeezed a part of Reva's personality into a box, forbidden a part of her personality from developing. The result was the "manic" episodes, which could have been channeled into creative outlets, given a less destructive family.

She was a fearless warrior, a woman determined not to let herself be overcome by the adversity life dealt her. Unfortunately, our greatest and most intractable enemies are often our parents.

She loved to cook and was creative at devising recipes, but once she had entered dialysis, she was too tired to cook on dialysis days and we usually ordered out.

In the early years of our marriage, when we were living in Elmwood Park, my mother came down from Rhode Island for a family wedding and stayed with us. Reva's parents came for dinner, which Reva cooked. I remember Reva's mother asking her suspiciously, "Where did you learn to cook American?" Her mother disapproved.

We still went out for dinner with friends after she became disabled, but one of my disappointments is that we could no longer participate in outdoor activities together. After 2005, when I was transferred to the *Northern Valley Suburbanite* in Cresskill, the towns I covered had environmental commissions and nature preserves, and I reported on these natural habitats. I regretted that Reva could not join me. Bird watching was largely a hobby of the past, although we enjoyed Allison Park overlooking the Palisades and areas along the Hudson River, which Reva could enjoy from her wheelchair.

From childhood, Reva identified strongly with Jewishness. She once told me when we were dating that Judaism meant life to her.

Her social life had been almost entirely among her fellow Jews. Had I not been Jewish, Reva would never have dated me.

But she was broadminded. She accompanied me to church before and after my conversion, and, as she wrote in her spiritual autobiography in Chapter 3 of this memoir, saw no contradiction in being Jewish and attending church. (She never took Communion, although she told me she had before I met her when it was offered by a Roman Catholic chaplain while she was in a psych ward.) She found the church services educational and was sometimes so moved by the sermons that she wept. She had friends among the parishioners and enjoyed the coffee hour after church on Sunday. But she attended the local synagogue when her dialysis schedule permitted. She lit Sabbath candles, covering her face while she prayed. Worship, to Reva, was not a perfunctory ritual but an emanation from her deep belief in God and his goodness.

I, as a convert to Christianity, have come to understand Jesus through Reva, a being wholly human and yet divine. For the flame of divinity shone in Reva.

The concept is not alien to Judaism. In Leviticus, God instructs the ancient Hebrews, "You shall be holy as I the Lord your God am holy."

CHAPTER TWENTY-SIX

WARNING RATTLE

Reva continued to work for Liberty Health Care and I for the *South Bergenite* and *ANSOM* through the spring and summer of 2004. Life, though traumatized, still had a regular rhythm.

In July 2004, Denise D., a forty-seven-year-old dialysis patient whom Reva and I knew, died. Denise lived in Carlstadt and had dialysis the same evenings as Reva. She drove herself to dialysis and home, but she often looked exhausted after the treatment. I had spoken on the phone with her brother about a week before her death in reference to a letter he had written to the *South Bergenite*. (Mona Bleak put me in charge of the editorial page when she was on vacation or otherwise absent. In addition to writing editorials on those occasions, I also chose and verified letters to the editor.) At that time, he told me that his sister was dying but was expected to live another two years. This did not happen.

Throughout her sixteen years in dialysis, Reva had known other patients who died during the course of treatments. One of those patients chose to die, to stop the treatments. She died within two weeks. No adult can legally be forced to undergo dialysis. Reva's hope was for a successful transplant, and she was waiting to be notified of an available kidney from one of the four hospitals where she had registered.

My perspective, at that time, on her dialysis and the planned transplant was that it was treatment for a chronic disease, like diabetes (which, incidentally, many dialysis patients have but Reva never did). I used to say to her, "Thank God, neither of us has cancer."

She was often tired on the day after dialysis. Not only did she have dialysis three evenings a week, but she worked three full days a week.

On a summer day in 2004, she called me from work. The University of Pennsylvania had called on her cell phone. A cadaver kidney that matched her blood and tissue type was available for her. She needed to be in Philadelphia that evening.

She left work early, drove home, and ate dinner. We planned to drive to Penn Station in Newark, and Reva would take the train to Philadelphia. I called my cousin Ted, who lived in Fair Lawn, and asked him to drive us in and wait with us.

I knew nobody in Philadelphia, except Reva's brother, who lived in an affluent suburb but who was distant from me. My perception was that he disliked me and would never have invited me to stay at his home, although Mona Bleak would have given me time off from work.

Perhaps one reason for his distance from me and apparent dislike is that Reva had registered at the University of Pennsylvania Hospital and not the hospital where he worked, Hahnemann Hospital.

I don't remember exactly why we made the choice to register at the University of Pennsylvania. A prospective transplant patient was, and perhaps still is, allowed to register in only one hospital per state. Perhaps we chose Penn because it is a major teaching hospital, like Columbia. Perhaps it was a way of asserting our independence. I did not know at the time, and Joe Brezin never told me, that Hahnemann also was a teaching hospital.

Whatever the reason, when she went to Penn to register, I did not go with her, although I drove her to Newark and picked her up. I was working, and this trip was for registration only. She stayed overnight at her brother's home. From what she told me later, the visit to her brother was less than pleasant. Would it have made a difference in the end if we had chosen Hahnemann Hospital? There is no way of knowing. In general, people choose large teaching hospitals for major, life-altering elective surgeries. Of the four hospitals where Reva registered, three were connected to Ivy League university medical schools. Hackensack was local.

Ted arrived at our building in the early evening. I went outside to meet him, but when we got back to the apartment, there was no sign of Reva. "I hope she didn't freak out," I said to Ted. But a few minutes later, Reva walked through the doorway. She had been looking for us. While I was downstairs with Ted, the University of Pennsylvania called to cancel the transplant. For some reason, which was not communicated to Reva, the kidney was no longer available, although we were on schedule. Perhaps a defect had been discovered in it or it was not a match for Reva. We never found out.

As I walked Ted to his car on that warm summer evening, I confessed my relief that the transplant was called off. It was my hope that when a kidney became available for Reva, it would be at Columbia or Hackensack, where I knew that I could be with her.

Dr. Ackad had even suggested that Reva register in Maryland. Arranging for hospitalization in distant states is for the wealthy, whose families can afford a prolonged hotel stay. We lived on our income and had no savings at that time. Sometimes we had to borrow money to pay the rent.

I had been hired by St. Peter's College in Jersey City to teach an English course in the fall. Mona Bleak was annoyed that I had accepted the job, which would keep me out of the office two afternoons a week. But most of the meetings that I covered were in the evening. Mona harassed all the reporters if they claimed overtime, although working overtime was inevitable. Ultimately, we worked overtime and claimed our regular hours.

However, I had also gone for an interview at Felician College in Lodi, like St Peter's, a Catholic institution, and was hired to teach there. The classes were on the same afternoons as the St. Peter's classes, so I withdrew from the St. Peter's assignment and accepted the one at Felician, which was much closer. I hadn't taught in several years and was eager to return to the classroom, and, of course, I was glad for the extra money.

CHAPTER TWENTY-SEVEN

BITE

On the afternoon of Friday September 24, 2004, I was at my desk at the *South Bergenite* when I received a call from Reva. It was Yom Kippur Eve, and Reva had left work early to prepare for Kol Nidre services. But the University of Pennsylvania had just called. Another kidney had become available. Once again, she had to be in Philadelphia that evening.

I informed Mona Bleak what was happening, left the office, and went home. I didn't call Ted this time because Ted, co-owner of Prozys with his father Milton, my father's surviving brother, was also studying to be a cantor and would be attending synagogue services that evening. Instead, I asked a coworker, a fellow reporter, Nancy R., who knew Reva.

Reva believed strongly in God and was committed to Judaism. But no rabbi I have ever known would counsel turning down this surgery because of the Jewish High Holidays. There are long waits for cadaver kidneys, although that apparently was less the case at the University of Pennsylvania than the other three hospitals where Reva had registered.

Later that afternoon, Reva, Nancy, and I left for Penn Station in Newark in Nancy's car.

Reva had called her brother, who was packing for a vacation in Hawaii with his wife, for which he was to leave the next day. Reva spoke to him again while we were waiting for the train at Penn Station. Joseph called Amtrak to pay for a single one-way ticket to Philadelphia, but for some reason, the transaction did not go through. The train was almost due, so I paid for the ticket with my Master Card, which I shared with Reva (we each had a card on the same account).

The card was almost maxed out. In fact, there was not even money left on it for a ticket for me if I had planned to accompany Reva. It was impossible for me to go down with her. I had no place to stay and not even enough money for a ticket. Reva went down alone, but she and I remained in cell phone contact. She had her phone and charger with her.

Months before we had agreed that if Yale or Penn should have a kidney, I would take her to the train but she would go to the hospital alone, as I lacked money, and also, I was at that time severely agoraphobic. I am still agoraphobic but less so.

In fairness to her brother, he frequently advised Reva and me on medical issues and had spoken on the phone with Dr. Ackad on several occasions. In fact, we came to rely on him for information about dialysis and transplants. As a result, we did not do as much research on our own as we should have. Joe Brezin also helped us financially, paying down payments on two cars and monthly installments until we were in a financial position to take over the installments ourselves. But his involvement did not go so far as postponing his vacation.

Reva was the bravest person I have ever known. But that night her mood was euphoric. She saw only that the next day she would have a new kidney and would no longer need dialysis.

I have never ceased to feel guilty that I didn't go down with her. Her brother was not there for her either. No one met her at the hospital. Although the University of Pennsylvania was not Joseph's hospital, he was her brother and lived in a Philadelphia suburb. But he also had planned a Hawaiian vacation.

I don't know if Joseph would have canceled his vacation if Reva had registered at Hahnemann Hospital instead of Penn, but it may have been best for Reva that she had not. The cadaver kidney was from a young man killed in a motor vehicle accident. The University of Pennsylvania got one kidney and Hahnemann, the other. Months later, Reva told me that her brother had informed her that the patient who got the kidney at Hahnemann developed sepsis and died. That fate could have been Reva's. She developed complications following the transplant, which will be related subsequently, but she did not die.

As we waited for the train at Penn Station, I had a sense of foreboding, a feeling that something wasn't right. Months later when I told Reva about this sense of foreboding, she said I should have said something at the time. Yet how could I dare to try to dissuade her from going for the surgery whose purpose was to give her a new kidney and relieve her from the need for dialysis, based on a premonition which I could not even articulate? It was a mood. But I did want her to wait for a kidney from Columbia or Hackensack so I could be with her, even though it meant that she would remain longer in dialysis. As it turned out, she remained in dialysis for the rest of her life.

When the train came, she got on, waved happily to us from the car and was gone.

Contending with my sense of foreboding was the feeling that I needed to trust the doctors. They were the experts, and we were following their advice. They would make everything come out all right, and she would return home, a healed woman no longer dependent on dialysis, although she would face a lifetime of antirejection drugs.

When I was back in our apartment, I called Reva. She was in the taxi on her way to the hospital. Her spirits were high. I spoke to her again when she was in the pre-op room. She had met the doctor, an Indian surgeon. She was operated on that night.

CHAPTER TWENTY-EIGHT
VENOM

Early in the morning on September 25, my phone rang. It was Reva. "Howie, Howie," she called. The surgery was over. The anesthesia was wearing off. She was in agony. She said she was lying on something burning hot.

My memory of the next few weeks is spotty. Reva remained at Penn. I spoke with her several times a day and also spoke to the nurses and, when they were available, the doctors. Most of the nurses, although not all, were rude and seemed to regard my calls as an annoyance. They were short and snippy to me. A few were more helpful. One of the more helpful ones told me that the transplant was "slow to wake up." Reva was still getting dialysis until the transplant started working.

It never did.

Eight days after the surgery, she called me on my cell phone. I was at my desk at the *South Bergenite*, and I went out to the park for the call. She told me she was about to have another operation. She sounded broken. The nephrologist then got on the phone. He said the transplant was not getting blood and had to be removed.

This was and remains the saddest phone call of my life. It was all in vain, and worse was to come.

I was also in cell phone contact with Reva's brother in Hawaii. Reva did have a regular visitor, however. Joe's sister-in-law, Rosalind, who lived in a Philadelphia suburb and was a minister at a nondenominational church, visited Reva often. Reva described her as a spiritual person. She was a comfort to Reva.

I attempted to visit Reva on a Sunday. I asked my cousin Ted to drive. We got about halfway down on the Garden State Parkway when panic hit me, and we had to turn back. Anybody who has not experienced phobias cannot imagine their power. It is like slamming into a brick wall. My agoraphobia is not as bad today, and I think today I could make it to Philadelphia with someone else driving. I know I can travel there by train, and a few years later I did, with Reva.

Much of this period, the fall 2004, is a blur.

I continued to work at the *South Bergenite*, and two afternoons a week I taught an introduction to literature course at Felician College. Felician was an unpleasant experience, and I taught there only one semester.

Following the failed transplant, Reva developed blood clots. I do not know if the blood clots prevented the transplant from receiving blood, nor do I know if the fact that the donor was resuscitated briefly, or an attempt was made to resuscitate him, caused or contributed to the transplant's failure. The heart pumps blood to the rest of the body. If the heart had stopped and then was revived or almost revived, could this have affected the kidney's ability to receive blood? I don't know the answer. I am not a medical doctor, and I don't know if medical doctors would have an answer. But the resuscitation or attempted resuscitation of the donor was presented to Reva as a risk factor when Penn called her that fateful Friday afternoon. Reva then called her brother and explained what she had been told and asked him whether she should attempt the transplant. "Go for it," Reva said he told her.

She told me during our phone conversations that her right leg was weeping, that is, suppurating. The surgeon had looked at it and said she had an infection in the skin of her leg and that a Doppler and biopsy were unnecessary. Later a dermatologist looked at it and told her to keep the leg elevated above her heart and not stand on it, but he said she could walk on it.

But Reva couldn't walk.

Her right leg and foot had become strangely contracted. A social worker from Penn arranged for her to go on disability and receive Medicaid services. The hospital wanted to keep her longer, but Reva wanted to return to New Jersey. Her brother, by then, had returned from Hawaii. Reva remembered Prospect Heights where she had worked in her first social work job, the only one in her aborted career as a social worker that medical conditions did not preclude her from working full-time. She arranged with the Penn social worker to be admitted to Prospect Heights.

In late October, her brother drove her from Penn to Prospect Heights in Hackensack. Reva told me that when they stopped for food, her brother brought her lunch to the car. She was unable to walk and had no wheelchair.

I met Reva at Prospect Heights. We had not seen each other for more than a month. I walked into her room and said, "Hello, sweetheart." She grabbed my head and pulled it to her and kissed me with all the passion, yearning, and love in her beautiful soul and body. Even her brother seemed moved.

He and I looked at Reva's right leg and foot. Both were contracted. The skin on her leg was hard and thick, like wood. It lacked the pliability of normal skin, like the skin on her left leg. Her brother did not know what the condition was. He speculated that it might be Weber-Christian disease.

At this time, however, Reva's right leg, though contracted, could reach the floor, and she was able to walk about forty steps with a walker and someone pushing a wheelchair behind her for safety. But over the years, as the contracture worsened, her right foot no longer reached the floor, and she was unable to walk, even with a walker. Her left leg had also begun gradually to contract, but at the time before her final illness in 2019 that led to her death, it was still stable, usable, and strong—and enabled her to transfer and remain relatively independent.

Her brother suggested that the right leg might be straightened manually while Reva was under general anesthesia; however, an orthopedist who was consulted said that straightening the leg, if successful, wouldn't last. The leg would contract again.

Through Medicare, Reva now had a private ambulance service to take her to and from medical appointments and dialysis. She resumed dialysis at Hackensack Hospital, but because of pain in her hip and leg, which was exacerbated during the three to four hours of dialysis when she could not turn on her side, she had to take Percocet before treatments.

CHAPTER TWENTY-NINE

REHAB

In the spring of 2005, Dr. Ackad told me that when he first saw Reva after she returned from the University of Pennsylvania, he thought she was going to die.

She survived another fifteen years, but they were difficult years, not the years she had anticipated. They were made tolerable to Reva because of her unyielding spirit, determination, courage, and compassion.

Reva was transferred at least once from Prospect Heights to Hackensack Hospital. It may have been after a stay in the hospital, which I think was to treat blood clots, that she was transferred to Regent Care Center, like Prospect Heights, a rehab facility in Hackensack.

She was in either Prospect Heights or Regent at least through Thanksgiving because I remember visiting her on Thanksgiving Day and being served dinner with her in her room. While at the rehab centers, she received physical therapy.

She was in Regent when I took her to a rheumatologist in Teaneck recommended by Dr. Ackad, Dr. Neil Gonter. A physical therapist showed me how to help Reva transfer from a wheelchair to the car.

Dr. Gonter was so astonished by Reva's condition, which he could not diagnose, that he called in his senior colleague. Dr. Gonter referred Reva to an academic rheumatologist at Robert Wood Johnson University Hospital in New Brunswick. Her ambulance service transported her for the outpatient visit. The rheumatologist offered the diagnosis of scleroderma and proposed a course of prednisone.

However, Joe Brezin had researched the condition and believed she was suffering from nephrogenic systemic fibrosis (NSF), a rare illness found only in patients with kidney disease.

A biopsy from Reva's right leg confirmed the diagnosis.

NSF was originally named nephrogenic fibrosing dermopathy (NFD) and was thought to affect the skin only, but the name was later changed to nephrogenic systemic fibrosis when physicians observed that the disease could invade internal organs and, in some cases, cause death.

About this disease, I can say little except to name it and describe Reva's physical condition. There was a lawsuit that has been resolved.

I continued to work at the *South Bergenite* and teach at Felician College until the fall semester ended. I produced my quota of stories and my police blotters and laid out my pages on Friday evenings. Because most municipal meetings were in the evening, I had time during the day to visit Reva. But my relationship with Mona Bleak had become increasingly difficult.

Mona Bleak wanted to fire me, but she had to be careful, I think, because I had been with North Jersey Media Group for seven years, had a good reputation, and had won awards from the New Jersey Press Association and the Society of Professional Journalists. Mona Bleak hesitated to fire me outright. She sent me two final warning letters. I responded with a letter to management.

On one occasion, she ordered me into her office where, among other complaints, she said I had been on the phone ordering a wheelchair.

She knew about Reva and, before the surgery, had met her. I had ordered a wheelchair because Reva would be coming home soon. All reporters made some personal calls.

My wife was lying disabled in a rehab center after a failed kidney transplant, and Mona Bleak was harassing me about a phone call for a wheelchair. I was holding my prescription reading glasses in my hands while she berated me, and I became so furious that I snapped the frame in two and threw the two pieces on the floor. When Mona Bleak added the incident to her complaints against me, she wrote that I had thrown objects around the office. She omitted mentioning that I had broken my own glasses.

Mona Bleak ordered me to meet with Ellen B., the company's

human resources director, and in late November I met with her at North Jersey Media Group's headquarters in Hackensack.

Ellen B. asked me some questions. I remember the first one. "Do you know why you are here?" I apparently answered her questions satisfactorily and, after I explained Reva's condition, she informed me that federal law allows an employee one week of paid disability leave for each year he or she has worked for the employer. The leave can be for the employee's care or for care of a family member. I had worked for NJMG for seven years, so I was eligible for seven weeks paid leave.

However, I did not then sign the papers for the leave but went back to the office and worked through the rest of the week. But I was certain that Mona Bleak intended to fire me that Friday after squeezing a week's work out of me. Once I was fired, it would be too late to apply for disability leave.

On early Friday afternoon, I left the office in a panic and drove as fast as I safely could to Hackensack, a distance of less than ten miles. I felt as if Mona Bleak were chasing me like a wild animal. I reached HR and signed the papers. I now had seven weeks leave, during which I intended to take care of Reva and look for another job.

I sent out résumés (I had begun sending them out weeks earlier) including to libraries, and I was interviewed for a position as reference librarian at Bloomfield Public Library, but I did not get the job.

Reva came home in December. She had a manual wheelchair and a walker. Grab bars and other specialized equipment had been installed in the bathroom. She also had a home health aide three days a week, the days she was not in dialysis. As she was no longer working, Dr. Ackad had switched her dialysis from the evening to midmorning. It is a testimony to Reva's skill as a social worker that Liberty Health Care held her job open for her until it became evident that she could not return to it.

Our building had an elevator but had two flights of steps to the front entrance. The rear entrance was also inaccessible to a wheelchair. But the ambulance service transported Reva to dialysis and medical appointments.

CHAPTER THIRTY

WARNING THE PUBLIC

The following essay was written by Reva, probably in 2005. The only discrepancy is the number of years that she says she was on lithium and the year she went off. If she had been on lithium for twenty-one years and went off in 1978, then she would have been put on it when she was five, as she was born in 1952. But this was not the case. Reva told me many times that she was on lithium for eighteen years. She was not on lithium but another drug when we began dating in 1985 when she was thirty-two. I believe she was taken off lithium just before. Therefore, I would estimate that she was on lithium from 1966, when she was fourteen, until 1984, a total of eighteen years.

***

WARNING THE PUBLIC
by REVA PROSNITZ

I awoke from my kidney transplant in burning pain on my back and legs. I urged the doctor to kill me because it hurt so much. He said, "You are not sick enough to kill." When I was transferred to my room, I asked the nurse to remove me from the burning pad. She did. She also said that I have been "schooled." I had my kidney operation at University of Pennsylvania Medical Center, a teaching hospital.

Eight days later, I called my husband in New Jersey telling him that they had to remove the new kidney, as it failed to work. It was a cadaver's kidney, and if it worked, it would last approximately ten years.

No new kidney, but that was not the end of my troubles. It appeared that I had blood clots and the doctors made me lie in bed or sit on a chair with my leg up. This lack of movement may have saved my life, but the doctors neglected to place my leg in a brace and I ended up having two contractures—one on my knee and one on my ankle. That means that my knee was and is stuck in a forty-five-degree angle and my ankle is stuck with the toe turned in. I am presently in a wheelchair and need two more operations to get me more ambulatory.

What else could have happened to me? I came down with a rare condition called NSF, Nephrogenic Systemic Fibrosis disease. I lost collagen on my skin and my skin is as hard as a rock. It is a scleroderma-like condition, but it comes from the kidneys. O.K. to top the cake, I was intubated during the transplant and lost a tooth. I still can't open my jaw enough to eat a decent sandwich.

Doctors. You have to be so careful. I got the call for the transplant as I was about to leave for synagogue on Yom Kippur. I, not a super-religious Jew, answered the phone. The nurse from U. Penn. said they have a cadaver that matches my blood type and tissue and the only thing wrong is that they had to jump start the heart. I called my brother, the nephrologist, and asked him if this was a problem. He said, "Go for it."

I went to Philadelphia with stars in my eyes and a hope to get off the kidney dialysis machine for good, but my hope got shattered.

I was working at my new career as a social worker when this episode in my life occurred. I graduated NYU about three years previously, and I really enjoyed my work. Now, I am in physical therapy part-time but the other operations are necessary.

How did my kidneys fail? That is a story of another iatrogenic disease. I took a medicine for twenty-one years called lithium. I had mood swings and was able to function with this medicine. I worked as a secretary and went to school at night. Then one day the psychiatrist stated that she just caught the blood toxicity level in my body in time, meaning I was lucky not to be completely poisoned and dead. She got me off lithium; however, it was too late for my kidneys. That was in 1978. In 2003, my kidneys failed.

Guess what, dear reader? The doctors in their infinite wisdom are still prescribing lithium. I realize that not everyone gets kidney failure from this metal, but I have met another kidney patient who recently died, and she also had taken lithium.

Is the cure better than the disease? Is having end-stage renal disease and being on dialysis, which only came from taking lithium, and listening to the wisdom of the doctors and getting a transplant that left me in this wheelchair, the way to go?

I know the answer to that and so do you. The answer is NO. The answer is to ask the doctors myriads of questions about medication, etc. before you take their advice.

In my social work practice, I came across a young man who was taking drugs. The psychiatrist thought that drugs were not the way to go, and I agreed. However, the way the doctor took this patient off of drugs was first to detox him and then prescribe lithium. I was itching to warn him, but I never was left alone with him.

Now, I feel it is my obligation to warn the public that lithium, the metal that is in batteries, may, indeed, disrupt your life by causing irreversible kidney damage.

Tragedies need not occur with knowledge and in-depth research before one leaps into medical modalities. Today, there are slick ads for medicines and hospitals. Doctors are getting money and vacations and other rewards to prescribe new medicines.

Open your eyes and beware of these oily ads. Don't despair of your medical condition, as there is plenty of good information out there on the Internet.

Always ask the prognosis and the success rate before an operation. Get to know your doctor. Never let a strange doctor touch you.

O.K., so what if you are a kid? You don't have much say as to what happens to you. I know this firsthand. When I was a "too-quiet" kid my parents took me to shrinks. I did have a physical symptom, though. I saw flashes of light, and many years later a psychiatric social worker said that I may have been epileptic (petit mal). But my parents were relentless. I went from one shrink to another. That in itself made me depressed. My depression did get very bad in high school, especially after my father talked to the guidance counselor, Mrs. Katz, and she said I would have to work harder than anybody else in order to go to college. I was doomed to work as a secretary for twenty-one years.

I tried twice to commit suicide. It was really a cry for help. What could my parents have done? They could have sent me to college, my dream. Instead, they preferred to send my brother to college and pay for his loans. Being a girl then in my particular family was not respected. Of course, I would get married and not need college.

CHAPTER THIRTY-ONE

STEPS AND STAIRS

My leave ended and I returned to the *South Bergenite* on January 17, 2005. The situation in the office was, if anything, worse, and I wrote to management requesting a transfer. My request was granted, and I was transferred to the *Northern Valley Suburbanite*, which was located in Cresskill, where it shared an office with several other weeklies. The *Northern Valley Suburbanite* published three editions: North, South, and Teaneck. I was assigned to cover three towns for the North edition: Closter, Norwood, and Demarest.

The change from the *South Bergenite* was dramatic. The office was large and felt like a newspaper office. The people I worked with, including the editors, were congenial.

Commuting, however, was a forty-five-minute drive each way, whereas I could walk from my home to the *South Bergenite* office. Rutherford is in the southern end of Bergen County, and Cresskill and the three towns I now covered are in the far northeast corner, not far from the New York State border.

Reva was now home. Although she was dependent on a wheelchair, she could walk forty or more steps with a walker. Following doctors' instructions, I followed her with a wheelchair while she walked in the hallway as often as she had the energy. Her right leg and right foot were contracted but the foot could touch the floor. Her left leg was then normal.

A home health aide came in three mornings a week, but Reva needed little help in dressing, grooming, and getting around the apartment. In time, she was able to cook for both of us on non-dialysis days. The aide functioned mainly as a housekeeper and companion for Reva.

Reva began a series of doctors' visits, both in New Jersey and

Manhattan, to see if anything could be done to remedy or ameliorate her disability. I will discuss these visits and their outcome in a subsequent chapter.

I often told her that she helped me as much as I helped her. I gave her physical care that she needed, but Reva provided me with incalculable emotional support.

I have noted that I suffered from agoraphobia. In fact, I suffered from a host of phobias and still do, but over the years I have learned strategies to live with them or live around them. One of the manifestations of my agoraphobia is a fear of driving when roads are deserted or driving alone on highways where there are no stores, gas stations, or people.

I did not always have these phobias. They crept up on me. I could not, in 2004, and still cannot, drive alone on the Garden State Parkway, but when I worked in the South Plainfield Public Library, I did so four days a week. As I noted earlier, when I taught at Seton Hall University in the 1990s, I drove through the streets of Newark and East Orange to get to the South Orange campus, a drive of almost an hour. If I had been able to take the Parkway, the commute time would have been halved.

I now had three towns to cover with most municipal meetings in the evening. I could not drive home to Rutherford after 9:00 p.m. on streets where almost every store was closed. Yet most meetings did not begin until 7:00 or 8:00 p.m.

It was not always so. In the late 1980s, when we lived in Elmwood Park, I had a part-time job in a call center (this was in the pre-Internet days) in the same office building in Cresskill where I now worked for the *Northern Valley Suburbanite*. I worked on Friday and Saturday from 6:00 p.m. until 2:00 a.m. and drove home alone in the dead of winter without a second thought and without a cellphone. Few people had cell phones in the late 1980s.

But the phobias would not allow me to do this any longer. Yet I had to cover those meetings.

It was a dilemma that I resolved using several strategies.

Sometimes I would listen to the tape-recorded meeting the next day in the clerk's office. Every town recorded meetings, but clerks of the various boards were not equally accessible. I also made a friend out of a council watcher in Closter, a man who went to every council meeting, sometimes spoke but never ran for office. I would leave my SONY cassette tape recorder with him before I drove home in the late afternoon and pick it up at his house the next morning with the council meeting taped. He never failed me.

And one strategy was to bring Reva with me. As long as Reva was in the car, I could stay the length the meeting, if necessary.

We lived on the third floor, and the elevator went to the lobby. But there remained two flights of steps to the street.

Reva would hang on to the railing, and I would hold her around her waist as she slowly descended a step at a time, putting the weight on her good leg. When she reached the landing, she would rest a while in the wheelchair, which I had positioned there. Then when she was ready, she went down the second flight to the street level.

I helped her into the car, put the wheelchair in the trunk, and we were off.

For Reva, it was a way of getting out. She had been cooped up in the apartment for weeks when she first accompanied me to a meeting. She left the apartment only for medical appointments and dialysis, traveling via ambulance service. I stopped on Park Avenue, Rutherford's main street, and bought her a Blimpie, which she ate in the parked car while observing the crowds around her. She felt happier. "This is the life," she said.

When we returned home later, I left Reva in her wheelchair in front of our building while I found a parking space on the street. Then we repeated the stairs in reverse. I supported her from behind as she went up a step at a time, slowly gripping the railing, again resting in her wheelchair on the landing.

Reva was always ready to help me. I can think of no time in our marriage or relationship before our marriage when she failed to help me if she could. She would walk on the ceiling for me.

CHAPTER THIRTY-TWO

AFTERMATH

"You really care about these people," Josephine, Reva's supervisor at the hospital for substance abusers in Newark, remarked incredulously.

Reva related this to me when she was interning at the hospital. One evening, as we lay in bed before sleep she said to me, "I want to take all this suffering I see and bring it to God and ask him what to do with it."

Reva's compassion, even for life's most wretched outcasts, was unusual. Reva cared deeply about the suffering that people experience and, sadly, this trait set her apart from many others. Compassion and caring ruled Reva, not greed and arrogance.

In the spring of 2005, after Reva had returned disabled from Pennsylvania, I observed a middle-aged man drive up to a Rutherford convenience store in a motorized wheelchair. He got out of the chair, leaving it outside the store, and walked inside. A short time later, he exited with his purchases and drove off in the chair. The sight of a man able to walk using a motorized wheelchair made me angry but also goaded me to action. I learned that Reva was eligible for a motorized wheelchair through Medicare. Vendors from a few companies came to our apartment. We chose a chair and a few weeks later it was delivered. The chair made life easier for Reva, although while we lived in Rutherford she could use it only in the apartment, as there was no ramp from the lobby to the street. When we moved from Rutherford in 2007 to a more accessible building, Reva was able to go out on her own. In time, we bought a ramp-van, a modified Toyota Sienna with both foot and hand controls, which Reva drove after taking lessons at the Kessler Institute and passing a state licensing test for driving with manual controls.

But to the time of her final hospitalization in the spring of 2019, Reva relied on motorized wheelchairs for getting around the apartment and traveling short distances outdoors. She rarely used her manual wheelchair. I wonder, in retrospect, if she depended too much on the motorized chair, especially after her right foot could no longer reach the floor and she was unable to walk with a walker. She had little exercise, beyond some physical therapy. If she had used the manual chair more, she would have improved her cardiovascular health. But she also needed to protect the fistula in her left arm, her lifeline to dialysis. Prolonged pressure on this arm, as from moving the left wheel of the manual chair, could put stress on the fistula.

For Reva, much of the next two years, from the spring of 2005 until 2007, was spent trying to unravel the mystery of NSF and to find a treatment to reverse, or at least to halt, the spread of this terrible disease that followed her failed kidney transplant.

However, as she was still able to manage the two flights of steps to and from our building lobby, we went out to parks and to restaurants for dinner with friends. Reva maintained her social work license, which had to be renewed every two years and which required course work. She took the courses online or by mail. She hoped to return to work as a social worker, and she did.

There is no cure for NSF, although there have been various experimental treatments ranging from thalidomide, the sedative that caused severe birth defects in the 1960s, to photopheresis, in which all the patient's blood is removed from his or her body, as in dialysis, treated with ultraviolet light and returned to the body. Dr. Ackad added his own experimental treatment, prescribing off-label one of the antirejection drugs used following a successful transplant. He claimed there was some softening of the skin on Reva's leg following a few months on this drug, but I didn't notice any change. In any case, it had no effect on her contractures.

We consulted a dermatologist at Columbia Presbyterian Hospital who had coauthored a paper on NSF, and another Columbia physician who was in charge of photopheresis. We were told that photopheresis had failed to produce significant improvement in patients. There seemed little to be done except to consider surgery.

Reva's spirits remained good after she adjusted to her changed condition. She went out, as I mentioned, played the piano, painted in water colors, wrote in her journal, read, and watched television. Most of all, we both continued to explore possible remedies.

The principal doctor treating Reva's disability was Dr. David L., a physiatrist who practiced in Englewood and taught at Columbia's medical school. Physiatrists should not be confused with psychiatrists, the monstrous source of all Reva's medical problems. A physiatrist is a physician specializing in physical rehabilitation. Physiatrists treat many of the same conditions that orthopedists do when they can be treated by nonsurgical methods. Dr. L. prescribed braces for Reva's right leg and foot, physical therapy, and referred Reva to Dr. Richard Cramer, a prominent orthopedist practicing at Columbia Presbyterian.

I went with Reva to her two consultations with Dr. Cramer. We were transported by her ambulance service. A plastic surgeon was present at the second consultation, as the skin on Reva's right leg was so unusual. Dr. Cramer had never operated on a patient with NSF. The surgery he proposed was the type he had done on polio patients. He said it would enable Reva to walk like the character Chester in the old television series, *Gunsmoke*, with her right leg straight instead of contracted.

Later, when we consulted with Dr. L. about the surgery, he advised against it. He said it involved installing a lot of hardware in Reva's leg and that the operation might paralyze her. We later consulted with another Columbia orthopedist who said that only a person who felt that life was unlivable without being able to walk would consent to the surgery which, he said, could leave Reva in constant and lifelong pain, although, perhaps, allowing her some limited ability to walk.

In the end we decided against surgery. As for the NSF, that was untreatable.

As Shakespeare said, "Rather [we] bear those ills we have than fly to others that we know not of."

Perhaps a semester or two of Shakespeare should be required in medical schools.

CHAPTER THIRTY-THREE

SAVED FROM THE SLAUGHTERHOUSE

It wasn't only Columbia physicians whom we consulted. I recall a visit to a surgeon in Manhattan whose office was located near the Hospital for Special Surgery, with which he was affiliated. He had written a book that was on sale in his office. Unfortunately, I could not buy it. I drove Reva in that day, but we were watching every nickel and dime. We were chronically short of money.

But I glanced through the book while we waited. It seemed to amplify the motto that hung on a wall of his waiting room: "There is no condition that cannot be made worse by surgery."

I do not remember the doctor's name or much about the visit other than that there were two medical students present. I recall, however, that the doctor urged caution in considering surgery.

The reality of the potential consequences of jumping into surgery was brought home a few weeks later and involved a part of Reva's body that was not related to her disability.

We were lying in bed one evening several months after Reva's return from Pennsylvania when she turned to me in alarm.

"Howie, feel my breasts," she said. I took one breast in my fingers and felt a hard lump near the nipple. The other breast also had a hard lump.

In the morning she made an appointment with Dr. Neil Share, who had been her gynecologist for more than twenty years. Dr. Share urged her to see a breast surgeon for a biopsy. He may have recommended one, but Reva had a friend who had been diagnosed with breast cancer and credited a breast surgeon practicing in Hackensack with saving her life. Reva made an appointment with the surgeon, a woman whom I will call Dr. M.

Dr. M. examined Reva's breasts and scheduled a biopsy to be performed in her office.

There are at least two types of breast biopsies: fine-needle aspiration and the more extensive, deep-core biopsy. Both are done under local anesthesia. Reva was scheduled for the deep-core biopsy.

I brought Reva to Dr. M.'s office for the biopsy, which was not done by Dr. M. but by an interventional radiologist, an Indian woman who worked with Dr. M.

However, when Dr. M.'s office scheduled the biopsy, no one had thought to ask Reva if she was taking a blood thinner. She was, in fact, taking coumadin at that time. Blood thinners have to be discontinued a week before a deep-core biopsy because of the risk of excessive bleeding. Fortunately, the radiologist asked before beginning the biopsy. The deep-core biopsy could not be done, and a fine-needle aspiration biopsy was substituted for it.

At Reva's request, I remained in the room during the biopsy. As I wheeled Reva out when it was finished, I observed a puzzling interaction between two nurses, one of whom had assisted at the biopsy. What I observed wasn't anything exceptional. As they spoke to Reva, giving her instructions to call in for the biopsy results, the nurses seemed sad and appeared to me as if they were holding something back. I became frightened that they knew that Reva had breast cancer. But how would they know until they had the pathologist's report? They appeared as if they would like to say something but could not. I also noticed that they exchanged glances. Of course, this is all conjecture on my part, yet I have always remembered those few minutes with the nurses.

The results of the biopsy came back and did not show any sign of cancer, but Dr. M. recommended excising a portion from each breast as a precaution, although there is no history of breast cancer in Reva's family that she knew of. Reva scheduled an appointment for the surgery at Hackensack Hospital, which has since been renamed Hackensack Meridian Hackensack University Medical Center (HMHUMC), and which is how I shall refer to it subsequently. Our understanding from Dr. M. was that only a small portion of each breast would be removed.

Yet both Reva and I had lingering doubts, as the biopsy was negative for cancer. The surgery was a few days away when Reva called Dr. Share's office to ask if she should seek a second opinion.

Dr. Share returned the call the following day when Reva was in dialysis, but I was home. I explained to Dr. Share why Reva had called. His response was emphatic. "She should absolutely get a second opinion," he said. He noted that the pathologist's report had no diagnosis. "She will hardly have any breasts left after this surgery." We had not realized before how extensive the surgery would be. He recommended a breast surgeon in Ridgewood for a second opinion.

When Reva came home and I informed her what Dr. Share advised, she called Dr. M.'s office to postpone the surgery, but the receptionist refused to give her a new date. "When people seek a second opinion, they usually do not return here," she said. I thought this a curious response.

We set up the appointment with Dr. B., the surgeon whom Dr. Share recommended. This time Reva discontinued coumadin for a week, and Dr. B. performed a deep-core biopsy. He also explained that women who have been bedridden for many weeks, as Reva had been, sometimes develop temporary hard nodules in their breasts, which are innocuous and resolve once the woman is active again.

The deep-core biopsy came back negative. There was no need for breast surgery, and Reva did not have it. The nodules resolved, as Dr. B. said they would and, for all her other medical woes, Reva never had trouble with her breasts again. I shudder to think how close she was to having another injury and insult to her body, this one accompanied by loss of a part of her femininity. I am grateful that she called Dr. Share, that I was home to take the call and that he, a doctor who had known Reva for many years, was unequivocal in advising her to get a second opinion. We were almost like sheep ready for slaughter, even though the biopsy showed no evidence of cancer, even though Dr. M. did not suggest that Reva return for a deep-core biopsy after discontinuing coumadin for a week, which seems to me what should have been the logical next step, not a rush to surgery. But hard lumps in the breast of a woman (or a man, for that matter) can be alarming.

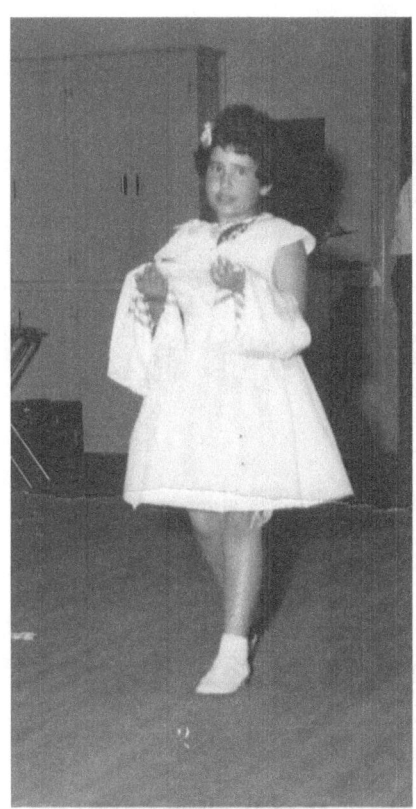

Reva at age eight at Joseph's Bar Mitzvah.

Reva as a teenager. Location unknown.

Civil wedding on January 29, 1988 in Fair Lawn Municipal Court. Judge Jonathan Harris is officiating. Reva's parents are in background.

Reva and Howard under the chuppa at their Jewish wedding on May 18, 1988. Rabbi Benjamin Yudin is officiating. Reva's parents are in the foreground.

Reva and Howard early in their marriage.

Reva bird watching at the Celery Farm in Allendale.

Reva and Howard at a wedding in Rhode Island.

Another photo from the Rhode Island Wedding

Reva at her NYU graduation. Washington Square Arch is in background, and the World Trade Center towers are visible in the distance.

Reva at the Nutley Family Service in the summer of 2001

Reva and Howard at home in 2018.

Another photo of Reva and Howard at home in 2018.

SSH Northeast New Jersey
96 Parkway
Rochelle Park NJ 07662

Prosnitz, Reva E
MRN: 5753, DOB: 11/2/1952, Sex: F
Acct #: 1506766
Adm: 8/20/2019, D/C: 8/27/2019

Prosnitz, Reva E (MR # 5753 / ACCT # 1506766) DOB: 11/02/1952

Procedure Notes (continued)

Procedures by Syed Raza I, MD at 8/26/2019 9:11 AM (continued) Version 1 of 1

Attribution Key
SR.1 - Syed Raza I, MD on 8/26/2019 9:11 AM

Procedures by Neha Chheda, MD at 8/23/2019 9:06 AM Version 1 of 1

Author: Neha Chheda, MD   Service: Nephrology   Author Type: Physician
Filed: 8/23/2019 9:09 AM   Date of Service: 8/23/2019 9:06 AM   Status: Signed
Editor: Neha Chheda, MD (Physician)

Pt seen and examined on dialysis
Tolerating current tx w/o any issues
Low grade fevers; hypotensive requiring low dose levophed; mild tachycardia; on vent - 50% fio2, 5 peep
Awake
Regular s1, s2
ctab anteriorly
abd soft
Ext warm; + edema

Labs reviewed
cxr w/ bibasilar infiltrates
+leukocytosis

A&P: 66yoWF with HTN, hypothyroidism, asthma, hx of DVT, bipolar disorder, hx of NSF wheelchair bound. a-fib on a/c, PADs/p multiple interventions in past. ESRD d/t lithium nephrotoxicity s/p failed renal transplant now on HD since 2013 most recently at Davita Maywood TTS via LUE AVF; per husband, pt was admitted to Holy Name Hospital in on 6/18/19 for LLE ischemia; she was being evaluated for limb salvaging procedures; course c/b cardiac arrest, VDRF, hemodynamic shock; initially weaned off vent and pressors; underwent LLE AKA on 6/25/19; was also found to have BL LE DVTs and underwent IVC filter placement on 6/25/19; underwent R thoracentesis for pleural effusion; course c/b another cardiac arrest ~2 weeks ago c/b VDRF and septic shock; wound growing VRE; unable to be weaned this time; course also notable for GIB, SBO; reportedly was also found to have free air in abdomen c/f perforated viscus; was considered high risk for surgical intervention; currently on TPN and bowel rest; transferred to Select on 8/20/19 for further management. We are consulted for management of ESRD.

1. ESRD on HD - MWF here

- HD today
- aiming for only 1L UF given hypotension and possible sepsis
- dose meds for gfr <10; avoid gadolinium

2. Anemia - hgb 7s; start epogen. Check iron stores

3. Phos low - d/t poor nutritional status; no need for binder

4. HTN - bp currently low; requiring levophed and midodrine. Will use albumin support during HD
[NC.1]

Attribution Key

Medical report from Reva's nephrologist dated August 26, 2019. The report states "ESRD d/t lithium nephrotoxicity." End State Renal Disease due to lithium nephrotoxicity.

CHAPTER THIRTY-FOUR

TEANECK

I covered Demarest, Closter, and Norwood for the *Northern Valley Suburbanite* from the spring of 2005 until the spring of 2006. I was then transferred to the Teaneck edition of the paper.

The Teaneck edition was published from the same Cresskill office as the two other *Suburbanite* editions. Although the transfer did not include a salary increase, it was, effectively, a promotion, as Teaneck, with a population of approximately 40,000, was the largest community covered by the *Suburbanite* and the only one to have its own edition. (The Teaneck edition of the *Northern Valley Suburbanite* later split off into its own weekly, *The Teaneck Suburbanite*.) I was the sole *Suburbanite* Teaneck reporter.

I reported on Teaneck for the next six years, until 2012, when I left North Jersey Media Group. I was responsible for four to five stories per week and the police blotter. I also wrote occasional editorials and, although the *Suburbanite* employed a full-time photographer, I bought a Canon digital camera and took many of the photos that accompanied my stories.

During the six years that I covered Teaneck, I won two first place awards from the New Jersey Press Association: for First Amendment Writing in 2007 and Business Writing in 2009. I also won awards from the NJPA and the Society of Professional Journalists for other stories. I won the NJPA First Amendment award for weeklies three times: first Place in 2007; second Place in 2002; and third Place in 2011.

Covering Teaneck was, for me, a wonderful gift. Teaneck is my home town, where I lived from age three until sixteen and attended Teaneck public schools. Although I grew up in a toxic home, the town itself was beautiful in the 1950s, and still is, although the demographics have changed considerably.

I covered politics, crime, schools, and just about everything else and wrote features. I also wrote a monthly Teaneck history column, "Teaneck Yesterday." Both the idea for the column and its title were my own.

As a columnist, I was permitted to have a headshot accompanying my column, but I chose not to. I feel that anonymity is an important asset to a reporter, and I did not want to be recognized on the street. Or harassed. During my entire newspaper career, I maintained an unpublished landline number.

Reva continued to accompany me to meetings when I needed her, but I was often able to obtain DVDs of the Teaneck council meetings the following day.

The building in Rutherford where we lived for sixteen years had gradually converted to condos. We were offered the opportunity to purchase our apartment, but we couldn't afford to, so it was sold to a couple who invested in real estate. For a few years, we rented the apartment from the new landlords without a problem. Then they informed us that they wanted us out so their daughter could move in.

This was a crisis, but it was also an opportunity to find a more accessible building for Reva. And we did. Rather Reva did. She perused apartment ads in newspapers and found an apartment in Hackensack, which, she was told when on the phone with the realtor, was wheelchair accessible.

But when I went to the building at 88 Clinton Place to meet with the rental agent, I observed that there were steps leading to the front entrance. When the agent arrived, I pointed this out to her. She took me to the side of the building where a driveway sloped to an area of parking spaces and garages and a side door to the lobby. The overhead sliding garage door that separated the driveway from the parking area was key-operated from a box reachable from the driver's seat of a car or from a wheelchair. There was one elevator in the building. The apartment was on the second floor, and the lobby was below it. This was a good arrangement for piano playing because no one would be living under us. It was a one-bedroom apartment, in contrast to the two bedrooms we had in Rutherford, but there was storage area in the basement for each apartment. The rent was about the same. We signed the lease and moved in 2007. Reva now had freedom to use her motorized wheelchair outdoors as well as indoors. She sometimes drove it to a movie theater in Teaneck. We were not far from the bridge that crosses the Hackensack River into Teaneck.

The major drawback was that the building was alongside the NJ Transit railroad tracks. At first, it was a novelty to hear the horns and bells and the trains as they rolled by, but after a while it became more than an annoyance, and I feel that the train noises have permanently diminished my hearing.

In some ways, the three years we lived at 88 Clinton Place were stable years that continued the sixteen years of growth, despite traumas and disappointments, that we experienced in our last years in Rutherford.

As I no longer had a separate room for an office, I set up the computer and phone in a corner of the living room. Vivian, Reva's home health aide, came in two mornings a week. I no longer needed Reva to accompany me to Teaneck meetings: my agoraphobia did not affect my driving at night in Teaneck. I could leave a council meeting after 11:00 p.m., drive on Cedar Lane, Teaneck's main business street, and arrive home in fifteen minutes. I was on familiar turf.

About six months after I turned sixty-five in 2007, Reva told me that she had heard on the radio that I could collect Social Security even though I still worked full-time. I had thought that a worker had to be retired to collect Social Security. I contacted the Social Security Administration, and I received a large retroactive check and, thereafter, a monthly check. After I began receiving the Social Security checks, we were able to keep our heads above water financially. Throughout our marriage, Reva worked quietly and unobtrusively supporting me in countless ways.

CHAPTER THIRTY-FIVE

RETURN TO WORK

A horse chestnut tree grew in front of our Rutherford apartment building. Unlike the fruit of the sweet chestnut tree, the horse chestnut fruit is poisonous.

On the grounds of 88 Clinton Place, a tree grew that shed unusual fruit. Using our *Audubon Society Field Guide to Trees*, we identified it as a black locust tree. I said to Reva that we were getting to know our neighbors' names.

But the joke underscored our loneliness.

We did get to know some of our human neighbors, including Mr. Fitzgerald, who lived next door and whose first name, Clyde, I didn't learn until after he died and I spoke to his daughter. The building's superintendent, Pedro, was a jovial, hardworking Mexican American who was always helpful to us. When he was sick, Reva visited him in Hackensack Meridian Hackensack University Medical Center. Reva would visit the sick, an imperative of Jesus in Christianity, a *mitzvah* in Judaism, and a virtuous act anywhere.

Once Reva began to adjust to her changed circumstances, a process that had no ending, she was eager to return to work. She began with the piano. She called local nursing homes and assisted living centers and offered to play and lead patients in singing and other recreational activities. Several area facilities responded. She auditioned and began to get gigs. She usually played once or twice a week. This was not a volunteer job but work that she was paid for. I remember encountering her in her motorized wheelchair on a cold winter day as she was returning home from a gig in a Hackensack nursing home. She was happy. She was smiling her wide, beautiful smile, piloting the chair with one hand and holding her music bag with the other.

In one of the assisted living facilities where she played, the piano was in a pit and was accessible only by walking down a few steps. There was no railing, and I came with her and held her while she managed the steps. I observed her presentation. She played, led the residents in singing, and afterwards socialized with them. She brought to the job her training as a social worker, her skill as a pianist, and her natural empathy for people, and she brightened the elderly residents' day.

But she wanted to go back to social work. It was the profession for which she had trained. She went for job counseling at the New Jersey Division of Vocational Rehabilitation (NJDVR) in Hackensack. After some workshops in interviewing and résumé building, she was sent on an interview at Plaza Adult Day Care Center in Fair Lawn. She was hired to work two afternoons a week for a total of approximately twelve hours. It was a part-time job and fewer hours per week than she had worked at Liberty Health Care, but that was as much as she could work at this time. She had dialysis three days a week. In addition, she was receiving monthly disability payments, and there was a limit on how much money she was allowed to earn. But the job was for a professional New Jersey licensed social worker, which Reva was.

She worked at Plaza for about three years, until 2012, when she resigned suddenly for reasons that will be explained subsequently. Although she later did volunteer work, Plaza was her last paying job.

She was happy working there, at least for the first two and a half years, and was lucky to have a caring and supportive supervisor, Laura B., a middle-aged social worker who, like Reva, began college later in life.

Fair Lawn today has a large immigrant Russian population, and the day care center was owned and operated by Russian immigrants. The center served several populations. There was a separate section for autistic teenagers. Reva did not work with this group. She worked with the adult clientele, which included both Americans and Russian immigrants, and some of the entertainment programs were in Russian. Reva worked with the American clients. Every client had a diagnosis and had been referred by a physician. Reva spent part of her day with the clients and part at her desk working on their charts.

Laura, a widow, was a friendly, sociable woman and she, Reva, and I met for dinner in local restaurants on several occasions. Most of our social life during these years consisted of dining with friends in restaurants.

Reva traveled to and from Plaza on Access Link, a bus service for the handicapped run by NJ Transit. Access Link picked her up at our apartment and took her home later. There was usually a window of about twenty minutes for the bus to arrive.

There were abundant flowers on the grounds of 88 Clinton Place, and I can still see Reva on a warm spring day sitting in her motorized wheelchair waiting for the Access Link bus. She always dressed well, which was one of the things I noticed about her when we first met in the group therapy sessions so many years ago. She would come from work, always wearing a nice outfit. She had a taste for colorful garments. She has been dead at this writing for two years, and I still have almost all her clothing.

Hackensack Meridian Hackensack University Medical Center sold its outpatient dialysis department to a private, for-profit dialysis company. With Americans living longer and kidney failure often a consequence of aging, dialysis has become a big business. It was inevitable that private companies would enter it, and private dialysis centers have sprung up nationwide. Reva no longer received dialysis at Johnson Hall, a building that was part of Hackensack Meridian Hackensack University Medical Center, but at a private dialysis center in Maywood, a town bordering Hackensack.

However, Dr. Ackad and his nephrology group remained her nephrologists and made rounds at the private dialysis center. The changes from outpatient hospital-based dialysis to a private, profit-making center were subtle, but there were some notable ones. Patients no longer had beds but sat in reclining chairs for the three-to-four-hour sessions. For Reva, this was uncomfortable because of her disability. In addition, Dr. Ackad could no longer order samples of Reva's blood from the dialysis line for any testing except nephrological or add an antibiotic to her line for treatment of a respiratory infection. He could no longer act as her internist or, as they say today, primary care provider. The dialysis center allowed only kidney tests and treatment, a limitation that fragmented the care of some very sick people, as most dialysis patients are.

The period in Reva's life from approximately 2007 to 2010 was relatively smooth, given her physical limitations. She saw a psychotherapist once a week in Teaneck. She worked two days a week and was in dialysis three days. I continued to work full-time for the *Suburbanite* and to write two monthly articles for the trade magazine *ANSOM*. I had also begun to teach again in the communication department of Fairleigh Dickinson University. Our financial problems were mitigated. A highlight of this period was the fiftieth reunion in 2010 of the Teaneck High School class of 1960. Reva and I attended the banquet in a hotel in Woodcliff Lake, where I saw people whom I hadn't seen for more than fifty years, as I attended Teaneck schools from kindergarten through the ninth grade but did not graduate from Teaneck High School. My family moved to Westwood when I was sixteen. However, I did not attend Westwood High School.

One evening soon after we moved to 88 Clinton Place, Reva was cooking supper and I was in the living room on the phone with a pharmacist obtaining information about one of her medicines, which she had asked me to do. I heard her scream. I rushed into the kitchen. She had spilled boiling water on her thigh and buttocks. Fortunately, the water did not hit her genitals or her bad leg. She was crying in pain. I called 911, and an ambulance transported her to the Hackensack Meridian Hackensack University Medical Center emergency room. I followed in my car.

She had suffered second-and third-degree burns. She was given a shot of morphine which eased her pain. A nurse tried to draw blood from her arm but was unsuccessful. Reva had small blood vessels, a result of her many years in dialysis. A highly skilled phlebotomist was usually needed to draw her blood.

At about 2:00 a.m., the ER doctor told me that she would be discharged. I protested. She had suffered severe burns over a wide area of her body. How could she even use the toilet with her buttocks burned? The doctor implied that one reason for discharging her was that the nurse had been unable to draw blood. I demanded that another nurse try. The second nurse succeeded. The doctor then relented and admitted her.

She spent about a week in Hackensack Meridian Hackensack University Medical Center in the newly built women's pavilion. She was given good care, including whirlpool baths. She was then sent to Wellington Care Center in Hackensack, one of the rehab centers where she had played the piano. Her ambulance service transported her to dialysis during the ten days that she was in Wellington.

I wrote a letter to the patient advocate of HMHUMC, in which I first praised the care she was given once she was admitted and then questioned the judgement of the doctor who wanted to discharge a severely burned patient.

To my surprise, the doctor who was head of the emergency department phoned me and said that the ER doctor thought I wanted Reva discharged. This was not so. Hackensack Meridian Hackensack University Medical Center ER was bad then. It has gotten much worse. We lived, and I still live, in a high-rise on Prospect Avenue, just blocks from the hospital, but I have learned that many of my neighbors will not go there.

CHAPTER THIRTY-SIX

GOOD FRIDAY

There was only one elevator at 88 Clinton Place, and the City of Hackensack and the building management determined that it needed extensive repairs and would be out of service for at least two weeks. The management staff, to its credit, was concerned about Reva. They knew she could not use the stairs in the five-story building and that she was in dialysis three days a week and worked two days a week. The company also managed Brookchester, a sprawling complex of garden apartments in New Milford, a town near Hackensack. Brookchester was built in the 1940s for returning veterans. It is one of the largest and was one of the first such complexes in the United States.

Teaneck also experienced a surge of apartment construction for veterans in the late 1940s. In fact, so many apartments were going up in Teaneck that the council enacted a moratorium on new apartment buildings, fearing, in the words of one councilman at the time, that the town would become an "apartment city."

The management moved Reva and me into a Brookchester apartment temporarily. We paid no rent, as we continued to pay our rent at 88 Clinton Place. The company also paid for moving us in and out and for a portable aluminum ramp that I rented, as there were a few steps from the street to the entrance of our temporary first floor apartment. All Brookchester apartments are either on the first or second floor.

The Brookchester apartment was smaller than our Clinton Place apartment, and we only took essential items with us, including our bed, computer, television, desk, couch, and kitchen utensils and appliances.

The ramp weighed seventy-five pounds and folded up into a unit that looked like an oversized suitcase. I put it out for Reva each time she left or came in, but I always brought it back inside. Metals like aluminum, as I learned from many police reports, are prime targets for theft.

At first, Reva adjusted well to our new surroundings. Our exile from 88 Clinton Place lasted close to a month before the elevator was finally repaired and inspected by the city. Vivian, Reva's home health aide, continued to come two mornings a week. (Reva worked in the afternoons.) But the complex was large and not close to stores and neighborhoods. Vivian accompanied Reva one morning to the New Milford Public Library, where Reva took out books, but otherwise she had little to do in her spare time and became depressed.

One night, I was awakened by the sound of voices in the living room. I discovered an angry Reva and two New Milford police officers. She had called 911 claiming that I had assaulted her. I had not and, indeed, as the police officers affirmed, had been asleep. But I sometimes sleep restlessly and might have bumped into her in my sleep or even flailed my arm. It is impossible to say because I have never witnessed my movements when I am asleep. The cops left, but Reva was beginning to show signs of a breakdown brought on, in part, by boredom and dislocation. Indeed, she ended up in Hackensack Meridian Hackensack University Medical Center's psych ward for a few days while we were living in Brookchester.

We were still there on Easter 2010, and I was a lector at Christ Episcopal Church in Hackensack at the evening Good Friday service. I had been attending Christ Church for about six months, sometimes with Reva, but she didn't come with me to the Good Friday service. I had become one of the church's lectors, but I was not yet a baptized Christian.

I had been searching for a faith for many years. To sum up as simply as possible how I came to Christ Episcopal: There is a sign outside the church that reads, "Wherever you are in your journey of faith you are welcome here." Welcome. The word means a lot to me. I have, unfortunately, been in many situations where I have not felt welcomed or have felt barely tolerated, like a poor, annoying relative. But Father Bill Parnell, the rector, and Father Phil Krug, the associate priest, and the entire congregation welcomed Reva and me. I even performed the role of Christ at a Palm Sunday Passion Play in 2011, and this was before I was baptized. (There wasn't any acting; the passion play was an oral presentation.) Although Reva remained Jewish to her death and had a Jewish funeral, she participated in my baptism at Christ Church in 2013. She did so out of love. At my request, the baptism was in the evening. I wanted a quiet ceremony, and we had only a few guests, all from the church. Fr. Michael Gerhardt, who had replaced Fr. Bill Parnell, who had become Archdeacon of Missions at the Episcopal Diocese of New York, baptized me and allowed Reva and me to choose the readings for the service. Reva read the great chapter on love, 1 Corinthians 13, and I read chapter two of Genesis, the story of the creation of Eve. Fr. Michael, at my request, read a Gospel passage about healing. The readings personalized my baptism.

Another personalization was a change that I requested in the text of the baptismal vows. Even when driving to my baptism that evening, I had qualms. Changing religions is not something done lightly. When Reva and I arrived at the church, I requested some substitutions in the language, and Fr. Michael complied. So I accepted Jesus as my role model and companion, which was substituted for savior. But the baptism was official. I have the certificate.

Afterward, everyone had coffee and a cake that Reva had brought. Although Reva remained Jewish, and devoutly Jewish, lighting candles on Friday nights and going to the synagogue as often as her dialysis schedule permitted, she had no problem with my conversion. In fact, sometimes when strangers asked her what her religion was, she replied, "Jewish Episcopalian." That usually shut them up. But I think she was partially serious. However, she often told me that she would never convert because of the experience of her parents in the Holocaust.

Reva had a deep identity as a Jew, but she had a greater identity as a human being who tried to do good for others. In my eulogy at her funeral, I said that she did good for many people but no one more than for me. Reva was often deeply moved by the sermons at church. She had a close relationship with Fr. Michael and had met privately with him before my baptism. Except for me, he was her most frequent visitor during her hospitalizations. She had a Jewish funeral conducted by Rabbi Simon Glustrom, the retired rabbi from Fair Lawn who lives in our building and who knew Reva, but Fr. Michael, at my invitation, delivered a nonreligious sermon that focused on Reva's courage and determination in the face of adversity. In Reva's case, these are not platitudes but truths.

She is buried in George Washington Memorial Park in Paramus, where I will be buried next to her. This is a nonsectarian cemetery that we chose together as the final destination of our bodies several years before Reva's last illness and her death.

Reva also had a close relationship with Fr. Jim Warnke, a legally blind priest associated with Christ Church who, like Reva, was a social worker. Fr. Jim's wife, Marie Warnke, had been a Teaneck council member before I began covering Teaneck for the *Suburbanite*, but she was a member of several town committees during the years I covered Teaneck, and I occasionally interviewed her.

Reva enjoyed the coffee hour after church and the various buffet lunches held on Sunday afternoons throughout the year. In our limited social life, the church activities played an important role. Reva had an almost mystical Jewish consciousness, but she also had an open mind. As she says in her spiritual autobiography in Chapter 3 of this memoir, she saw no conflict in attending Jewish and Episcopal services. However, she was sometimes called to read from the Torah in the synagogue, but she never took communion or participated in the healing services at the church. The latter, which used to be part of the weekly service, was another reason I came to worship at Christ Church.

The first service I attended there in the 1990s was a healing service. Fr. Mark Beckwith, the rector at the time (he later became bishop of the Newark diocese), laid his hands on anyone who came up to the alter for healing. He said that the healing touch could be transferred to others.

I did not go up to the alter, but when I got home that Sunday, I laid my hands on Reva's back over her kidneys. This was several years before she entered dialysis. When her creatinine was tested later that month, it had dropped, a healthy sign for someone with kidney disease.

Who can explain these things?

CHAPTER THIRTY-SEVEN

RETURN TO PHILADELPHIA

My mother was born in Elizabeth, New Jersey to Russian-Jewish immigrant parents. My father was born in the Bronx, New York to an American-born father and a German-born mother. Both were Jewish. Both my parents, on occasion, used Yiddish words and phrases, my mother more than my father, and the expressions were usually derisive or scatological. Yiddish seemed to me a vulgar tongue.

But Reva would sing beautiful Yiddish songs her mother taught her. One song was about the moon as a gift from God to lovers. Another was a riddle song in which a student tests his prospective bride's cleverness.

I loved to hear Reva sing these songs, which were in a Yiddish so unlike the phrases and fragments I grew up with. When I was anxious or sleepless, I would ask her to sing me the song about the moon or the riddle song, and she would always comply. I have listened to these songs on the Internet, but no one sings them as beautifully as Reva did.

In her journal, she wrote that I was the *narisher bokher*, the foolish student of the riddle song.

We moved from Brookchester back to Clinton Place, and in 2010 we moved into a larger apartment in another building in Hackensack, away from the trains.

I still live in this building as of this writing in December 2021, although I moved into a smaller apartment after Reva's death.

Reva continued to work two afternoons a week at Plaza Adult Day Care. I continued to work full-time for the *Suburbanite*, teach part-time at Fairleigh Dickinson University, and write two articles a month for *ANSOM*. However, in 2012, *ANSOM* ceased publication.

The magazine had already shrunk from a big, splashy monthly to a much slimmer publication that came out in print eight times a year with four additional issues appearing only on the Internet. Long the bible of the army and navy store, military surplus, and outdoor store industry with an international circulation, *ANSOM* became an early casualty of the decline of print media. I had written on the average of two articles a month for *ANSOM* from 1997 to 2012.

One of the curiosities about writing for *ANSOM* is that the experience humanized the army and navy store industry to me. Although my family owned army and navy stores and I had worked in them, even when I was in elementary school (often without pay as a punishment from my father) and in later life when I needed a job, I never felt any affection for the business or regarded it as anything more than a way of earning some money when I didn't have other work. Although my father was a partner until his early death in 1961, neither my mother, nor I, nor my siblings ever had any ownership in the business, and according to my mother, my father's share of the ownership did not pass to any of us but to the other partners: his father and two brothers.

But writing about the industry and interviewing retailers, wholesalers, and manufacturers from all regions of the country gave it a humanity that my family never did. I even discovered a romance in its history and learned about the variety of surplus and army and navy stores—from those that double as gun shops, mainly in the South, to stores that sell only authentic surplus, to stores catering to the blue-collar worker, and to those that resemble museums of military memorabilia. Writing for *ANSOM* brought me the belated respect of my father's brother Milton, who, with his son Ted, was the last owner of Prozys. The business subscribed to *ANSOM* and Milton read my articles, and it was Ted who first showed me a copy after I returned from an unsuccessful interview in Manhattan for a job with a hardware industry trade magazine.

After we moved to our new apartment, we bought a ramp-van so Reva could travel more easily. This was a modified Toyota Sienna van with the middle row of seats removed and an automated ramp installed that descended from the rear passenger's side door. Now Reva could travel with her motorized wheelchair. There was no longer a need for me to help her into our Hyundai sedan, fold up her manual wheelchair, and pack it in the trunk.

The next step was for her to learn to drive using hand controls and obtain a manual control driver's license. She took lessons at Kessler Institute in Saddle Brook and passed the state test. I then brought the ramp-van back to the dealer and hand controls were installed. Reva could now drive the van independently, and I could still drive it using standard foot controls.

Like most New Jersey teenagers, Reva initially obtained her driver's license at seventeen and drove until she became disabled following her surgery at the University of Pennsylvania. Now she could drive again.

She drove to malls, to the Teaneck Library, to the supermarket (where she would ask an employee to help load the vehicle), and to meet with her friends. A group of women who had graduated with Reva from Fair Lawn High School met every few months for dinner in restaurants in Bergen and Passaic counties, and Reva drove herself to join them. For the last four years of her life, Reva took art lessons every Monday at the Art Center of Northern New Jersey in New Milford. I knew Reva had a talent for the visual arts and had often urged her to take lessons, but she would respond that the piano was her creativity. To her great joy, she finally relented and studied art for all-too-brief a period. Reva usually drove herself to art school. When I had hip surgery in 2016, Reva drove and did the errands.

In July 2012, we traveled to Philadelphia for the wedding of her niece, her brother's younger daughter.

Minute and careful planning was essential for a successful trip. I overcame my travel phobia, or at least suspended it: I knew we would be traveling in an air-conditioned train and that the ride was less than an hour. And I knew how badly Reva wanted to go.

The wedding was scheduled for Saturday evening. She had dialysis Friday evening, and Saturday morning we took a taxi from our building to Penn Station in Newark. It was necessary to book a specific train at a specific time both to Philadelphia and back because Amtrak had to supply an employee with a ramp so Reva could board and leave the train in her wheelchair. Because we traveled by taxi to Newark,

Reva took her manual rather than motorized wheelchair. When we arrived in Philadelphia, we took a taxi to the hotel, and the wheelchair went in the trunk. We attended the wedding, and Sunday morning her brother hosted a brunch. On Sunday afternoon, we took a cab to the historic district, but it was so crowded that we took another cab to the Philadelphia Museum of Art, where we spent the rest of the day. We stayed over at the hotel Sunday night, and on Monday morning we returned to New Jersey. While at the hotel, I conducted an interview by phone and on the train ride home, wrote a story for the *Suburbanite* on my laptop. As soon as we arrived in Hackensack, I drove Reva to dialysis. Hemodialysis patients cannot go safely for more than two days without a treatment.

To the seasoned traveler, these may seem like petty details and an insignificant trip, but to us it was a victory: I overcame a major phobia and Reva got to Philadelphia for her niece's wedding. A bonus was the Philadelphia Museum. When someone disabled and in dialysis is accompanied by someone suffering from anxiety and phobias, it is a little like the blind leading the blind. Travel requires careful preparation.

CHAPTER THIRTY-EIGHT

PLAZA

The Philadelphia wedding was in July 2012. In mid-August, my editor at the *Suburbanite*, C.K., phoned and told me that she wanted me to come to the Cresskill office on August 22 and to bring my company laptop. I asked her if I was getting fired. She said no. I asked her if anyone else would be at the meeting. She said that G.F., the publisher of the weekly division, would be there.

I had been working from home for more than two years. Many reporters at North Jersey Media Group were now so-called "mojos," mobile journalists, and worked from home or from wherever they could park their laptops. The computer age no longer required the presence of the reporter in the office.

C.K. was a young, recently married woman who was now pregnant. She would be taking a maternity leave. She had been my editor for about three years. She was adept at computers and layout, and I no longer participated in the latter. As I wrote much better than she did and was a careful proofreader of my own work (Reva also proofread my drafts and her quick eyes often found errors I had overlooked), C.K. did not edit my work much except on occasions when a story required clearance from the legal department.

G.F. was an older woman who rarely showed up in a weekly newspaper office unless there was bad news. So I was apprehensive about the meeting.

On Aug. 22, 2012, I came to the Cresskill office with the laptop. "Your job has been eliminated," C.K. announced cheerfully to me. As C.K. was now editor of three additional weeklies (their editor having been fired by the company), and was about to go on maternity leave, the company decided to appoint a managing editor for her papers.

The managing editor would double as Teaneck reporter. When I suggested that I be appointed managing editor, G.F. told me that I did not have the experience.

She also told me that I would receive three months' severance pay, the maximum allowed by NJMG, if I signed a severance agreement. "I don't want to go so quietly," I said, and took the papers with me but did not sign them that day. (I later signed them and mailed them to human resources.) I remember the silence of the two women as I walked out. They didn't wish me good luck or commend me for the decade and a half that I worked for NJMG, winning more than a dozen press awards, including two first place awards from the New Jersey Press Association. The scene reminded me of the evening some twenty-five years earlier when the Passaic Public Library Board of Trustees, led by Ben Gold, accepted my resignation.

I called Reva from the car and told her what had happened. I described it as a mixed blessing. For many months, I had thought about requesting a change from full-time to part-time status, but I never took any action. NJMG let me go a month after my seventieth birthday. I had Medicare, as did Reva because she was a hemodialysis patient, so I no longer depended on NJMG for medical insurance, and I continued to teach at Fairleigh Dickinson University.

The cold manner in which I was let go and the apparent lack of appreciation for my years at NJMG rankle me to this day. The Borg family, which had owned NJMG for almost a century, has since sold the company to Gannett, and the iconic headquarters building at 150 River Street in Hackensack has been demolished. But I will never forget the casual way I was dropped. Let it suffice to say that I have never looked at a copy of the *Teaneck Suburbanite* since, and I have bought a copy of the *Record* less than a dozen times in the nine years since I left the company. I also refuse to subscribe to the on-line edition, so I am not abreast of local news, but that's fine with me.

Reva continued to work two days a week at Plaza, and I continued to teach at Fairleigh Dickinson. But Reva would soon leave her job.

Laura B., her supervisor, had already left. A much younger social worker was hired to take Laura's place. This young woman wanted Reva on the floor mingling with clients her entire workday. This was difficult for someone in a wheelchair. Reva sometimes had to wheel after a male client while holding his walker and alert him when the man neglected to take it to the men's room. Reva's new supervisor took from Reva, not only her charts, but her desk. Another young woman, who was not a social worker, was hired who now worked on clients' charts at Reva's former desk.

It was humiliating to Reva to have professional work removed from her and given to a nonprofessional, although the woman who now did the charts knew Russian and had that advantage in documenting the Russian clients.

Reva was a modest and humble person, but she had worked hard for her social work degree. Having her desk taken from her and her professional work given to a nonprofessional was a blow to her pride.

Laura had been a friend to Reva. The social worker who took Laura's place maintained a strictly business relationship.

Reva had also begun developing additional health problems. She had a Stage 1 pressure sore from the wheelchair. However, she took care of it, seeing a wound care specialist and her dermatologist regularly, and the sore never advanced beyond Stage 1 until her final illness years later. But it was painful for her to sit in the wheelchair for many hours.

She had told me that she intended to resign soon. "It may be sooner than you think," she said, before leaving for work one day.

Indeed, it was. That day Reva resigned.

She had made up her mind, she later told me. She confronted her supervisor, who denied speaking to her in a harsh, authoritarian tone, which Reva complained to me she had. Plaza's owner offered to let Reva use his desk, but Reva was determined. The staff hastily convened a party for her, sending out for flowers and food. She was moved by all this and recorded it on a tape recorder she carried with her. She gave a little speech bidding farewell to her clients, mentioning many by name. Reva's gentle manner was appreciated by the clients, and for several years after she left, she and Laura would meet with some of them in restaurants on birthdays and holidays. Reva maintained her friendship with Laura to the end.

Although Reva later played the piano as a volunteer in the lobby of the cancer center of Hackensack Meridian Hackensack University Medical Center, Plaza was her last paying job. She later had misgivings about her decision to leave and tried to get the job back. But there had been a fire in an adjacent part of the building, and fumes still permeated the day care wing. The owner did not think it would be healthy for Reva to return.

Reva took on-line courses and renewed her social work license every two years, as the State of New Jersey requires, and she sent out résumés and was still hoping to resume her career at the time of her final hospitalization.

But at other times she expressed the desire to retire. There was a weariness in her voice. New and encroaching health problems were emerging. Sadly, her career as a social worker lasted only five years, most of it, part-time.

CHAPTER THIRTY-NINE

HACKENSACK MERIDIAN HACKENSACK UNIVERSITY MEDICAL CENTER

Reva left her job at Plaza in 2013. I must now write about the final six years of her life, years of stress and increasing health problems through which Reva remained creative and active almost until the end. Her final illness and early death were unexpected and, I believe, preventable. Her killer was psychiatry, which claimed her as a victim when she was fourteen and she was put on lithium, which ultimately destroyed her kidneys. Death, in the form of psychiatry and American medicine, took Reva as its own. Her major illnesses were iatrogenic. Were it not for lithium, she would be here with me now, perhaps sitting on the couch next to me reading; she would have been cycling and swimming through this long summer of 2020, instead of lying in the grave. Psychiatry and American medicine killed her, while generating billions of dollars for doctors and hospital CEOs.

American medicine crucified her as surely as, according to the Gospels, Pontius Pilate crucified Jesus.

Hackensack Meridian Hackensack University Medical Center played a large role in the last years of Reva's life. It is a grim specter three blocks from where Reva and I lived and where I now live alone. As I have written, many of my neighbors on Prospect Avenue, where the hospital is located, will not go there. One neighbor who had breast cancer surgery at Hackensack Meridian Hackensack University Medical Center swears she will never return there. She went to Englewood Hospital for her chemotherapy. I am inserting below two emails that I sent to Senator Loretta Weinberg, the New Jersey state senator who represented the district where Reva and I lived.

These emails, sent four years apart, barely begin to describe the horror of this hospital's emergency room and psychiatric facility.

The first email is from 2018, and the circumstances involved Reva's infected right foot. The second email was sent several years earlier. My experience with Hackensack Meridian Hackensack University Medical Center made me reluctant to have Reva transferred there in July 2019 from Holy Name Hospital in Teaneck. These circumstances will be narrated later.

Concerning the second email, Reva told me afterwards that Dr. Ackad, her nephrologist at the time, said that if she went through another such ordeal, she would die.

Dear Senator Weinberg:

I need your help ASAP. Your office has helped me in the past with problems related to Hackensack University Medical Center. Yesterday afternoon, July 5, at 5:30 p.m., my wife, Reva Prosnitz, was sent over to the hospital for admission by her podiatrist, Dr. Chioddo (Dr. Edward Harris's, office, 20 Prospect Ave., Hackensack) for an infected foot. The doctor wanted her admitted to the hospital for IV antibiotics and possible incision and drainage of the wound. The only way to be admitted to that hospital is through the ER. We arrived at the ER waiting room at 5:30 p.m. Thurs. July 5. As of this morning, 11 a.m. July 6, my wife is still in the ER. She is in the treatment area. I spoke to her on the phone a few minutes ago. She told me that she saw a doctor for the first time at about 10 this morning. She has been rotting in the ER for 17 hours. She is a hemodialysis patient and has not been given any of her medications. She is disabled and dependent on a wheelchair and has been unsuccessful in attempting to attract someone's attention to help her to the bathroom. She has been ignored (although they did begin IV antibiotics).

I had grave misgivings, based on past experience, when the doctor wanted her to enter HUMC, but this is the hospital where he works from. It is a horrible hospital, a horrible ER that should be investigated by the state. Please help my wife in getting humane treatment. No human being should be treated this way.

I am willing to give written and/or oral testimony about the practices of HUMC as my wife and I have experienced them. But it is more urgent to help my wife. My mobile phone number is xxx-xxx-xxxx.

Sincerely,
Howard Prosnitz

Dear Senator Weinberg:

I spoke to D. [Sen. Weinberg's chief of staff] earlier today. I had brought my wife, Reva Prosnitz, (DOB 11/2/52) to the emergency room of Hackensack University Medical Center at 11 a.m. Monday Nov. 5. She is bipolar and was in an unstable state. HUMC has an in-patient psychiatric unit on the sixth floor of the St. John Building. In fact, Reva was an in-patient there from Oct. 24–Oct. 30.

She was still in the ER waiting for a bed in 6 St. John at 11 p.m. on Nov. 5. She did not even have a room in the ER. She was on a stretcher next to the nurses' station in the noisy, brightly lit ER. The nurses told me that she would be admitted to 6 St. John and was waiting for a bed. She was kept there all night, more than 24 hours after she came to the ER. This morning, Nov. 6, the nurse told me she had no sleep during the night. She was taken to dialysis in-patient this morning (she is a hemodialysis patient). She is now on 6 St. John and she called me a few minutes ago. She is profoundly exhausted from this ordeal. She is disabled and depends on a wheelchair. The nurse tells me they have ordered one for her, but she does not have one now. She can't even get to the bathroom. They have given her no food, but she told me what she wants now is rest. Why do people face such an ordeal when they enter this hospital? How can a person be restored to mental health when she is deprived of sleep, forced to lie awake all night on a stretcher in the hallway of a noisy, brightly lit ER?

When she was a patient in 6 St. John last week, from the time she was admitted, I requested on numerous occasions to speak to her doctor. I did not receive a call until Oct. 28, five days after she was admitted.

She has no wheelchair. The bathrooms on this unit are tiny and she needs the assistance of two female aids to use them, although normally she can use a handicapped bathroom on her own. There is no handicapped shower on this unit and she was unable to bathe during the six days she was there last week. When she was a patient on 6 St. John several years ago, she was brought downstairs to another floor where she could shower in a handicapped equipped shower. But apparently no one offered to bring her there last week.

Most of all, she needs rest. She told me that when she was there last week, the hallways were noisy at night and the nurses were clicking all night at a computer station right outside her room. Her greatest need right now is a quiet place to sleep to restore her mental health and prevent deterioration of her physical health.

I have also contacted the NJ Dept. of Health about some of these issues.

Reva and I will be grateful to you for whatever help you can give us.

Sincerely,
Howard Prosnitz

CHAPTER FORTY

ART SCHOOL

Senator Weinberg's office contacted the Consumer Affairs Department at Hackensack Meridian Hackensack University Medical Center, and a representative of that department contacted me. Thereafter, Reva's physical treatment on 6 St. John improved, and she was able to take a shower. As for the horrible experience in the ER, that was done. I complained to the State. I am sure that there are people who, experiencing chest pains, would rather risk a heart attack than go to the Hackensack Meridian Hackensack University Medical Center ER, and I can't blame them. Fortunately, there are other ERs in the area.

I no longer taught at Fairleigh Dickenson but taught public speaking at Montclair State University. In 2013, I began writing monthly articles for a trade magazine, *Surplus Today*, which was the successor to *ANSOM*. But *Surplus Today* paid me less than half of what *ANSOM* had paid me, and I was assigned only one article a month. My request for a raise was denied. I was informed that the magazine paid all writers the same rate. I wrote for *Surplus Today* for about two years but did not enjoy the work. In addition to being underpaid, I felt uncomfortable calling my former *ANSOM* contacts for interviews. The army navy/military surplus industry had changed, as had retail in general. For example, when I began writing for *ANSOM*, there were three army and navy stores in Hackensack, including my family's store. Today there is none. Military surplus sales now are mainly through the Internet. In 2015, *Surplus Today* changed its format and even its name, and I was dropped as a writer. I was not unhappy.

Reva, having been discharged from Hackensack Meridian Hackensack University Medical Center, continued in dialysis, volunteered playing the piano, and emailed her résumé for social work jobs. I advised her to always include in her cover letter the fact that she was disabled and in a wheelchair, but that she drove and had her own transportation.

There are many things I regret in our marriage, things I did not do for Reva. For example, she wanted to travel. This is difficult when someone is disabled and in dialysis but not impossible, and we had been planning a vacation. We planned to visit Washington DC but dropped the idea after Trump's election. We planned to go to Williamsburg, Virginia, and in the last year of Reva's life but before the crisis that brought her into the hospital, we were planning to go to Cape May, and I think we could have pulled this one off but for ensuing events. A vacation would mean careful planning, travel by train, and arranging with the dialysis center for Reva's dialysis in one of its other facilities. The company had centers nationwide, but had to be informed at least six weeks in advance for vacation scheduling.

But except for our honeymoon in Canada when we first married, the wedding in Philadelphia and another wedding in Williamsburg, Brooklyn, we traveled little, although we frequently went into Manhattan both before and after Reva became disabled, but more often before. Reva loved the ocean and wanted to see it again. I regret that I didn't take her to the New Jersey shore. My failure here was because of my agoraphobia, which had intensified.

But as I consider my many failures in our marriage, and I know that Reva loved me despite them, I take credit for one thing I did right when Reva and I faced a crisis in late August 2015.

The crisis was not substantially different from ones she had faced since she was a teenager: hospitalization in a psychiatric facility, in this case 6 St. John at HMHUMC. But it didn't happen.

Reva had been seeing a psychiatrist at HMHUMC's psychiatric outpatient department, which was located about two miles from the hospital in a building on Route 17 that also housed a gym that seemed to be jointly run by HMHUMC and the New York Giants football team. HMHUMC advertised its gym as "Powered by the Giants," an unusual arrangement for a hospital.

The gym occupied about half the building, and the psychiatric clinic and some other HMHUMC outpatient departments, the other half.

The psychiatrist, whom I will call Dr. B., was an Indian or Pakistani whose medical degree was from Spartan Health Science University, a for-profit medical school located in Santa Lucia. According to a 2003 article in the *Hartford Courant*, the school comprised "four classrooms, one lab and three old cadavers" and was located near a brewery.

For years, the *Courant* article says, governing officials of Santa Lucia have refused to license Spartan grads or allow the school's students to train in local hospitals out of "deep skepticism" of the school's standards. Six US states, including Texas and California, would not license Spartan graduates at the time the article was written.

But New Jersey licenses them and HMHUMC employs them.

Reva was also in psychotherapy with a middle-aged female social worker at the HMHUMC outpatient clinic.

She was in a hyper mood when I brought her for her regular appointment with the social worker and the psychiatrist. They called me into the consulting room. Reva must go immediately to the ER at HMHUMC to be evaluated for admission to 6 St. John, they said. She apparently wasn't so erratic that they would call an ambulance, but I had to take her to the hospital. "Trust us," the social worker said.

Reva seemed compliant and drove her motorized chair into the rear of the van. It was late afternoon on a late August day.

The gym/outpatient facility had an exit from its parking lot onto Essex Street. The hospital is located on Essex Street and Prospect Avenue.

As I drove Reva up the Essex Street hill, I thought of the sleepless night she had spent in the ER, which I described in the previous chapter.

"Do you want to go to the hospital?" I asked her.

"No," she said.

"Will you be alright at home?"

"Yes."

I made a left turn off Essex and brought her home.

When we reached our apartment, I showed her a brochure that had come in the mail a few days earlier from the Art Center of Northern New Jersey, which is located in New Milford, announcing its fall classes. I had long recognized Reva's talented hands and admired watercolors she had painted and had urged her to enroll in one of the art schools in Bergen County. This time she heeded my advice and the next day registered for a course in watercolors given on Monday afternoons.

This began a course of study that continued up to her admission to Holy Name Hospital in June 2019. Every Monday, year-round, except for holidays and breaks between semesters, she took a lesson at the Art Center of Northern New Jersey. The first semester was watercolors, but later she studied drawing from live models and drawing still lifes. She studied under the same teacher for the four years and usually drove herself to the school and home. Sometimes, when she was tired or the weather was very bad, I drove her.

I could observe the parking lot of our building from our bedroom window and would take pleasure in seeing her drive into the parking space at 5:00 p.m., electronically lower the ramp from inside the van and drive her chair down, holding her big, red art bag with one arm. When a car was parked in the space next to the passenger's side, she would call me from the van to park the vehicle, as the adjacent car prevented her from parking the van and lowering the ramp.

We set up a long table (she didn't want an easel) facing a large window in our living room. After the watercolors course, she usually worked in pastels, charcoal, and pencils. As I have mentioned, Reva was a modest and humble person, but I remember rare moments of pride. We were driving to an art supply store and she knew just what she wanted. "I know my pencils," she said. She was acquiring new knowledge and learning a new craft.

Just before she was admitted to the hospital in 2019, from which she never returned, she chose two pictures to be evaluated for entry in a summer-long, county-wide juried art show at the school.

After she entered the hospital, I had the pictures—one in pastels and the other in pastels and charcoal—professionally framed and brought them to the school. On July 14, 2019, Bastille Day, I received a call from the school that the pictures had been accepted into the exhibit. Reva, at the time, appeared to be recovering and had been moved from the ICU to a regular medical floor. I visited her and told her the news. "I'm so proud of myself," she said.

The pictures today hang above the piano, reminding me always of Reva's creativity.

CHAPTER FORTY-ONE

HEALTH CONCERNS

After more than a decade in dialysis and disabled from a rare disease she acquired following an unsuccessful kidney transplant in 2004, Reva developed other health problems.

She had experienced shortness of breath and was in treatment with a pulmonologist beginning in 2012 or earlier. She used a nebulizer twice a day and carried albuterol with her in case of emergencies. I remember buying a plastic replacement part for her nebulizer at a drug store in Philadelphia when we were there for the 2012 wedding.

The pulmonologist also found that fluid had accumulated on one side of her chest cavity. An interventional radiologist drained the fluid in the outpatient department of HMHUMC. Reva was conscious during the procedure; only a local anesthetic was necessary. But the radiologist said that the fluid would return periodically. There was talk of putting a permanent catheter in one side of Reva's chest and teaching me to drain the fluid at home or having a visiting nurse drain it. The decision, as I recall, was left to Dr. Howard Weizman, who was now Reva's nephrologist, Dr. Ackad having retired. Dr. Weizman was a member of the same nephrology group.

Dr. Weizman had Reva come in for some extra dialysis treatments but, as best I remember, rejected the proposal to insert a catheter. As I recall from what Reva told me, Dr. Weizman's opinion was that normal dialysis three days a week would rid her body of the excess fluid.

The pulmonologist eventually diagnosed Reva with pulmonary hypertension, took her off the nebulizer (she still used albuterol when needed), and referred her to a heart failure specialist at the HMHUMC.

I had never heard of pulmonary hypertension. As best I understand the disease, it has nothing to do with the overall blood pressure of the body as measured by the sphygmomanometer, the standard blood pressure machine that we are all familiar with. In fact, Reva's blood pressure, like that of most dialysis patients, was low. Dialysis lowers blood pressure.

On dialysis days she would take her blood pressure before leaving for the treatment. If it was below a certain number, she would take an oral medicine to raise it. She would often need a second dose during dialysis.

Although I bought a book on pulmonary hypertension during the summer of 2019 when Reva was in the ICU at Holy Name Hospital, hoping that when she came home we could use what we learned to work with her doctors, I have only a rudimentary knowledge about the disease. Since Reva never returned home, we never had a chance to study the book.

As I understand it, however, the disease raises the arterial blood pressure of the lungs, putting stress on the heart. In severe cases, it causes heart failure.

According to her brother, Reva had end-stage pulmonary hypertension when she entered Holy Name in June 2019. He said that pulmonary hypertension occurs in some long-term dialysis patients.

The senior doctor at the outpatient heart failure group at HMHUMC, to which the pulmonologist referred Reva, was American and a respected American-trained physician. But there was a long wait for an appointment with him. Instead, she saw one of the other cardiologists in the group, an Indian-trained, Indian doctor, Dr. Rao.

Dr. Rao performed cardiac catheterization, among other tests, on Reva. He prescribed sildenafil, which is the generic of Viagra. This drug apparently increases blood flow to certain parts of the body, including the penis in men and the heart in both sexes.

Reva saw Dr. Rao every few months, and he continued to prescribe sildenafil. But Reva developed tinnitus. She then read the brochure from the pharmacy that accompanies the drug and discovered that tinnitus and visual disturbances were permanent side effects from long-term use of sildenafil. She described her tinnitus as like "crickets" in her ears. She was, understandably, disturbed by it and sometimes had trouble sleeping because of it. She also complained of visual problems but did not elaborate. Dr. Rao never warned her about tinnitus, Reva said, and she urged me to find a lawyer so that she could sue him. At the same time, she acknowledged that she should have read the prescribing information before taking the drug. Reva stopped taking sildenafil and refused to see Dr. Rao again. I do not remember if I sought out a lawyer. Her brother, according to Reva (I seldom spoke directly to him on the phone), felt that a lawsuit against the manufacturer of the drug would be more appropriate. But events cascaded rapidly and dwarfed the injury to her hearing.

I went with Reva to Dr. Scott Pomerantz, her ophthalmologist and mine, for the visual problems she spoke about. I was with her during the eye exam and was astonished to discover that she could not read the letters on the screen, even when they were greatly magnified, with her right eye. Dr. Pomerantz examined the eye and said that Reva had experienced what he described as a "stroke" of the optic nerve in her right eye. She had lost most of the vision of that eye. The examination also revealed that she had glaucoma in both eyes. The glaucoma was treatable with eye drops, which Reva used twice a day and which kept her eye pressures in the normal range. But the loss of most of the vision in her right eye was permanent. Dr. Pomerantz sent us to a retina specialist, who confirmed the diagnosis.

Reva believed the stroke in her optic nerve ("stroke" is the metaphor that Dr. Pomerantz used-- she had not experienced a cerebral stroke) was caused by the sildenafil, but both ophthalmologists, Dr. Pomerantz and the retina specialist, said that it was more likely caused by an episode of blood pressure fluctuation during dialysis. However, several articles from medical journals that appear on the Internet link long-term use of sildenafil to ocular nerve damage.

Under these circumstances, with much or most of the vision lost from one eye, Reva's achievement in producing two art works in the late spring of 2019 that were accepted into an exhibit is even more remarkable. She was still able to drive, as New Jersey law allows a person with vision in only one eye to drive.

After Reva dropped Dr. Rao, I contacted Columbia Presbyterian Hospital and made an appointment for her with Dr. Erika

Berman-Rosenzweig, the head of the pulmonary hypertension division at the hospital. I brought Reva into Columbia Presbyterian for testing, which included extensive blood work, a pulmonary function test, and an echocardiogram that lasted more than an hour. After the results of the testing were in, we went back to the hospital the following week for a consultation with Dr. Berman-Rosenzweig.

I was in the room with Reva during the consultation and examination. Dr. Berman-Rosenzweig said that Reva's pulmonary hypertension was mild. In fact, Reva was confused as to whether, according to Dr. Berman-Rosenzweig, she had pulmonary hypertension at all. The extensive echocardiogram was, according to Dr. Berman-Rosenweig's report, "essentially normal." Dr. Berman-Rosenzweig agreed that Reva should not take sildenafil, but she did not prescribe any other medication. Our instructions were to return in six months for a follow-up visit.

But we could not keep that appointment, and Reva never saw Dr. Berman-Rosenzweig again. If she had been able to, she might be alive today. But an event occurred that made the appointment impossible, a dastardly event that was avoidable and that, I believe, ultimately led to Reva's death.

CHAPTER FORTY-TWO

THE LURKING PRESENCE

Death is a lurking presence in a dialysis unit. A number of people who traveled with Reva through dialysis over the years, friends of hers, died on the journey—not attached to the machine, not in view of their fellow patients, but at home or in the hospital. I knew some of them.

Reva's dialysis days were Tuesday, Thursday, and Saturday. Weekdays, Bergen County Transportation, a free service for the elderly and handicapped, transported her. On Saturdays I did, and when I picked Reva up after dialysis, I would often drive one of her fellow patients home. Many dialysis patients depended on Access Link, NJ Transit's bus service for the handicapped. But the wait times can be long.

One woman lived alone in Hackensack, and I often drove her home on Saturdays when I picked up Reva. I remember going up to her apartment with her while Reva waited in the van. The woman was light-headed after the treatment, a not-uncommon reaction, and I escorted her to be sure of her safety. She once called me at home when she was due for some tests at HMHUMC but was having trouble on the phone with the scheduler. She asked me to intervene. I did so, identifying myself to the scheduler as a friend of the woman. She died a few months later.

I have written in a previous chapter about Denise D. of Carlstadt, whom we knew when we lived in Rutherford before Reva became disabled. She had a tough, fighting-Irish spirit and drove herself to and from dialysis, which was then in Johnson Hall at Hackensack Meridian Hackensack University Medical Center. She died at forty-seven. Reva told me that her access site had become infected.

And there was a woman who lived in Hackensack who chose death. She lived alone, had no family, and was partially blind. She simply stopped coming to dialysis and died within weeks. No adult can legally be forced to undergo dialysis, just as no adult can be forced to undergo chemotherapy for cancer. But in cancer treatment, there is at least hope for remission. Dialysis offers no cure, except as a transition to a transplant. It is, at best, a stasis, a continual dependence on a machine.

Reva told me that the dialysis staff didn't inform other patients why people disappeared or stopped coming, but word would get out and sometimes a nurse would tell Reva privately when she asked about someone's absence. While Reva was in the ICU at Holy Name Hospital, a fellow dialysis patient, a friend of Reva's (Reva made friends easily), called to find out what happened to her. After Reva's death, the woman and her daughter put a tribute to Reva on the funeral home website. I still keep in touch with them, as I do with some other people who knew Reva. It gives me a feeling of closeness to her.

A man whom both Reva and I knew who was in dialysis at a different center than Reva's, and later in another state after he moved with his wife, died when doctors were no longer able to find a stable access site for treatment. But he had other health issues, including a serious one that was iatrogenic in origin. So many diseases and deaths are iatrogenic. The reasons for this are complex, but money certainly plays a part. A century ago, doctors did not have the knowledge or tools to cure as many sick people as they do today. Now they have more knowledge and high-tech machines, but people die unnecessarily in their care. Of course, many people recover. But greed, lack of oversight, poor education in second- and third-rate medical schools, and a self-perpetuating and self-protecting system—a thick white wall— contribute to the problem.

When we lived in Rutherford and Reva was getting dialysis in the evening, I often drove a Korean-American woman home who lived in town and went to dialysis at the same time as Reva. The woman had her own flower shop in Manhattan, and five days a week, including dialysis days and the day after dialysis, she took the bus to the city and worked in her shop. But it was too much for her. She didn't die, but she suffered a stroke. Afterwards, she had to give up her business. I would still see her in Rutherford walking with a cane. She recognized me, but since the stroke she no longer spoke English, only Korean. She had been bilingual before.

These are a few of the people Reva knew who died or became disabled while in dialysis. It is true that dialysis keeps people alive who otherwise would die. Without it, toxins would accumulate in the body of someone with end-stage renal disease and the person would die of uremic poisoning, sometimes in days, sometimes months. Wolfgang Amadeus Mozart, US President Chester A. Arthur, and the actress Jean Harlow are among prominent people who died from ESRD before there was dialysis. Dialysis and transplants are lifesaving. But years ago, an excellent doctor, who had graduated Phi Beta Kappa from Cornell and earned his medical degree from Cornell Medical College, advised me that it is better to prevent a disease than to treat it. This should be obvious. It is common sense. But unfortunately, it isn't always the way of medicine today. There is more money to be made treating a disease once it has developed than in counseling a patient on how to prevent it.

I haven't seen much effort by physicians toward preventative medicine: working with a patient to change his or her life style to halt or ameliorate a disease rather than prescribing powerful, dangerous drugs that produce other diseases, or performing risky and often unnecessary procedures and surgeries, or—as in Reva's case—forcing a vulnerable adolescent to take a poisonous psychiatric drug.

When Reva would come home from dialysis, she was hungry and would eat a meal, which she would order out. She was too exhausted to cook. Then she would sleep for several hours. I remember how she used to ride her wheelchair into our apartment and call out, "I'm home." I will never hear her say that again. She knew her home and mine, and she knew that I was her home and she was my home. Without her, I am homeless.

CHAPTER FORTY-THREE

S

Reva often had her Saturday dialysis in the afternoon instead of the morning, when she had her weekday dialysis. She made this arrangement so she could attend Sabbath synagogue services. I regret that I never accompanied her, as she often accompanied me to church on Sundays. Indeed, she liked the church services, and some Sundays when I was tired and didn't want to go, she urged me on. She also said she didn't have many social contacts because of her disability and schedule, and the coffee hour after church provided some social life. The church collected nonperishable food, which was transported to the local food pantry on Monday. Reva would always make sure we came with canned and packaged foods.

The synagogue is only a few blocks from our apartment building. I would usually drive Reva and pick her up or she would come home herself in her motorized wheelchair. She would have lunch at the synagogue after the service: white fish, smoked salmon, hummus, challah, and crackers. The salty ethnic fish wasn't good for her, but she loved it. After she returned home, I would drive her to dialysis and pick her up in the late afternoon when she was done.

On Saturday afternoon, June 23, 2018, I picked Reva up from dialysis. She seemed subdued. We ordered supper out, as we almost always did on her dialysis days, but she said little throughout the evening. Later we went to bed. At about 6:30 Sunday morning, Reva woke me. She had been trying to sleep on the living room couch but had little sleep. She had extreme burning pain in her right foot. I saw that it was hugely swollen. She told me what had happened. Toward the end of the Saturday dialysis treatment, she asked a technician, whom I will identify only as S, to please straighten out her blanket. S, a young

Latino male, roughly pulled the blanket over her right foot. The skin on her right foot was now on fire. Reva's right leg was her disabled leg: it was contracted and no longer reached the floor. As I mentioned in Chapter 28, the disease, nephrogenic systemic fibrosis, was first called nephrogenic fibrosing dermopathy because it appeared to affect only the skin. Later it was discovered that, like scleroderma, it could invade internal organs. The skin on Reva's right leg and foot was thin, stiff, woody, and fragile. Her left leg was her good leg that kept her functioning and made it possible for her to transfer and drive and live relatively independently. Now she was crying in agony from the pain in her right foot.

I dressed and we drove to the emergency room of Holy Name Hospital in Teaneck. There she was given oxycodone, which partially relieved the pain. She spent the entire Sunday in the Holy Name ER, undergoing both a venous Doppler and an arterial Doppler on her right leg. No blood clots were discovered but, according to the hospital records, the findings were inconclusive. She was given a prescription for oxycodone and discharged.

Sunday night she slept in her big quantum wheelchair which allowed her to lean back and elevate her legs. Even with oxycodone, the pain was too intense for her to sleep in bed.

On Monday, I brought her to Dr. Edward Harris, a podiatrist in Hackensack whom she had seen previously. Her right foot was a bulging, red, swollen mass. Dr. Harris diagnosed second- and third-degree burns, like rope burns, brought on by S's pulling the blanket. He put medicine on the foot, bandaged it, and put Reva on antibiotics.

She saw Dr. Harris or his partner, Dr. Warren Chiodo, every few days and they debrided the dead skin from the foot. The injury might not have been as severe to someone with normal skin, but the skin on Reva's right leg and foot was not normal. She was in great pain even when taking the maximum allowable dosage of oxycodone. Dr. Chiodo considered an MRI for further diagnosis but decided against it because it could not be done without putting pressure on Reva's foot, which would have caused her intolerable pain.

I was with Reva at her appointment with Dr. Chiodo in the late afternoon of July 8, when he said that she needed to be admitted to the hospital. However, he also said that the antibiotics seemed to be working and that she would probably not need surgery. Reva was still in great pain.

My 2018 email to Senator Weinberg quoted in Chapter 38 refers to this ER admission. The podiatrists were located in a medical building adjacent to HMHUMC, the only local hospital where they practiced. I brought Reva to the ER in the early evening. At HMHUMC, it is necessary to go through the ER for admission to the hospital except for prescheduled surgery.

She was admitted to HMHUMC and her overall care was supervised by a hospital internist, but Dr. Chiodo came several days a week to debride the dead skin from the foot. The internist made a diagnosis of peripheral arterial disease and scheduled an angiogram of her right leg and foot, but Dr. Massimo Napolitano, Reva's vascular surgeon, overruled it. (Hemodialysis patients who have a fistula need a vascular surgeon, both to create the fistula and maintain it. Reva had a good relationship with "Dr. Nap" and trusted him.) I was glad it wasn't done. I felt that it was an unnecessary test on her disabled leg that could be dangerous.

In addition to the antibiotics and oxycodone, she was receiving blood thinners. The blisters on her foot gradually began to subside, and on July 17 she was transferred to Prospect Heights, the same rehab center where she had her first and only full-time social work job and where she returned as a patient when she left the University of Pennsylvania Hospital, disabled following her failed kidney transplant.

A private ambulance service transported her three days a week from Prospect Heights to the dialysis center. Dr. Chiodo or one of his associates continued to treat her foot while she was in Prospect Heights. Over time, her condition improved, and on August 8 she was discharged home. The social worker at Prospect Heights had ordered a hospital bed, which was installed in our living room, and a visiting nurse came two or three days a week to clean and dress Reva's foot which, by late August, was almost healed. But the brutal burns inflicted by S had tragic consequences.

CHAPTER FORTY-FOUR

INTO THE DARK

There is an apparent randomness to life. Sometimes our choice of a seat in a classroom as a child or a conference table as an adult, our decision to attend a social event or to strike up a conversation with a stranger, has life-changing consequences.

And somewhere we may make the wrong turn without knowing it, and one seemingly insignificant step leads to another, and ultimately to our undoing.

And sometimes the precipitating event is not under our control.

"If I had done this or not done that" tortures us. At least it tortures me concerning Reva's life in the years we were together and, especially, the last two years of her life.

I had to cancel the six-month follow-up visit Reva had scheduled with Dr. Berman-Rosenzweig because Reva was in Hackensack Meridian Hackensack University Medical Center. Pulmonary hypertension is a serious disease that, left untreated, can cause congestive heart failure and death. In January 2018, Dr. Berman-Rosenzweig had diagnosed Reva with minimal if any pulmonary hypertension and a relatively normal echocardiogram. If S had not brutally pulled the blanket from Reva's foot, producing third degree burns and subsequent infections, Reva would have been able to keep the follow-up appointment and, if her pulmonary hypertension had worsened, Dr. Berman-Rosenzweig would have caught it in time and treated it. As I wrote earlier, Joe Brezin said her pulmonary hypertension had become end-stage by July 2019, when she was in Holy Name Hospital. But for S, she might be alive today.

After Reva had resumed dialysis at the dialysis center, she and I met with the center's director and made a complaint about S. I showed the director photos I had taken of Reva's foot. The director said she had warned S not to go near Reva's chair or have any contact with her.

I also called a personal injury and malpractice law firm and spoke to the retired emergency room physician who screened potential cases. The doctor conferred with one of the law partners, and I was told to find out if the blanket-pulling episode had been caught on video. Otherwise, I would have no proof. I inquired from the dialysis center about surveillance videos but was given an ambivalent response. Apparently, surveillance footage existed but did not clearly show S's actions. However, by mid-August, Reva's foot had almost healed. New skin had replaced the burnt skin, and there was only one small, raised pink pustule on the foot. A lawsuit did not seem likely. The foot appeared to have healed, and Reva had no lost time from work because she was not working.

But the healing of Reva's right foot was only an interlude. In pulling the blanket, S had uncovered the door to her death.

In late August of 2018, Reva complained of pain in her good, left leg. We suspected a sprained ankle as Reva had had one a few years earlier and knew how painful it could be. On Saturday, September 1, 2018, she took the maximum amount of tramadol, but in the evening, she still had pain. I called New Jersey Poison Control to find out if it was safe for her to take more tramadol. Our primary care doctor had Sunday hours, but Reva had to get through the night. Poison Control advised against taking any more tramadol until Sunday. I felt Reva's left calf. It was cool.

We went to bed, but Reva awakened me at about 1:00 a.m. She had called 911, and EMTs were in the apartment. They took her to Hackensack Meridian Hackensack University Medical Center. I did not accompany her. I knew an ER visit to HMHUMC could take hours, if not days, and I also thought that whatever she had was not serious. Perhaps it was a sprained ankle. Her calf was cool but not icy.

I went back to bed but kept my cell phone next to me. Reva had hers. At about 7:00 a.m., she called me. It was hard at first to understand what was going on. She said they had done all kinds of tests and wanted to operate on her. She was doubtful that she needed an operation. She wanted to leave. I told her to just get in her wheelchair and come home. (The hospital is three blocks from our apartment.) Then I remembered that the EMTs had transported her on a stretcher, and she did not have her wheelchair with her. At this point, the doctor got on the phone, Dr. Kristin Cook, a vascular surgeon and a member of Dr. Napolitano's practice. Dr. Cook said that Reva had no arterial circulation below the knee in her left leg and that unless they operated soon, she would lose the leg.

I dressed and walked quickly to the hospital. Dr. Cook, who looked to be in her late thirties, was with Reva in her ER room. Reva called her brother in California, where it was about 5:00 a.m. Joe Brezin spoke first to Reva and then to Dr. Cook. The situation was serious. Reva needed surgery to save the leg, her one good leg, which gave her independence. Among other tests that night, Reva had both a venous and arterial Doppler. The problem was in the arteries of the leg. They were blocked.

We all agreed that surgery was urgent. Dr. Cook explained the surgery and the risks involved, including the risk of death. Neither Reva nor I had a living will. Dr. Cook asked Reva if she wanted to be resuscitated in case she went into cardiac arrest. Reva looked at me and said emphatically, "Yes, I want to live." "Then you want extraordinary measures?" I asked. Extraordinary measures were my understanding of resuscitation and life support. "Yes," she said again.

In the months that followed, I always remembered Reva's affirmation and her emphasis. When she was no longer conscious and the doctors, including her brother, were urging me to let her go, stop dialysis, and remove the breathing and feeding tubes, I would not. I would have betrayed Reva if I had. As long as there was hope for her recovery and as long as her pain was controlled, I would not consent to her death. She clearly did not want me to.

CHAPTER FORTY-FIVE

SUNDAY MORNING

Reva signed the consent for surgery, and Dr. Cook left the ER cubicle to prepare. A young female anesthesiologist soon entered and asked Reva some questions and briefly discussed anesthesia with her. They decided on general anesthesia. Spinal anesthesia is an option for an operation below the waist, but this was to be a long operation. General anesthesia was the wiser choice, I think, and indeed, the anesthesiologist never mentioned spinal anesthesia.

Soon a patient transporter arrived and wheeled Reva in her ER bed into a large elevator. Only Reva, the patient transporter, and I were in the elevator. I was standing behind Reva's head and she couldn't see me. "Howie, are you here?" she called out. "I'm right behind you, sweetheart," I replied.

The elevator reached the surgical suite. I kissed Reva, and the patient transporter wheeled her down the corridor to the operating room.

A hospital surgical suite is an eerily quiet place on a Sunday morning. I was told where the OR waiting room was, the room where relatives and friends of patients undergoing surgery wait. I had been in this room before, when Reva had the initial surgery to create her fistula and when she had her fistula repaired. At that time, it was filled with people, and there was a receptionist to provide information. Now the room was empty except for me. There was no one behind the receptionist's desk. It was a large room with chairs and sofas and magazines. I prepared to wait out Reva's surgery. It was about 8:30 in the morning.

I called Fr. Michael Gerhardt, the priest at Christ Episcopal Church, which I attended, often with Reva, to let him know what had happened. Then I tried unsuccessfully to sleep on a sofa. I saw there was a television and turned it on. After about an hour, a couple came in, stayed briefly and left. I didn't speak to them.

About two hours passed, and I saw Dr. Cook coming down the corridor. I went out to meet her. "Were you able to save her leg?" I asked. "We're not there yet," she replied. She said she was on her way to get stents.

I went down to the lobby and had a cup of coffee and some breakfast and then returned to the waiting room. After another two hours, Dr. Cook came in. She said she had been able to open one of the arteries in Reva's leg. The leg has three arteries, she explained, but one is all that is needed. Stents had been inserted to keep the artery open, and Reva had been transported to the recovery room. I thanked God for the successful operation.

Reva was later moved from the recovery room to a bed on a medical floor. I did not get to see her until Sunday evening or Monday. I was grateful for the success of her surgery but was surprised that her voice had changed dramatically. Instead of sweet musical tones, she now spoke in the barely audible voice of a young child. I questioned a nurse. "I don't know what her voice was like before," the nurse replied snippily. But what did I expect? This was, after all, Hackensack Meridian Hackensack University Medical Center. One must expect rudeness from the staff.

It later became apparent that the change in Reva's voice was temporary, the result of intubation during the surgery. A few days later, her voice had returned to normal.

A second operation was usually done a few days after the first, if the first was successful, Dr. Cook told us Sunday morning in the ER. This operation was less important and, at the time, Dr. Cook said that she would probably not do it because of Reva's overall health problems. I am not sure what the second operation was for. I think it involved the inner calf. But Dr. Cook said it was not essential.

However, after the initial operation, she decided that Reva was strong enough to withstand the second surgery, and it was done two or three days later. This operation was less complex and shorter than the one on Sunday morning, and Dr. Cook said that Reva would receive only a mild anesthesia and would not have to be intubated.

Reva went for the second surgery, but when I called the hospital some hours later to find out when I could visit her, I was told she was still in the recovery room. When I called again two hours later, she was still there. In fact, she was in the recovery room until evening, longer than she had been after the first surgery.

I learned that Reva had gone into atrial fibrillation during the surgery.

Eventually, she was returned to her hospital bed. She was now on cardizem, a drug to regulate her heart rhythm. Otherwise, the second surgery seemed to have been successful.

After a few more days in HMHUMC, she was once again transferred to Prospect Heights.

Prospect Heights has since been swallowed by HMHUMC. It has, with other local rehab centers and nursing homes, become part of the hospital's mushrooming network, but at that time it was independently owned by the same owner who had hired Reva as a social worker fourteen years earlier.

One advantage for Reva of recuperating in Prospect Heights is that it is three blocks from our home. But I found it difficult and sometimes impossible to reach the nurses' station by phone. Calls went unanswered. While she was there, I had to be, in effect, her case manager, coordinating her care myself, or at least, making sure that none of it was neglected. She had many health issues, including glaucoma. I had to make sure that she had her eye drops and that the nurses put them in her eyes, morning and evening, as Reva was instructed to do by her ophthalmologist. I didn't want her to leave a hospital or a rehab center blind. On the positive side, Prospect Heights was clean and had large rooms for patients, and Reva had good occupational and physical therapy.

On October 15, while she was still at Prospect Heights, her ambulance service transported her to Dr. Cook's office in Hackensack to have the remaining stiches removed. I met her there. The stiches were supposed to dissolve, but some did not. Dr. Cook did a bedside Doppler of Reva's left leg, and the sound of circulating blood was clear.

"I didn't hear all that before the surgery," Dr. Cook said.

Reva had Dr. Cook's permission for physical therapy and worked hard at it. I observed her more than once. She seemed to have full use of her left leg, had recovered from the burns on her right foot, and was still able to drive. We confirmed this while she was at Prospect Heights. I brought the ramp-van to the front of the building. Physical therapists were standing by, as were Fr. Michael Gerhardt and I. Reva transferred to her motorized wheelchair, which I had brought in the van, drove it up the ramp and scrambled and climbed into the driver's seat. On Oct. 26, 2018, she was discharged home. We did not know that she had less than a year to live.

CHAPTER FORTY-SIX

INFERNO

Reva had numerous health problems, and almost all stemmed from lithium, first prescribed for her by Dr. Nathan S. Kline in 1966 when she was fourteen. Kline was then experimenting with lithium on people incarcerated in Rockland State Hospital in Orangeburg, New York, but Reva's parents brought her to Kline's Manhattan office. Reva was never in Rockland State or any other state hospital.

Subsequent psychiatrists continued to prescribe lithium for Reva. She told me that she was on lithium for eighteen years. She had been switched to another toxic medicine, tegretol, by the time we began dating when she was thirty-two, which would mean that she had been recently taken off lithium. She told me that a psychiatrist at the public mental health clinic she attended told her that they had caught the kidney disease "just in time." But they hadn't. Blood testing was apparently sporadic at the clinic, and she was taken off lithium only after it was obvious that her kidneys had begun to fail irreversibly.

Although her death certificate lists septic shock as the primary cause of death, the seeds of her death were sown decades earlier by lithium.

A record from her nephrologist dated August 23, 2019, less than two weeks before she died, reports, "ESRD d/t lithium nephrotoxicity," End Stage Renal Disease due to lithium nephrotoxicity. There is no cure for ESRD and no treatment except dialysis or transplant. Reva had both.

Had her parents left her alone to grow as an American girl born in America, the only American-born member of her family, she would have had her chance of surviving and thriving.

As mentioned in Chapter 24, while she was dying in the ICUs during the long summer of 2019, her brother told me during a phone call to his San Clemente, California home where he had retired, that he felt badly to be losing the last member of his European family.

But Reva was born in Paterson, New Jersey. She was no more European than I am, and I was born in Newark, New Jersey.

Yet although she was born in America, she could not prove it. She had no birth certificate. Her parents saw to that and kept her legally nameless. This story has been told earlier in this memoir. If I gave Reva nothing else, I gave her a legal name, which she did not have from age two until we married when she was thirty-five. No one in that "European family" cared enough about her to give her a name. Yet Reva's love was so great that it included her parents and brother.

But I believe that the event that directly precipitated her death was the brutal blanket pulling by S.

The burns that S inflicted on Reva were to her right foot, her contracted foot. But the months that she lay bedridden and inactive in HMHUMC and Prospect Heights as a result of the burns caused, I believe, the arterial blockage in her good left leg.

And it was a good leg. It was a beautiful, strong, and muscular leg because she depended on it—for transferring, driving, remaining independent. Even if she hadn't died, S committed a violent assault against her.

On Thanksgiving 2018, Reva cooked chicken instead of the conventional turkey. We spent the day together, just the two of us. From the time I was a teenager, I have spent more Thanksgivings alone than with other people. But I had not spent one alone for thirty years. I have spent the holiday with Reva. Since she became disabled in 2005, we spent three Thanksgivings with another family who had an accessible, one-story house. In the first fifteen years of our marriage, before Reva became disabled, we also spent three, perhaps four, Thanksgivings with others. I have spent more Thanksgivings alone or with Reva than I have with others, and those with Reva been good Thanksgivings. I would rather have been with her than anyone else.

Reva began outpatient physical therapy at Hackensack Meridian Hackensack University Medical Center and started to return to her normal routine. She drove and went shopping and registered for the spring semester at art school. She sent out her résumé for social work jobs, although almost always through online resources. I noted in my journal that she seemed to be excited, although this is to be expected after the months of hospitalization, surgery, and rehabilitation.

On Dec. 11, 2018, at Dr. Cook's advice, Reva checked into the HMHUMC ER at 6:00 p.m. Dopplers performed on her earlier in the day revealed some small blood clots and stenosis, that is, narrowing of blood vessels. Dr. Cook thought it would be sufficient to keep her in the ER overnight and administer an IV of heparin to dissolve the clots. I left Reva at about 11:00 p.m.

At about 1:00 a.m., I got a phone call from a nurse saying that she was unable to find a vein for the IV. She said a doctor would try. About an hour later I got a call from a barely intelligible foreign-accented woman, the doctor, who said that she also was unable to find a vein. It apparently never occurred to these medical professionals to call a phlebotomist or anesthesiologist skilled in finding veins. Reva had small blood vessels. This was from stenosis and is one of the effects of many years in hemodialysis.

In the morning, I called Reva before leaving to teach my class. She had had a sleepless night on a gurney in the hallway of the noisy, brightly lit ER and did not receive the treatment because the ER staff could not find a vein and had not bothered to page someone who could. Her nephrologist, Dr. Weizman, though on the HMHUMC staff, had not even been informed that she was in the ER. I called Dr. Cook, who had spoken to Reva. Dr. Cook said it would be safe to discharge her and that she could have angioplasty as an outpatient on Wednesday. Reva had been sent from the ER to dialysis, but when she returned four hours later there was no order for food or drink for her. And no discharge order. She had not eaten or drunk since 6:00 p.m. the night before, and it was now midafternoon. The nurse refused to give Reva food or water because there was no doctor's order. Dr. Cook called the ER and said that the ER doctor could discharge Reva. But when I returned from work and went to the ER, I could not locate the ER doctor assigned to her, nor could the nurses, who refused to feed her or discharge her because the ER doctor had left no order. The Hackensack Meridian Hackensack University Medical Center emergency room is a god-awful place, a circle out of Dante's Hell. People lie for hours on gurneys in hallways; patient rooms are unused. Once when I was there with Reva, an adult diagnosed with measles was lying on a gurney surrounded by other patients on gurneys. No effort was made to isolate him. Reva was without food or water or any of her usual medications since she was admitted at 6:00 p.m. Her nephrologist, who was on the HMHUMC staff, was not informed she was in the hospital even though she had dialysis the next day. Is it any wonder that years before, Dr. Ackad said she could die from that ER? She signed out Against Medical Advice (AMA). That was the only way she could get out of there. The final indignity came as I was wheeling Reva out in her wheelchair and we were challenged by a security guard at the exit. "Do you have your discharge papers?" he demanded. I asked him, "Is this a prison?" Reva never returned to that ER, nor have I. I would rather die. Months later when she was in the Holy Name Hospital ICU, her brother tried to arrange for her transfer to the ICU at HMHUMC. I consented to the transfer, but there were no beds. For six days we waited for a bed. I thought of all the bad experiences of HMHUMC and I, as Reva's next of kin (Reva was still sedated and unconscious), canceled the proposed transfer. I have little good to say about Hackensack Meridian Hackensack University Medical Center.

CHAPTER FORTY-SEVEN

LAST SPRING

Sometime during Reva's hospitalizations, first for the burn on her right foot and later for the arterial blockage in her left leg, I bought her a small stuffed lion in the HMHUMC gift shop.

It was a sweet-looking lion, not at all ferocious. She kept the lion with her in the hospitals and rehab center. It was her Columbia lion, a proxy for me, who she thought of as her real Columbia lion. (I graduated from Columbia, but my leonine quality is limited to a roar.) The lion gave her comfort. After she came home, she took it with her to dialysis. "You don't know how much it has helped me," she told me. I was with her when I was physically not.

I brought the lion to her when she was in the ICU in Holy Name Hospital in June 2019. It remained with her in the two other hospitals to which she was transferred that summer. It was on her death bed during the last weeks of her life when she was unconscious and unaware of it. When she died in the afternoon of September 10, 2019, in St. Joseph's Hospital in Paterson, I was in her room with Fr. Jim Warnke, the legally blind Episcopal priest and social worker to whom Reva had confided her fear of losing her leg. I had one hour to gather her belongings. I discarded the lion. It would have been contaminated after months in hospitals.

During those last weeks of her life, she had had a tracheotomy and would have been unable to speak even if she had been conscious. She did become conscious for short periods, and I will never forget the look of woe in her eyes. She moved her lips as if she wanted to say something but no sound came out.

On Wednesday Dec. 12, 2018, Reva returned to HMHUMC for the outpatient angioplasty. The lion was on the bed with her in the prep room. I waited with her. Doctor Cook came in briefly and then left to scrub.

We liked Dr. Cook and trusted her. Perhaps the trust was misplaced. She was the emergency vascular surgeon on call in the early hours of September 2, when Reva called 911, and she was a member of Dr. Napolitano's group. She was young, but not too young. She was American and trained in an American medical school. She also seemed caring. There was no reason for me to doubt her skill, and there is still no reason, except that Reva died, that the surgery and angioplasties that Dr. Cook performed didn't last. But that could have been because of Reva's condition.

I asked Dr. Cook if I could scrub and be present in the procedure room, but she said there wasn't enough room. So after the transporter took Reva, I waited in the procedure waiting room, which was not the same room as the surgery waiting room, where I had waited alone three months earlier while Reva underwent surgery.

Reva later described the angioplasty to me. It was done under a local anesthesia. She was conscious throughout the procedure and responded to questions from Dr. Cook. A small incision was made in her groin, and a scope was passed into an artery of her left leg. A camera at the end of the scope allowed the surgeon to visualize the interior of the artery. Dr. Cook enlarged the artery and inserted new stents. After returning from the recovery room, Reva could have gone home, but as she was a dialysis patient, she stayed in the hospital overnight so that she could have dialysis immediately after the procedure to wash out the contrast medium.

The procedure was apparently successful, and Reva left the hospital the next day.

She resumed her life. She returned to the art school for the spring semester and to a book club once a month in Hackensack that she had joined more than a year before. Most of the members of the book club were blind and obtained books on tape through the state library for the blind. Reva obtained print copies from local libraries. She continued to go to dialysis three days a week, and she resumed physical therapy. She asked me to help her find a social work job, but all I could do was to make suggestions about her résumé. I had no connections in the social work world. She had more physical problems now and, because her right leg had continued to contract and could no longer reach the floor, she had been unable to use a walker for several years, so she had little cardiovascular exercise.

In the early spring of 2019, we went to two cinema telecasts from the Met Opera: *Adriana Lecouvreur* and *Die Walküre*. We did little else together recreationally except to see a few movies and visit parks and the local zoo. However, she often accompanied me to church and enjoyed the coffee hour afterwards. She also went to the synagogue on Saturday mornings, as often as her dialysis schedule permitted. Her pressure sore, although it remained Stage 1, had become increasingly painful, and she treated it with various creams and ointments recommended by her wound care doctor and her dermatologist. She also bought a special pillow for the wheelchair. Most nights she slept with me, but some nights she could sleep comfortably only in the hospital bed in the living room. But she always preferred to sleep in our bed together. She played the piano as a volunteer at the HMHUMC cancer center, and she looked forward to her Fair Lawn High School reunion in October, 2019.

In April, her brother visited from California. He did not stay with us but, by choice, in a hotel that had a gym. But we all went for dinner at an Italian restaurant in Teaneck. He had brought Reva some gifts, including a new Dell laptop. The HP laptop I had bought her no longer worked. He spent Monday setting it up in our apartment, while Reva was at art school. After he had returned home to California, she expressed disappointment that the three of us didn't go anywhere. Her bother, in fact, had wanted to take us to a chamber music concert in Manhattan, but I had some health issues of my own at the time that were not related to agoraphobia, and I was reluctant to travel. Reva also wanted her brother to drive us to the shore. She loved the ocean. But we didn't go. I had no way of knowing that this would be her last opportunity to see the ocean. There are many things I wish we had done, but we did some things.

Reva's main focus in her last spring was entering her first art show, the annual juried Bergen County Senior Art Exhibit, which was held at the Art Center of Northern New Jersey. She worked on several pieces for the show, eventually choosing two: an owl and a portrait of a lady.

CHAPTER FORTY-EIGHT
MIXED NEWS

Joe Brezin visited from Saturday, April 20 to Monday, April 22. We had dinner with him Saturday evening. A few days earlier, Dr. Cook had performed a second angioplasty on Reva's left leg. Reva had again been experiencing pain.

Although the procedure was scheduled for late morning, Dr. Cook was at a hospital in Hudson County for most of the day. I waited with Reva for hours in the prep room. Another woman doctor from Dr. Napolitano's group, a doctor of osteopathy, offered to do the procedure instead of Cook, but we declined. We trusted Cook. I, personally, have misgivings about osteopaths, especially those who practice specialties, but this is only my opinion. Osteopathy seems to me a back door to a medical practice.

Finally, in the late afternoon, Cook arrived. Once again, I waited in the procedure waiting room. At about 7:00 p.m., Cook entered.

"I have good news and bad news," she said. Then she qualified: "At least pessimistic news."

The good news was that she had been able to open two arteries in Reva's leg. One was an artery she had been unable to open during the surgery on Sept 2, 2018.

The bad or pessimistic news she put bluntly. "She will lose the leg in one to five years."

Cook explained that Reva's arteries were small and the stents became occluded.

I do not recall my emotions at the time, but I imagine they were mixed. I was happy that Reva now had two functioning arteries in the leg, and I felt that we had time. Dr. Cook said one to five years. I believed that Reva could hold onto her leg and prove Cook wrong.

We would get a second opinion, but it didn't seem imminent. We had some weeks or months to find a way for Reva to save her leg, I thought.

I went to the recovery room. Reva seemed in good spirits, and once again, she stayed overnight in the hospital, getting dialysis that evening. I picked her up in the morning.

If Dr. Cook had thought that the time range might be shorter than a year, she should have said so. Then we would have rapidly sought out a second opinion. And a third and fourth, if necessary. Unfortunately, I took her literally.

An incident later in the spring may have hastened the tragic outcome, although there does not seem to be a logical connection.

Reva's emotions often became elevated in the spring: "Manic" is the word that she had been taught to use. Her emotions would flood out reason. She would be swept up by the light, the warming air, and the birds' singing, just as one might be swept up listening to a Beethoven symphony. But imagine the listener so enthralled that she jumps out of her seat and onto the podium, pushes the conductor aside, and conducts the orchestra herself.

Reva had difficulty putting a boundary or buffer zone between her emotions and the expectations of the world. She seemed to lack a filter for her emotions. Her emotional and creative life had been so stifled by her parents, especially her mother, that she never learned as a teenager and young adult how to channel her emotions. Or perhaps her emotional range exceeded the norm and needed more space than I or anyone could give her. And being dependent on a wheelchair, she was unable to temper her emotions by physically exhausting herself through exercise.

In May 2019, she went into a hypermanic state. These states usually lasted no more than a week, but they could be severe and she would sleep little. In fact, sleeplessness was both a trigger to the manic state and a consequence of it. After she had come down from the May mania, for which she was hospitalized in a psych ward, she told me that she had gone off depekote on her own. She had been taking only 500 mg a day, not even a therapeutic dose, according to one social worker, but it is often not a good idea to stop a medication abruptly.

On a rainy May morning, one of Reva's dialysis days, I woke up early and found that she wasn't in bed beside me. She wasn't in the hospital bed in the living room either. In fact, she wasn't in the apartment, nor was her large quantum wheelchair. But I wasn't worried at first. I presumed Reva had gone to the restaurant across the street for breakfast. Then I saw her mobile phone on a table. She would never, in a reasonable state of mind, leave the apartment without her mobile phone. For someone in a wheelchair, a mobile phone is essential. In addition, I knew that the wheelchair battery was low on charge.

I called the doorman in the lobby and was told she had gone out a while ago. I began to panic, and in my panic, I could not find the remote to the ramp-van but only the key to the Hyundai, a regular sedan that cannot accommodate a motorized wheelchair. I took the Hyundai and began searching for her.

She was not due in dialysis until ten and it was before eight. The dialysis center is only about three miles from where we lived. I drove along Prospect Avenue and then west down Essex Street to the dialysis center, observing the sidewalks. There was no sign of her. I called the center, but she wasn't there. I drove back up Essex Street, a hill, and I saw her emerge from a Duane Reade drug store at the corner of Essex and Prospect carrying bags with items she had just purchased. She started down the hill in her quantum chair to the dialysis center. I turned around in a parking lot and drove alongside her in the rain. If I had had the van, I could have brought her inside, but the chair could not fit in the car. But I kept alongside her, and she gave me her purchases, which I put in the car.

Essex Street in Hackensack and Maywood, west of Hackensack, is heavy with vehicular traffic. But west of the Duane Reade and a small strip mall at Prospect and Essex, there are no stores on the north side of the street, and that is the side where Reva was driving her wheelchair. It is the side of Essex Street where the dialysis center is located. Because of the absence of businesses, there are few pedestrians in this area, especially in the rain, especially at 7:30 in the morning.

The distance between Prospect Avenue and the dialysis center is approximately two miles, but Essex Street turns uphill to form a bridge over Route 17. The dialysis center is located on the other side of the bridge. Reva's wheelchair would not go up that hill. It lacked charge. It stopped.

If I had not been alongside her, she, without a mobile phone, might have been stranded in the rain for hours on that sidewalk where few pedestrians walk.

Although I could shift the quantum wheelchair gears to manual and push the chair on a level surface with Reva seated in it, I could not push her up a hill. I had noticed some cops on a side street patrolling roadwork. I walked over to them and explained the situation. They radioed headquarters, and a cop met us at the foot of the bridge. He knew us. When we lived in Rutherford, he worked part-time for one of the ambulance companies that transported Reva. He pushed the heavy quantum chair with Reva in it up the hill and into the dialysis center. It was a physically demanding job, even for a young police officer. Reva was now safe, although it wasn't yet 8:00 a.m. and she had two hours to wait in the waiting room for dialysis, but she said she had eaten breakfast. After some social conversation, the cop left and then I left, promising to return soon with the charger for her chair so it could be charged while she was getting dialysis.

But it was unnecessary. Soon after I arrived home, the center called. Reva had been wheeling herself around the waiting room and was in a manic state. The center had called an ambulance to transport her to the hospital. The hospital was Holy Name in Teaneck, at Reva's request. She wasn't so insane as to let them take her to Hackensack Meridian Hackensack University Medical Center.

CHAPTER FORTY-NINE

DARKENING CLOUDS

Reva was taken to the Holy Name ER and from there was admitted voluntarily to the hospital's small psych unit. She was in Holy Name from Tuesday until Saturday. During those five days, she did not see a doctor, other than a nephrologist, Dr. Roberto Singer, who supervised her dialysis. A nurse practitioner, Donald Mazzo, was in charge of her psychiatric care. On Wednesday, Mazzo phoned to inform me that Reva had signed a forty-eight-hour release. Mazzo said Reva was still manic and that he would have her committed unless she rescinded the release. That evening, when I visited her, I persuaded her to rescind it. She was discharged three days later. Mazzo had put her back on depakote but did not prescribe additional psychiatric drugs out of that vast, murderous arsenal.

Reva returned home. Her energy was focused on entering the art show. She asked my opinion between a landscape and the portrait. I chose the portrait.

She also went for physical therapy for her left leg at HMHUMC outpatient physical therapy department, as prescribed by Dr. Cook. The goal of the therapy was both to increase the blood circulation in the leg and to slow or possibly halt the contracture of this, her one good leg, which had slowly begun to contract as a result of the nephrogenic systemic fibrosis that had crippled her.

But in early June, she again began to experience pain in her left leg. She entered HMHUMC ER in the early morning hours of Sunday, June 9, 2019, and was admitted to the hospital.

Her room was a spacious, private room in the relatively new Women's Hospital, where she had been a patient in 2010 after she burned herself while cooking. At that time, she had good care, but this time her care was horrific, diametrically the opposite of what it had been in 2010.

Dr. Cook was on vacation the week of June 9, but Reva had a previously scheduled appointment with her in her office on Friday, June 14, her first day back.

When I visited Reva on Monday, she informed me that the doctors were planning to amputate her left leg. I had expected they would do another angioplasty. Just after she told me this, one of the doctors, a fellow (that is, a physician, a step beyond a resident, who is studying a specialty within a specialty), walked into the room. He began to introduce himself, but I exploded.

In retrospect, I regret my verbal outburst, but my anger was not directed at the doctor but at what they were planning to do to Reva.

"You will not cut off her leg," I asserted. I went on for some time, pointing out that the left leg was Reva's only good leg and that the hospital should do another angioplasty. The hospital should make every attempt to save her leg.

Then I sat on a chair opposite the doctor and gave him a chance to speak.

I don't remember his response, except that he seemed quiet. I requested that one of the senior doctors in Dr. Napolitano's group phone me the next day. A fellow is, after all, still in the learning process, although he or she may be board certified in the specialty.

The following day, the woman osteopath telephoned me. She was standing in for Cook while Cook was on vacation. This time I was calm. I heard her out. She said that too many angioplasties are dangerous, that they can injure the kidneys and other organs. I pointed out that Reva's kidneys were already nonfunctioning. But she was adamant. They would not do an angioplasty, and If Reva would not agree to amputation, she would have to be discharged. Amputation was the only treatment they would offer.

I spoke to Reva. As she had the appointment with Dr. Cook on Friday, and as she was not in excruciating pain (she was getting oxycodone when needed), she chose to be discharged and see Dr. Cook. She was getting a heparin drip, but she called her brother who said that when the heparin drip was discontinued, she could immediately go back to Eliquis and Plavix, oral blood thinners, which she had been taking and which, he said, would be as effective as heparin.

An internist, an Indian doctor with a thick accent whom I never met but spoke to on the phone, was in charge of Reva's overall care in the hospital. Reva was initially scheduled to be discharged on Wednesday, June 12, but her blood pressure was too low. So she remained until Thursday. What happened on Thursday is described below in a letter I sent to both the hospital administration and the New Jersey Department of Health and Senior Services. I have changed the name of the nurse, the hospital representative mentioned in the first paragraph, and the hospital room number but made no other changes.

000 Prospect Ave. Apt 00-0.
Hackensack, NJ 07601
June 18, 2019

Department of Patient Experience
Hackensack University Medical Center
30 Prospect Ave.
Hackensack, NJ 07601

Dear Patient Experience Representative:

This is a complaint against Hackensack University Medical Center. The complaint concerns both my wife, Reva Prosnitz, and me. I am sending, under separate cover, a statement by my wife authorizing me to make this complaint. I have previously made this complaint, in part, on the telephone to Marissa Rodriguez of your department.

My wife entered the emergency room of Hackensack University Medical Center in the early morning hours of June 9. From the ER she was admitted to Room 26F of the Women's Pavilion, where she remained until her discharge on June 13.

She went to the ER by ambulance with pain and coldness in her left leg. She previously had arterial surgery and angioplasty on this leg at HUMC.

This complaint is not about treatment of her medical issues but is focused on abusive nursing and support care she received, particularly from one nurse, Jennifer. I was also subjected to abuse from this nurse.

My wife is wheelchair bound. Although she has circulation problems in her left leg (PAD), her right leg is contracted, and she depends on a wheelchair and her left leg to transfer from the wheelchair to bed, toilet etc. During the entire time that she was in HUMC, she was confined to bed. No wheelchair was provided for her in the room.

On Wed. June 11, she informed me that she had not been washed since she was admitted. I informed the staff and an aide gave her a sponge bath that day.

My wife is a hemodialysis patient and receives dialysis on Tuesday, Thursday and Saturday. On June 13, the day of her discharge, she was transported from her room to the in-patient dialysis unit at 6 a.m. She was not given breakfast nor was she given any food in dialysis.

When I called the nurses station, I was informed that she was to be discharged, and I arrived at her room at approximately noon. I was informed that she was still in the dialysis unit. I then went to the diagnostic center on the first floor of 20 Prospect Avenue for a chest X-ray and an X-ray of my right elbow that had been ordered by my physicians. These X-rays, including the time it took me to walk from the women's hospital to 20 Prospect, took about a half hour. I then went to our apartment on Prospect Avenue, about three blocks from the hospital, to retrieve my wife's wheelchair so she could leave the hospital.

I returned to the hospital with the wheelchair at approximately 1:30 p.m., expecting my wife ready to leave. Instead, I found her in her room, still in her hospital gown and none of her belongings packed. As she depends on a wheelchair, and no wheelchair was provided for her, she could not pack her own belongings. She had not been given any lunch after she returned from dialysis. She had no food the entire day until after she left the hospital at about 3 p.m. However, Reva informed me that Nurse Jennifer gave her Miralax when she returned from dialysis. She was given a laxative but no food. She vomited several times after she returned home.

At my insistence, some staff helped dress her and pack her clothes and belongings. Jennifer checked closets and drawers for her belongings. When I began checking the closets and drawers myself, Jennifer threatened to call security on me. Why should I take Jennifer's word that all Reva's belongings were packed? Reva has a cell phone, partial dentures, headset radio and other small items that could be left behind. I feel that Reva was subjected to patient abuse by Nurse Jennifer and that I was subjected to visitor abuse. It is not unreasonable for a relative or a patient, if the patient is able, to check drawers and closets to make sure that all possessions are packed. Some years ago, my wife's personal wheelchair was stolen from her bedside at HUMC. Only after I made a complaint to the Hackensack Police Department did the hospital replace it with one of its own wheelchairs. Jennifer's manner to me was threatening and abusive. I felt that we were being given the bum's rush. I was merely checking drawers and closets for Reva's possessions when Jennifer threatened, more than once, to call security on me. In addition, she packed the discharge papers. Only at my insistence did she, reluctantly, go over them with us orally, as is customary, and I had questions.

This nurse Jennifer should be disciplined. Reva has been in dialysis since 2003. When patients return from dialysis, they are usually ravenously hungry. Yet Reva was given no food either before or after dialysis. This is cruelty.

Reva, who is a mild mannered and soft person who looks for the best even in bad situations, described HUMC as "foul." Her stay there was horrible. Neither she nor I will ever return to HUMC except, with extreme caution, for certain outpatient services, such as imaging. Neither of us will ever again enter the ER or spend a night under the roof of this hospital. I have made previous complaints to the state about HUMC.

I am sending a copy of this complaint to the New Jersey Department of Health and Senior Services.

Sincerely,
Howard Prosnitz
cc: New Jersey Department of Health and Senior Services

And I have never returned to HUMC, and never will, except for certain outpatient services.

CHAPTER FIFTY

HOLY NAME

On Friday June 14, I accompanied Reva to her appointment with Dr. Cook. Her leg was cool but not icy. She was in pain, but the pain was not as severe as it had been before the September 2 surgery. Dr. Cook explained that the stents were not holding because Reva's blood vessels were small. The narrowing of the blood vessels was the result of more than a decade of hemodialysis.

Cook said that if she were to amputate, it would be above the knee because of Reva's contractures. Amputation above the knee makes a prosthetic device more difficult to fit and use, and Reva might become entirely wheelchair-bound, unable to transfer by herself and unable to drive. But Cook offered to do one more angioplasty. "But next week," she said. She did not sound optimistic.

Then she mentioned a doctor at Holy Name Hospital, Dr. John Rundback, an interventional radiologist who specialized in limb salvaging. Cook said that while she would put in two stents, Rundback's methods were more aggressive, and he might put in a half dozen.

I recognized Dr. Rundback's name. Years earlier, I had interviewed him for Holy Name's magazine. I was then covering Teaneck for North Jersey Media Group, and Holy Name's PR department hired me to write a couple of freelance articles without byline about the hospital's interventional radiology program. Rundback was one of the doctors I interviewed.

Dr. Cook had introduced some hope. We declined her offer to do another angioplasty, and as soon as we got home, I called Dr. Rundback's office, which is in Holy Name, and scheduled an appointment for Reva.

I had interviewed Rundback in 2007, more than ten years before

Reva's current crisis. Reva had become so involved with Hackensack Meridian Hackensack University Medical Center doctors that I had forgotten about Rundback and had failed to associate him with Reva's condition until Cook mentioned his name.

Rundback saw patients only on Tuesdays. The earliest appointment the staff could give Reva was on June 25. But over the weekend, Reva's pain became more intense, and she had to use both Tylenol and oxycodone to sleep. I can still see her clutching her left leg to her chest in pain. On Monday I called Dr. Rundback's office, explained the situation, and we were given an appointment for the following day.

I was scheduled to teach one course for the fall 2019 semester in the communication department at William Paterson University, where I had been teaching for several years. This was a two-and-a-half-hour course that met once a week on Wednesday afternoons. I had also been hired to teach two sections of a freshman writing course for the fall semester at Ramapo College. These were morning classes meeting four days a week at 8:00 a.m.

In May, Reva had accompanied me to my interview at Ramapo. That is, she had driven up with me. She waited in a public area on the summer recess-quiet campus while I was interviewed by the dean.

Ramapo College is located in Mahwah at the northern tip of Bergen County, a rustic (for Bergen County) area. I had signed the contract to teach the two courses, and all that remained prior to teaching them was filling out some paperwork and getting my ID at Ramapo's HR department. I had an appointment scheduled for Tuesday, the day I took Reva to Dr. Rundback, but I called and rescheduled the appointment for Wednesday. I didn't realize at the time that I had all summer to fill out the forms, which took about ten minutes. I found this out later. I have long blamed myself for what happened to Reva on Wednesday in my absence, but I have come today to realize that my presence at Holy Name would probably not have prevented it.

On Tuesday morning, I brought Reva to her appointment with Dr. Rundback at Holy Name. He examined Reva's leg and decided to admit her and perform the procedure on Wednesday. Reva wanted him to speak with her brother, and she called him and gave the phone to Rundback. The speaker was on, so we could hear Joe Brezin's end of the conversation. Rundback explained that he had a choice between two procedures. The first was to attempt to divert blood from a vein into an artery. If that was unsuccessful, he would do a regular angioplasty. Joe Brezin agreed with the approach. I heard him say, "At last we have someone who knows what he is doing." I don't know if Joe Brezin lacked confidence in Dr. Cook, whom he had only spoken to on the phone, or if he was misogynistic about female surgeons. I think it was neither. Rundback had an international reputation, and his videos are on YouTube, which Joe Brezin had watched. (We informed him on Friday that we had made an appointment with Rundback.) Rundback's entire medical practice was limb salvaging.

And Reva's left leg, I believe, was salvageable. Although it was cold and she was experiencing pain, especially at night, the skin color was normal. There was no sign of gangrene. If there had been, I am sure that Dr. Rundback would not have gone ahead with the procedure.

I waited with Reva until a volunteer (not this time a patient transporter) wheeled her to her room. It was a Tuesday, and she would have dialysis that evening in Holy Name after being examined by Dr. Singer. I told Reva I would return in the evening. She asked me to bring her the stuffed lion.

CHAPTER FIFTY-ONE

LIGHTNING BOLT

I visited Reva in the early evening, but I forgot the lion. Would it have made a difference if I had remembered it? Would the tragedy have been averted? Logically and scientifically, it does not seem so. But I regret not bringing it.

Reva was in dialysis when I arrived, the only patient in the dialysis room. I spoke to her, but her answer did not make sense. She then shut her eyes and seemed to fall immediately to sleep. But she phoned me later when dialysis was over and she sounded normal. She had just eaten her dinner, a turkey sandwich.

She was scheduled for the procedure on Wednesday, but we didn't know what time. She had given me permission to go up to Ramapo in the morning to sign the papers for HR. As I wrote previously, I had all summer to sign those papers and obtain my ID, but I didn't know that. I had been given the appointment by HR for Tuesday, which I rescheduled for Wednesday. Besides, we did not know what time Dr. Rundback would do the procedure. I remember waiting with Reva all day at HMHUMC for Dr. Cook. It wouldn't take me long at Ramapo, and I expected to be at Holy Name by noon. Reva, I thought, might still be waiting for the procedure. Besides, angioplasty is not surgery but a procedure done under a local anesthetic.

Would it have made a difference if I had been with her before the procedure to calm her anxieties? If I had called HR and rescheduled my appointment? I have been haunted by these and similar questions for more than two years. The answer is that I don't know. Reva was the bravest person I have ever known and she covered her fears.

Reva called me early Wednesday morning and sounded well. She said she had not gotten breakfast. I told her that was because she was to have a procedure.

The trip from Hackensack to Ramapo College takes about a half hour straight up Route 17. But the malls and stores on Route 17 end in Ridgewood. Thereafter, until Ramsey, both sides of the highway are bordered by woods. Because of my agoraphobia, I cannot drive alone in areas where there are no stores, no gas stations, no people. So I took an alternate route to Mahwah, which goes through a populated suburban area but takes longer.

I was driving through Ramsey, the town just south of Mahwah, when my mobile phone rang. It was a doctor from Holy Name. At first, I expected him to tell me that the procedure was over and Reva was recovering normally. But that is not what he said.

The doctor was not Dr. Rundback but an ICU doctor. Dr. Rundback had been unable even to begin the procedure. They were moving Reva from the stretcher to the procedure table when she said, "I can't breathe."

"Her eyes rolled backward and she lost her blood pressure," the doctor said. She went into cardiac arrest. She was resuscitated after three minutes and was now sedated and unconscious in the ICU.

I drove into a parking lot. I called Ramapo HR and left a voicemail canceling my appointment and explaining that my wife was ill in the hospital. Then I called Joe Brezin and told him what had happened. "My God," he said.

I turned around and drove to Holy Name.

When I arrived in the lobby, I gave my name and told the receptionist that my wife was in the ICU. She asked me to wait. Soon two doctors came to meet me, Dr. Feldman, a cardiologist, and Dr. Moss, a pulmonologist, the doctor who had called me in Ramsey. They escorted me to the ICU. I stood outside the door of Reva's room. I could see her with tubes going into her body, but that first day I did not enter her room. It was too much for me. I did not have the courage.

Dr. Feldman said that most patients do not leave the ICU alive. He recommended that I prepare for end-of-life care for Reva. From the outset, from Reva's first day in Holy Name, the doctors seemed to have written her off. They seemed to be preparing for her death.

There was no steady critical care doctor or intensivist in the Holy Name ICU. Patients were assigned to GPs, internists, and family practitioners who came in before or after their regular office hours. Dr. William Leland, the doctor assigned to Reva, was a family practitioner, an American from New Jersey with a medical degree from a Caribbean medical school. We had come there for Dr. Rundback, who had an international reputation. Now Reva was in the ICU, and the procedure to save her leg had not been done.

I broke down outside her room and pleaded with the doctors to save her. But I did not enter her room that day.

She was in medical shock, they told me. Her cardiac arrest had lasted approximately three minutes.

That night I spoke to Joe Brezin. He said that the threshold for brain damage following a cardiac arrest is usually five minutes.

CHAPTER FIFTY-TWO

ICU

I do not remember how I spent that Wednesday evening, nor is it recorded in my journal, where there is a gap of about a week during this unsettling period.

I returned to the ICU Thursday, and this time I entered Reva's room. She was attached to a respirator and there was a tube down her throat. There were other tubes running from her body to machines. She was unconscious, but this was because she was receiving a continuous infusion of a sedative so that she could tolerate the intubation.

I crawled onto her bed. I covered her with my body. I cried, "Reevee, it's me, Howie. Don't leave me!" I pleaded over and over, "Reevee, don't leave me!" Throughout our marriage, I called her Reevee very seldom. I almost always called her Reva. Reevee was a special name. But drugged and unconscious as she was, I believe she heard me. In July, when she was no longer intubated and there were signs of hope for her recovery, she called me on her mobile phone and left a voicemail. "Howie, it's Reevee. Someone helped me with the phone. I hope you're having a nice day." I haven't erased the message. She had forgotten how to use her phone or was unable to manipulate the keys. But in calling herself Reevee, I believe she had been partially conscious of me that day in June. Often, the doctors who treated her in Holy Name discussed her condition in her room when she was unconscious, and sometimes when she was conscious, as if she were a piece of furniture. An exception was Dr. Singer, the nephrologist, a thin, pale, elderly man and a native of Argentina. The first or second day that Reva was in the ICU, he called me out into the hallway. "Your wife is very sick," he said. Dr. Singer was a man of few words, but I believe he took good care of Reva and treated her with respect, even when she was unconscious.

Joe Brezin was arranging to fly in, but the earliest flight he could book would bring him to Newark on Sunday. Reva was given dialysis on a portable dialysis machine in her ICU room on her usual three days. But Reva required an infusion of norepinephrine during dialysis to keep her blood pressure up. Norepinephrine is a vasoconstrictor used to treat life-threatening low blood pressure. Reva was given a dose when she went into medical shock following her cardiac arrest and continued on it during dialysis.

Long-term dialysis lowers blood pressure. When she was home, Reva would take her blood pressure before leaving for dialysis. If it was under a certain number, she would take 10 mg of midodrine, an oral drug that raises blood pressure. Whether or not she needed midodrine on a given morning, she took the bottle with her to dialysis. Sometimes she would need her first dose during the treatment. Sometimes she would need a second dose. But she never needed midodrine on non-dialysis days.

During the five days that she was in HMHUMC before she entered Holy Name, the Indian internist in charge of her overall care prescribed only 5 mg doses of midodrine for dialysis. Although Dr. Howard Weizman, her nephrologist, was on the staff of HMHUMC and was overseeing her dialysis he, or another doctor in his group, apparently did not correct the dosage error. The internist would not let her leave Wednesday because her blood pressure was too low. There seems to have been little coordination in Reva's care at Hackensack Meridian Hackensack University Medical Center.

During the three months that Reva was in Holy Name and two other hospitals until her death on September 10, 2019, I visited her twice a day, even when she was nonresponsive. I missed only one day when I had a cold. I wasn't working during the summer. Sometime in July, I drove up to Ramapo and signed the HR papers. The process took fifteen minutes. But I never taught the courses. Reva's condition worsened, and I resigned from Ramapo in late August just after the semester began. I knew I could never teach four mornings a week while Reva was fighting death.

In the evenings, it was crucial for my mental health to make phone calls. Every evening, I spoke with at least one other person, but I cannot now remember everyone I spoke with. I spoke often with my brother, who lives in Rhode Island, and with his wife, but to none of my other relatives except my cousin Eric, a physician and retired nephrologist with whom I had two long conversations about Reva's condition. I spoke to Fr. Michael Gerhardt and Fr. Jim Warnke of Christ Episcopal Church and to Rabbi Simon Glustrom, who lives in our building and who would later preside at Reva's funeral. I spoke to members of the church, and I spoke to friends, including a friend whose wife died in 2013. And I spoke to the nurses on the ICU. I found that the best time to call nurses is after midnight, when they have less to do. Without those phone calls, I don't know how I would have gotten through this period.

From the time Reva was first hospitalized in HMHUMC until her death, I made certain that the nurses inserted the drops in her eyes that the ophthalmologist had prescribed for glaucoma. As none of the four hospital pharmacies had one of the two medicines, I continued to refill the prescription and bring it to the nurses. I remember the two bottles in a sealed bag hanging from a wall hook in her ICU rooms. I never lost hope in Reva's recovery until the end, and I did not want her to leave the hospital blind.

Perhaps I was focused on the eye drops because it was something I could control and understand. The rest was beyond my comprehension.

I read *The Professor's House* and reread *My Antonia* by Willa Cather. I thought Cather would be calming. After Reva had regained consciousness, at the advice of a therapist, I began reading *My Antonia* aloud to her. The therapist thought that reading aloud to Reva would help her regain full cognition. But Reva didn't want me to, so I stopped.

During the first week that Reva was in Holy Name, I prayed and hoped that not only would she come out of the cardiac arrest intact, but that the procedure on her leg could still be performed. She had come through so much already.

CHAPTER FIFTY-THREE

AMPUTATION

Reva was admitted to the ICU of Holy Name Hospital on Wednesday June 19, 2019. I entered her room for the first time on Thursday June 20. I continued my vigil at her bedside twice a day, going home for lunch. She remained sedated and unconscious.

Dr. Leland was in charge of her overall care. Dr. Moss and his colleague, Dr. Okas, were her pulmonologists. Dr. Feldman was her cardiologist, but Dr. Feldman rarely looked in on her, at least when I was there, which was most of the day. He described the right ventricle of Reva's heart to me, visualized on ultrasound, as like "a piece of skin." The functioning of the right ventricle is affected by pulmonary hypertension.

On Saturday evening June 22, I observed a new doctor looking at Reva's chart. I was informed that this was the surgeon, Dr. Nicholas Thaddus. I didn't speak to Dr. Thaddus that evening. He seemed rather gruff to the ICU staff.

When I returned for my second shift at Reva's bedside Sunday afternoon, Joe Brezin was in her room. His flight had arrived in Newark a few hours earlier. He had booked reservations at the same hotel where he stayed in May. It had a gym, and it was near the Jewish cemetery where his and Reva's parents are buried.

That evening, or it may have been a subsequent day, he remarked to me that Reva was breathing on her own. She was still intubated and unconscious, but the nurses had titrated the respirator down so that she was no longer dependent on it.

Joe made friends quickly with Leland, and was soon greeting him warmly as Bill. He also made friends with the two pulmonologists. Feldman was seldom around. Joe told me later, after he had returned to California, that Feldman did not return his phone calls. Joe was concerned about treating Reva's pulmonary hypertension, which he said had become end-stage, and he sent an email or fax to Dr. Berman-Rosenzweig, the pulmonary hypertension specialist at Columbia, seeking information about treating the disease. I believe that on another occasion he also sought to have Reva transferred to Columbia. In the email he identified himself as Reva's brother and as a retired nephrologist. The rest of the email is written in technical medical language. I don't know if Berman-Rosenzweig ever replied, but Reva was never transferred to Columbia.

He also sought to have her transferred to the ICU at HMHUMC. Holy Name is a small community hospital. HMHUMC is larger and has equipment in its ICU for 24-hour-a-day slow, continuous dialysis, which Joe Brezin said would benefit Reva. Holy Name did not have this equipment. As Reva's next of kin, I consented to the transfer, and Leland found a colleague at HMHUMC who would take Reva as a patient. The problem was that HMHUMC had no vacant ICU beds. A week went by, and there were still no vacant beds. This was shocking to me, as I could not imagine a hospital not having an ICU bed available. And this was in June 2019, almost a year before the outbreak of the Covid-19 pandemic. HMHUMC seems to have benefitted from the closing of many nearby hospitals. Pascack Valley in Westwood; Beth Israel and Passaic General in Passaic; Barnert Hospital, where Reva was born, in Paterson; and United Hospital, where I was born, in Newark (it was then Presbyterian Hospital) are some of the hospitals that once served Bergen County residents that are now demolished, shuttered, or part of HMHUMC.

In the six days that he stayed in New Jersey, Joe would arrive early in the morning so he could catch the doctors on their rounds, which they made individually. He had inquired about doctors' meetings, in which he wanted to participate. But the ICU had none. He was, however, in close contact with Leland in the hospital and later, when he was back in California, by text and email.

I would not look at Reva's leg, but I was told by Joe, Leland and the nurses that it had become mottled and gangrenous. There appeared to be no choice but to amputate.

I was formally introduced to Dr. Thaddus, who seemed less gruff, and, following instructions from Joe, I signed the consent for surgery, as Reva was unconscious and unable to.

I remember the two transporters arriving in the ICU. I kissed Reva's forehead a dozen or more times, going from one side to the other. I could not kiss her lips or face because of the tube down her throat. I prayed for her. Then the transporters took her to the operating room.

Reva had visitors, both when she was unconscious and after she had awakened. Fr. Jim Warnke, the legally blind Episcopal priest and LCSW to whom Reva had confided her fear of amputation, came the second day she was in the ICU and often thereafter. His home was just behind the hospital. And Rosalind, Joe's sister-in-law and a minister at a small nondenominational church in Pennsylvania, drove up twice. As I mentioned previously, Rosalind had visited Reva in 2004 while she was at the University of Pennsylvania Hospital. On both occasions that Rosalind visited Reva at Holy Name, Reva was sedated and unconscious.

Fr. Michael Gerhardt was her most frequent visitor except for me. Nuns prayed over Reva and representatives from a Jewish organization brought grape juice and candles on Friday afternoons, although Reva couldn't use them. On different occasions, a Lubavitch Rabbi, a Roman Catholic Priest, and a hospital chaplain associated with the Polish National Catholic Church prayed over her. Her niece, Laura, Joe's daughter, and Laura's husband, Steven, visited, but Reva was unconscious.

The surgery removed Reva's left leg from above the knee. It appeared to have been performed without complications. But the records of the surgery were missing from the 300–400 pages of medical records that I obtained from Holy Name following Reva's death. I have since acquired the surgical records.

We came to Holy Name to save Reva's leg. Instead, she lost her leg and, ultimately, her life.

Fifteen years earlier, she went to the University of Pennsylvania for a kidney transplant so she could be free of dialysis. The transplant had to be removed in less than a week, as it failed to receive blood, and Reva returned to New Jersey in a wheelchair, on dialysis, and permanently disabled.

She was not lucky. She was lithiumed by her parents, but they were not the first parents to be taken in by the charlatanry of psychiatry. My parents were also taken in, and my life was damaged. But, unlike Reva, I escaped physical destruction. The moral responsibility of her parents lies both in consenting to her poisoning and in creating the conditions in Reva's childhood and adolescence that caused her emotional breakdowns.

CHAPTER FIFTY-FOUR

WAKING

There are gaps in my journal for 2019. The impact of events was so cataclysmic that regular journal keeping was neglected. I have to rely primarily on my memory to sort through the multiplicity of events, and my recollection of their sequence may not be entirely accurate.

Reva was never awake during her brother's visit. The surgery was in the early evening on Thursday June 27, and he left on Saturday, after staying six days. She remained sedated until the following week.

Holy Name had a luncheonette on the ground floor. The employee cafeteria was closed to the public.

At HMHUMC, employees and visitors shared the same basement cafeteria. One thing to be said in HMHUMC's favor: For a hospital, the food was good. More power to the concession. But the visitor's luncheonette at Holy Name had indifferent food and worse coffee.

One day while we were in Reva's room, Joe Brezin asked if he could get me a cup of coffee. I suggested that we go to a nearby Dunkin Donuts. He agreed but seemed surprised and disconcerted.

We were brothers-in-law, but I was not close to him. I did not really know him except through Reva. I thought we could clear out our heads if we had coffee outside the hospital, but I could see his discomfort and backed down.

Reva was moving the respirator with one-hundred percent her own breath, and a nurse withdrew the breathing tube. But she was still sedated. Then one day, while I was in the room, the nurse turned off the sedation.

Joe Brezin had said she was sedated with propofal. The nurse said it would wear off quickly, and she would wake soon.

And, indeed, Reva soon opened her eyes. I said to her, "Sweetheart, it's Howie. They took the breathing tube out, but don't try to speak yet. Let your voice rest." I well-remembered the horrible, squeaky sound she made in HMHUMC after her September 2, 2018 surgery. But she began to speak immediately, and to my surprise, though her voice was drowsy, it was the same sweet, melodious voice I had known.

"Where am I?" These were her first words.

"You are in Holy Name Hospital," I replied.

"Oh,"

The "Oh," in print looks insignificant, but it was the inflection that mattered. It was a slightly drawn out "Oh" that showed recognition of a familiar place. She had been in Holy Name many times, mainly in the ER, and she recognized where she was. It was if she had awakened from a deep sleep to normality. It was no longer normality as she had known it, but there seemed to be no change in her cognition or personality, except that she was very tired.

She spoke for the next few days, but very softly. Sometimes I had to bend over and put my ear almost to her mouth to hear her. But she made sense and spoke in full sentences.

I remember her saying, with emphasis on the last word, "I feel so *weak*."

She told me about a book a nurse had recommended, *The Artist's Way*. She had been talking to the nurse about her art lessons.

I told her I had the book and had done some of the exercises in it. She looked forward to reading it when she came home.

After Reva's death, Marjorie J., a friend from Christ Episcopal Church, told me that when she visited Reva in Holy Name, Reva commented that Marjorie had had her hair cut. Indeed, she had, and Marjorie said that few people had noticed it.

Marjorie, a widow and a warden at the church, had her own sorrows. The body of her youngest daughter, Mary, is buried in the same cemetery as Reva's body, not far from Reva's grave and mine. Mary had a form of blood cancer as a teenager, but it went into remission. She graduated college and social work school and became a social worker in the pediatric oncology department at HMHUMC. She married and had two children. Then the cancer returned, this time to her brain. She died at thirty-eight leaving behind her husband and her children, aged four and six.

Marjorie was a steadfast friend and support to me during Reva's final months, attending meetings with me, at my request, with the ICU doctors at SELECT Hospital and St. Joseph's Hospital.

Occasionally Reva would say something that didn't make sense. Once she said, out of the blue, "planche urea." I asked her what she said, and she said louder and with some show of irritation, "planche urea," spelling out, "planche." I may have asked her what she meant, but I don't recall or have a journal entry with her reply.

The BUN (blood urea nitrogen) level is a part of the standard blood test that measures kidney functions. Reva's was obviously abnormal. But planche? It means plank or board in French, and Reva knew French, having studied it in high school and college.

I had three years of college French, but on our honeymoon in Quebec, when dining in a restaurant where the waitress spoke no English, my mind went blank, and Reva successfully took over the verbal transaction.

To this day, I do not know what she meant by "planche urea."

I brought her magazines and a few books, but she didn't read them. But she did watch television. She still slept a lot.

She no longer needed the norepinephrine for dialysis. Her blood pressure was on the low side, but Dr. Singer found it acceptable. As I recall, the only intravenous line she now had was for a heparin drip.

She was on a soft diet because there was concern about her ability to swallow, and she seemed to have lost, at least temporarily, some dexterity of her hands. Sometimes I fed her; sometimes a nurse or an aide. But sometimes she fed herself. But she was not able to use her mobile phone by herself and needed help to make a call.

One of the people she called was Pattie C., a classmate from Fair Lawn High School who still lived in Fair Lawn. Reva and I used to occasionally have dinner with Pattie and her husband Rich. Dining in restaurants with other couples or with friends was our chief way of socializing.

The Fair Lawn High Class of 1969 reunion was in October, and

Reva had been looking forward to it. She was still looking forward to it and discussed with Pattie shopping for a dress. With some amusement, she spoke to me about my having to buy underwear and women's clothing for her in the future.

I had promised myself that I would never mention the amputation to Reva, and I never did. But she knew that she had lost her leg, and she seemed to accept it. She used the word, "stump" for what remained of her left leg, a word I cannot say.

Once she threw off her bedclothes and asked me to look at her naked. I did. She was, had been, and will always be, my woman. Nothing can change that. "Love is not love which alters when it alteration finds."

One day I came to the Holy Name lobby for my pass to the ICU. I was told Reva was no longer there but had been moved to an intermediate floor.

CHAPTER FIFTY-FIVE

INTERMEDIATE FLOOR

While she was still in the ICU, improving and becoming more alert, Reva was restless to resume her life. "I can't lie here like this. I need panties. I want to get dressed," she told me.

Adjacent to Holy Name's lobby luncheonette is a garden with tables and benches where staff and visitors can sit and eat. Once Reva's condition had stabilized and she was transferred to the intermediate floor, I asked Dr. Leland if aides could dress her and put her in a wheelchair and if I could bring her out to the garden to sit for a half hour or an hour. The heparin drip could go with her on a pole or perhaps be discontinued for a short while. I felt that some time in the sunlight, outside the walls of the hospital, would benefit Reva, both physically and psychologically. But Leland rejected my suggestion.

He didn't give me a reason, but I would like to believe that he thought it was not medically advisable. Perhaps there were liability issues. But I know that there are all sorts of concerns other than the welfare of the patient that influence medical decisions, and chief among these is money. It is possible that insurance, in Reva's case Medicare and our secondary insurer, would no longer pay for her hospitalization if she could sit outside for an hour in a wheelchair. The insurer might decide that if a patient can sit outside on the hospital grounds, the patient was no longer eligible to be treated in an acute-care hospital. Patients no longer remain in hospitals until they are well enough to be discharged home. A vast industry of subacute hospitals and rehab centers has sprung up. Then there is something even more obscure: the Long-Term Acute Care Hospital (LTACH), which the *New York Times,* in a September 17, 2019 article (an article published just seven days after Reva's death) called "an afterworld of medical care. "It is truly a hidden segment even to most people in health care," a physician is quoted as saying. Unfortunately, Reva was ultimately transferred to one of these shadowy for-profit facilities from which few patients return home: they die or go to nursing homes.

It wasn't long after Reva was transferred to the intermediate floor that Leland began harassing me about insurance. He said that Medicare would pay only if the hospital were treating Reva for an acute disease. By late July, Leland and other doctors were attempting to get Reva out of Holy Name any way possible, it seemed to me, including by death. I will write more about this in in a subsequent chapter when I discuss a doctor at Holy Name whom I refer to only as Dr. Death.

A major part of this problem was not so much Leland but the American medical system.

But for now, Reva was on an intermediate floor and things were looking up. She was weak, but she was alert and cognitive, though confined to bed. On Bastille Day, July 14, 2019, I received a call from the Art Center of Northern New Jersey, where Reva had been studying, informing me that the two pastels that she had entered in the annual senior art exhibit sponsored by the Bergen County Freeholders had been accepted. We had planned to attend the opening of the exhibit. That, of course, was now impossible. When I visited Reva later in the day and told her the news, she was happy.

"I'm so proud of myself," she said.

It was unusual for Reva to feel or express pride. She was a humble person in the best sense of the word, humility as a virtue. And she had no false humility. In a world of boasters and braggarts, Reva, a truly gifted person, felt lowly. This hurt her, too. It was how she was brought up—to regard herself as unimportant. But she also knew that there was a light inside her that she wanted to shine. And it did shine.

I never read Reva's journals when she was alive, although she had given me permission to do so in the last two years of her life: I had asked her because I wanted to understand her better. But I did not read them then. I regarded her journals as private. But when we still lived in Rutherford, before she became disabled, I found a loose page from one of her journals in which she had written, "I can make things grow." She knew she was more than a clerk-typist. She knew in her heart she wasn't meant to be a drugged-up mental patient. But she had been forced by her parents to hide her light.

One day when I visited her, Reva said ruefully "I missed your birthday."

"No, you didn't," I replied." My birthday is July 25th and it was mid-July. The weeks in the hospital left her less aware of the calendar. When I visited her on July 25th, she presented me with a birthday card she had made with the help of an aide. Reva loved to celebrate birthdays. I thanked her for the card and kissed her, but I did not take the card home. By this time Reva was back in the ICU and had developed an infection at the amputation site. The infection was not airborne, so a mask was not required when visiting her, but visitors had to wear disposable gloves and a gown. I left the card in her room because of possible contamination from the infection site.

Another time I visited her, Reva said mournfully, "I lost my wedding ring." She had observed that it was no longer on her finger.

"No, you didn't," I said. I explained that I was in the room while she was still sedated when a nurse removed it from her finger and gave it to me. Her fingers had swollen, and the nurse said that if the ring weren't removed, it might have to be cut off later.

"I have it in a safe place at home," I said.

"That's grand news," Reva replied.

This was how Reva talked. Her personality was intact. I noticed, however, that she was calling me Howard. She called me Howard throughout our courtship and into our first year of marriage when she confessed to me that she had always wanted to call me Howie. Thereafter, for more than thirty years, I was Howie to her. I asked her to call me Howie again, and she did.

She seemed to be growing stronger, but she was actually frail. The grand work of her parents was nearing completion. The shadow of the Nazis that they brought with them to America and cast onto Reva instead of celebrating a second chance at life and escape from destruction would soon envelope and conquer her. I, too, would become their victim

CHAPTER FIFTY-SIX

PLANCHE UREA

Planche urea. What did Reva mean? There is no doubt that she was not rambling incoherently, that she meant what she said. When I asked her to repeat it, she said it in a louder, more assertive voice, and she spelled "planche" at my request, but she never explained why she said it.

According to *Cassell's New French-English/English-French Dictionary*, an indispensable book in my college French courses more than forty years ago and one that I have hung onto, *planche*, as I noted in Chapter 53, means "board" or "plank." *Cassell's* lists a number of similar meanings, like "shelf," and gives several examples of idiomatic usage. The last example is *"s'appuyer sur une planche pourrie,"* "to lean upon a broken reed."

Planche pourrie. Is this what she said? She spelled out only *planche*. *Pourrie* (accented on the second syllable), means rotten, bad.

Did she actually say *planche pourrie*, referring to her left leg? *Pourrie. Urea.* The vowel sounds are the same except for the third syllable of urea, which does not exist in the two-syllable *pourrie*. Did she say or mean *planche pourrie*, rotten board, referring to her left leg? Was the reality of what happened to her so awful that beneath her calm demeanor she could express the horror only by distancing it? By saying it in another language?

Was she thinking, or perhaps, not even consciously thinking, was she subconsciously haunted by the "evil eye" that the long-ago high school French teacher gave her that, according to Reva, was one reason she dropped out of the academic program in which she was succeeding and switched to a business curriculum?

Even more painful to me is the use of *planch pourrie* in the phrase quoted above, *"s'appuyer sur une planche pourrie."* Was I the rotted reed that Reva had leaned on? I don't think she meant that. I hope she didn't mean that. She may have never come across that phrase. But she had a *planche pourrie* and now she had no *planche*, no left leg, and she had a *planche pourrie* for a right leg.

I wish I could ask her why she said that. I can't. There may be more to the story of the French teacher than Reva told me. There is always more to the stories that we tell and that we are told by others.

I will never know what she meant.

CHAPTER FIFTY-SEVEN

FIRST DO NO HARM

Reva was admitted to Holy Name Hospital on June 18, 2019, for a procedure to attempt to save her left leg. The procedure was to be performed by Dr. John Rundback, head of Holy Name's limb-salvaging department. But Reva went into cardiac arrest before Dr. Rundback could begin the procedure. Reva had never gone into cardiac arrest before. The procedure could not be done, and everything went downhill to her death three months later.

After Reva was resuscitated and moved to the ICU (she was kept sedated because a breathing tube had been inserted in her trachea), a CT scan of her lungs revealed that she had aspiration pneumonia. She had unknowingly entered the hospital with it. A physical exam given the evening before the procedure apparently did not include a chest X-ray. After Reva's death, I consulted a well-known malpractice and personal injury law firm. Dr. Runcelli, a retired ER physician who screened potential malpractice cases for the firm, reviewed Reva's Holy Name medical records, which I had obtained from the hospital. It was Dr. Runcelli who informed me of the aspiration pneumonia diagnosis. He said that the aspiration pneumonia probably caused Reva's cardiac arrest. Aspiration pneumonia is often fatal, he said, but Reva had recovered from it with two intravenous antibiotics.

I would, therefore, speculate that if the aspiration pneumonia caused the cardiac arrest, as Dr. Runcelli said it probably did, then if Reva had not entered Holy Name Hospital with aspiration pneumonia, she would not have suffered cardiac arrest, and Dr. Rundback would have been able to perform the procedure, and Reva might be alive today with a functioning left leg. It is true that Reva had two previous angioplasties performed by Dr. Cook and, though successful for a while, the arteries became blocked within a few months. But those angioplasties were performed by a vascular surgeon whose practice includes a variety of surgeries and procedures and who lacked the expertise in limb salvaging of Dr. Rundback, an interventional radiologist with an international reputation for limb salvaging, which was the focus of his practice. But for the aspiration pneumonia, Reva might be here with me today.

But what caused Reva's aspiration pneumonia? She had been in HMHUMC for four days the previous week, and it apparently wasn't diagnosed there. It wasn't diagnosed there because, I believe, it was caused there, although I would never be able to prove this in court.

Aspiration pneumonia differs from bacterial and viral pneumonia. It occurs when a person aspirates a foreign body into one of his or her lungs. Small pieces of food are often the culprit, but so is vomit.

On June 13, 2019, Reva's last day in HMHUMC, she was, as I related in a previous chapter, taken to dialysis early in the morning without breakfast. Then she was given no food on her return. Instead, the nurse, whom I have called Jennifer, gave her Miralax, a laxative. She had no food the entire day until she came home. Almost as soon as she entered the door of our apartment at about 4:00 p.m., she vomited.

It is possible that Reva, tired from the four days in the hospital, hungry, and having been without food but given a laxative, aspirated some vomit into a lung. Reva might be alive today and have a functioning left leg but for her last day in HMHUMC and Nurse Jennifer. Of course, this is conjecture, and as I was the only witness except for Reva to Reva's profuse vomiting, and Reva is no longer alive, it can never be proved.

But the iatrogenic disease that was the source of almost all of Reva's other ailments began decades earlier, long before I knew her, when her parents brought her to Dr. Nathan S. Kline in Manhattan who was experimenting with lithium for so called "bipolar disorder" on defenseless patients in Rockland State Hospital. Dr. Kline put her on lithium when, according to Reva, she was fourteen years old. I have told this story earlier in this memoir, but it cannot be told too often. It is a warning that Reva wanted to communicate to others. (See Chapter 30.) She was kept on lithium for eighteen years. Various psychiatrists in the clinics she went to kept her on the toxin. Her blood was infrequently monitored at these public clinics, although lithium has long been known to cause kidney disease. She never saw an individual counselor for psychotherapy until after we married. Her parents, apparently, would not pay for one. I do not know if Reva ever had health insurance from her decade-plus of clerk-typist jobs. As I wrote in an earlier chapter, even the nephrologist she saw before we married worked out of a public clinic.

Reva was a social worker, and I have her *DSM IV* that she used at NYU's social work school. This is the *Diagnostic and Statistical Manual* that psychiatrists and other mental health professionals use to make diagnoses and submit bills to insurance companies. What is most remarkable about this manual is the absence of science. In any other branch of medicine, there are lab tests, imaging studies, biopsies, and an array of scientific tests and measurements to diagnose disease. When I was in my twenties, I saw a doctor because I was feeling tired and thought I might have the flu. But my temperature was normal. I remember Dr. Burke saying, "I would not make a diagnosis of the flu in the absence of a fever." A simple home diagnostic tool, the thermometer, provides valuable medical information. But go through all 886 pages of *DSM IV* and the hundreds of diagnoses and you will not find a single scientific medical test. Psychiatrists make diagnoses from their subjective impressions. I have not seen the *DSM 5*, but from what I have read about it, it goes further in pathologizing everyday life without scientific evidence.

For LCSWs and others who offer talk therapy, the DSM can do little or no physical harm. But psychiatrists prescribe dangerous somatic treatments, including drugs, without any scientific basis, as was the case of my beloved wife, who was prescribed a drug that ultimately killed her when she was in the midst of discovering her real life. No other branch of medicine is as unscientific as psychiatry.

Professor Andrew Scull, a distinguished sociologist and historian of psychiatry, in *Psychiatry and its Discontents* (University of California Press, 2019), quotes neurophysiologist Robert Morrison who, in 1948 wrote, "There have been several times recently that I have felt that leaders of American psychiatry are trying to establish the truth on the basis of majority vote. This is, of course, quite contrary to the usual scientific procedure of submitting evidence which can stand on its own merit in a candid world."

Scull continues in his own words. "It would remain a device, however, that organized psychiatry would repeatedly resort to all the way to the present. It would be the basis, for example, on which the profession would decide that homosexuality was no longer a mental illness, and it has underpinned, indeed been the defining feature, of each successive version of the American Psychiatric Association's *Diagnostic and Statistical Manual* from the third edition published in 1980 all the way to the fifth edition released in 2013."

It is my contention that psychiatry has done immeasurable harm to many people and should be removed from the curricula of medical schools. I most keenly feel the harm it did to Reva, but I have known others whose lives were damaged and whose potential and talents were snuffed out by psychiatry. Mental illness is a metaphor and a dangerous one. Every human being is different and has unique abilities.

"In my Father's house are many mansions."

CHAPTER FIFTY-EIGHT

LTACH

Reva was now on an intermediate floor, and Dr. Leland was seeking to discharge her to another facility. According to an email he sent to Joe Brezin and copied to me, she was more alert and improving. The only IV she was on was a heparin drip. I continued to visit her twice daily. On a rainy day in late July, I visited her and intended to inspect a rehab center in Teaneck afterwards. Joe Brezin, now back in California, advised me to pay particular attention to the gym. However, while I was visiting Reva, a social worker entered her room and informed us that Dr. Leland wanted to discharge Reva, not to a rehab center, but to an LTACH, a Long-Term Acute Care Hospital. "The doctor doesn't think she is ready yet for a rehab center," the social worker said. I had never heard of this type of hospital. Few people have, according to the previously cited *New York Times* article. There was only one in Bergen County that provided dialysis, SELECT Hospital in Rochelle Park, a town about five miles west of Hackensack.

So I changed my plans. After I finished visiting Reva, I drove to SELECT instead of the rehab center.

SELECT is a nationwide, for-profit chain of LTACHs. There are a number of lawsuits that have been filed against the chain, according to Google. But I did not have the time to look at Google that day. I drove directly to the Rochelle Park location.

As I mentioned, it was raining, and the large parking lot was muddy in places. The SELECT hospital in Rochelle Park occupies one floor in a building that contains a nursing home. Three or four other buildings, including another nursing home, comprise a medical complex. One parking lot serves the entire campus, which is located adjacent to a residential area. All parking spaces in the lot, which I circled several times, were filled. I finally found the single unoccupied space, one reserved for handicapped parking. We had a handicapped placard on the van, but I usually did not park in handicapped spaces when I was driving alone. In fact, it is illegal to do so. The placard was not for me but for Reva. But I had no choice, and I parked in the space.

I wondered how I would be able to visit Reva twice a day as I had been when the parking lot was filled to capacity with vehicles of people working in or visiting the complex.

SELECT has free valet parking, I found out weeks later, but neither the social worker at Holy Name nor the person who escorted me on my tour of SELECT informed me of this. Parking may seem an insignificant issue when choosing a hospital; not so when the spouse visits every day, usually twice a day.

I took the elevator to the second floor, where SELECT hospital is located, introduced myself at the nurses' station, and explained the reason for my visit. I requested a tour. An administrator, not a nurse, was assigned to escort me. Since the entire hospital occupied only one floor, the tour didn't take long.

My escort said that dialysis was given to patients in their rooms and, at my request, she named some of the nephrologists who supervised dialysis at the hospital. I didn't recognize any of the names. Weeks later, I learned that Dr. Weizman's group, Reva's regular nephrologists, was among the SELECT nephrologists. Had I known this on the day I made the tour, it would have given me a greater sense of legitimacy about this medical facility that I had never heard of, despite having lived in Bergen County most of my life. I spoke to two young physical therapists and asked to see the gym. There was none. At the end of a corridor was a rack that held a few pieces of PT equipment: balls and lightweight dumbbells, but nothing that could significantly strengthen Reva's upper body. There was not even a room for physical therapy. Such physical therapy as was offered was in the patients' rooms. My impression of SELECT was negative: it certainly did not offer the physical therapy that Joe Brezin had advised.

When I returned to Holy Name the following day, I discussed my findings with Reva and communicated to Dr. Leland, through the social worker, that Reva would prefer to be transferred to a rehab center like Prospect Heights when she was ready. Leland faxed her records to Prospect Heights, which accepted her for transfer once she was off the heparin drip.

Perhaps Reva would have been better off if she had been transferred to SELECT at that time. She could have been transferred even while on the drip, as SELECT is not a rehab facility. But there was missing information, especially about parking and dialysis doctors. Had I been adequately informed, I would have felt more confident in her transfer to SELECT and might have advised Reva to sign the necessary papers. But I was given incomplete information. Missing information is as dangerous as misinformation.

It is significant that almost all my conversations with doctors at Holy Name, with two exceptions, were impromptu, with both the doctor and I standing or the doctor seated at a computer behind the nurses' station, where I had interrupted him. There was rarely a time when we were seated face-to-face for a planned discussion with Reva in Reva's room or, during those times when Reva was unresponsive, in a separate room. The two exceptions that I remember were a discussion with Leland, Reva, Joe Brezin (by speaker phone), and me when Reva was on a regular medical floor and a discussion between me and a doctor whom I call Dr. Death. This interaction will be described later.

I also do not know why the staff turned to me to make decisions about Reva's care rather than to Reva, who was now fully conscious and cognizant. I discussed all the medical issues with Reva, and when the staff handed me papers to sign, I gave them to Reva. I transmitted to Reva only my observations and findings. I had signed papers on her behalf only when she was sedated and unable to respond.

Dr. Thaddus, the surgeon who had amputated her leg, still had not removed the staples. It was his decision, I was told, to leave them in longer. A few days after my tour of SELECT, Reva was moved from the intermediate floor to a regular medical floor.

CHAPTER FIFTY-NINE

GOD SAVE ME FOR I AM ONLY A WOMAN

On July 15, Reva was moved from the intermediate floor to a room on the sixth floor, a regular medical floor. The following day, Leland, Reva, Joe Brezin (on the phone from California), and I had a conference in Reva's room about the next step in her care. Although Reva was awake and alert, she said little.

Leland suggested that Reva be evaluated by Kessler Institute in Saddle Brook, and, if accepted, go to Kessler for a week of intensive rehabilitation and then to a subacute facility. This was an upbeat plan, but I had misgivings, although I did not articulate them. I knew that Kessler requires patients to do several hours a day of intensive physical and occupational therapy, and I didn't see how Reva, in her weakened condition, could comply. This plan collapsed anyway when Dr. Moss, the pulmonologist, reported that an X-ray of Reva's lungs showed a large amount of fluid that needed to be drained.

After I had left the hospital and was in my car, a nurse called and said that Dr. Singer wanted to move Reva to the ICU temporarily to give her two hours of dialysis in an attempt to remove the fluids through dialysis instead of drainage. Singer wanted to dialyze Reva in the ICU because Reva's systolic blood pressure had dropped to 81. He wanted to have the norepinephrine ready if she needed it. She got through the first hour without norepinephrine, but then her BP dropped and the drug had to be administered intravenously. Norepinephrine is a vasoconstrictor that works, to the best of my understanding, by causing the blood vessels to constrict, thereby raising the blood pressure. I went back to the hospital to see Reva in the ICU. She was alert but, as I wrote in my journal later, "It is very depressing. We don't know what is to come next."

Joe Brezin informed me that Leland, at his request, was attempting to transfer Reva to HMHUMC. As previously mentioned, Joe Brezin had also faxed a letter to Dr. Rosenzweig-Berman, head of pulmonary hypertension at Columbia, whom Reva had seen as an outpatient. But Reva had been unable to keep the six-month follow up visit because she was in HMHUMC as a result of the injury to her right foot inflicted on her by S. I have a copy of the letter that Joe faxed to Dr. Rosenzweig-Berman. I don't know if he ever got a response, but Reva was never transferred to Columbia.

Joe Brezin also spoke to Dr. Rao, the Indian pulmonary hypertension and congestive heart failure specialist who had treated Reva as an outpatient at HMHUMC and had performed cardiac catheterization on her. As I wrote previously, Dr. Rao had prescribed a generic form of Viagra for Reva, which increased the blood flow to her lungs but gave her tinnitus. Reva had dropped Dr. Rao and urged me to find a malpractice lawyer so she could sue him. It was after Reva discontinued Dr. Rao that we went to Columbia to see Dr. Rosenzweig-Berman

According to Joe Brezin, Dr. Rao told him that HMHUMC could do no more for Reva than Holy Name was doing. When I questioned Joe about Dr. Rao's judgement and whether we could go to someone higher up at HMHUMC, he said that Dr. Rao was speaking for the hospital.

Reva remained at Holy Name which, despite having pretty flowers growing on its grounds and a religious tradition, is a small community hospital with limited facilities.

Leland was eager to get Reva out, it seemed to me, dead or alive. He complained to me that Medicare wouldn't pay unless Holy Name were treating her for a specific disease.

She was fighting death, but I guess that wasn't specific enough for him or for Medicare. I found it interesting to observe, in my many weeks visiting Reva in the ICU, that the customary position for doctors was not at patients' bedsides but behind computers.

Reva remained in the ICU in late July, as it was necessary now to use norepinephrine during dialysis. There is a note in Dr. Thaddus's report of the amputation that says that the stump was getting only marginal blood supply after the surgery. Reva's heart seemed not to be pumping enough blood. The cause of her reduced heart function may have been pulmonary hypertension and the fifteen years she had been dependent on a wheelchair, the last five of which her right foot could not reach the floor and she could not walk even with a walker. She had had little cardiovascular exercise in years.

I noticed that she was becoming lethargic and was eating less.

Members of the clergy of different faiths came to pray with her and over her. A rabbi came from the Lubavitch Hasidim bringing with him a pair of tefillin for me. I put them on, following his instructions, for the first time in more than thirty years. He then recited, line by line, the Hebrew prayers, which I repeated and Reva repeated as well, in a surprisingly loud and assertive voice. The rabbi came to the ICU at least once more, and I am still in contact with him.

Reva also prayed a Yiddish prayer, which she had often told me (and her mother told me as well) that her mother prayed while waiting in line at a concentration camp to be assessed by an SS officer. After the assessment, the women were sent either to the death chamber or to a work camp. Her mother, who was married to her first husband, said a prayer in Yiddish which translates as, "God save me for I am only a woman." According to her mother, after uttering the prayer, she heard a voice telling her to throw away her wedding ring. She did, and when she reached the SS officer, she was sent to a work camp. She believed that if she had presented herself as married woman, she would have gone to the death chamber.

Reva cherished her wedding ring. She was buried with it on her left ring finger, as I will be buried with mine. In the ICU, more than once when I was with her, she would say in Yiddish, "God save me for I am only a woman."

CHAPTER SIXTY

LIMBO

One day in late July when I visited Reva, there was a sign on the door of her ICU room that said gloves and a gown were required of all her visitors. Disposable gloves and gowns were in a dispenser outside her room. Her amputation site had become infected with Vancomycin Resistant Enterococcus (VRE), a hospital-acquired infection that is usually spread by the hands of health care workers. The infection was not airborne, so face masks were not required. An infectious disease doctor had looked at her leg but had not prescribed anything.

Reva remained weak, but she was conscious and her speech intelligible. Her blood pressure had risen, and she no longer required norepinephrine for dialysis.

Her brother had told me on the phone to hope for the best but be prepared for the worst. I heard these words again six weeks later from an ICU doctor at St. Joseph's Hospital, where Reva died.

I encountered Dr. Leland in the hallway, and he urged me to put Reva in hospice and end-of-life care. In Reva's case, death would come swiftly, as hospice would include discontinuing dialysis, as well as all other medicines except those to relive pain and terror. As Reva was alert and cognizant, I don't know why he didn't ask Reva what she wanted.

Leland said that she had so many medical problems that she would go from one hospital to another and live a few months, at the most.

I was outraged. Reva was a fighter and would continue to fight.

I returned to her room where Dr. Singer was examining her for dialysis the next day. I told Reva and Dr. Singer what Leland had said. Dr. Singer said calmly, "Don't worry. Just say no." Reva agreed. She wanted to live. Twice, before the September 2, 2018 surgery in

HMHUMC and now in the ICU of Holy Name, she affirmed her desire to fight for her life.

In August, just before she was finally transferred to SELECT, I told a SELECT nurse who came to Holy Name to answer my questions about the LTACH that I had come to consider the word "hospice" an obscenity and never wanted to hear it again.

Doctors are trained and paid very well to heal or at least ameliorate disease. Sometimes they cannot. The good ones fight nature and sometimes the patient dies anyway. But to ask a patient or a patient's close relative to surrender is like demanding that an army surrender on a battlefield. Armies sometimes surrender to save lives. But it is the opposite when a doctor asks a patient or a patient's next of kin to surrender. The doctor suffers no consequences and the patient dies.

After Reva's death, her doctors, including her nephrologist, knew she had died, yet I received only one condolence card from a medical professional and that was from our dentist. I was also handed a condolence card signed by the nurses and staff of our primary care doctor during a visit there. Doctors don't get paid to send condolence cards.

And they have no right to ask a patient's next of kin to surrender the patient when the patient is awake and lucid and capable of making her own decision.

Who is to determine quality of life?

In August, after Reva was transferred to SELECT, I put my finger in her hand and she squeezed it hard. She didn't want to let go. She knew me and expressed her love for me, as I expressed my love for her. If I had let her die in Holy Name, that moment would not have occurred.

And I was honoring her wishes clearly articulated to me by her before her surgery on September 2, 2018: She wanted to live. She wanted to be resuscitated. She wanted extraordinary measures.

And she did not seem to be in pain. On August 21, her first day in SELECT, I was in her room when the doctor examined her and tested her to see if she followed commands. She could not speak because of the breathing tube. (She was no longer sedated, however. The SELECT doctor said that patients get used to a breathing tube.) He asked her to raise her arm, which she did. Then he asked her if she was in pain, and she shook her head.

In Holy Name in late July, when I met with Dr. Death, a palliative care doctor who will otherwise remain nameless, a young man garbed in a lab coat with a stethoscope jauntily swinging from his neck, I felt myself pressured into signing a consent to withdraw treatments from Reva, which would quickly end her life. I would not do it, but I gave Dr. Death permission to prescribe morphine, if Reva needed it for pain, and sedatives, if she needed them. I also allowed myself to be pressured into signing a DNR (Do Not Resuscitate) order, which I later rescinded at the advice of the surgeon, Dr. Thaddus. Reva, by this time, had suffered her second cardiac arrest and was intubated, sedated, and unconscious.

Indeed, if I had authorized discontinuing dialysis, which Dr. Death urged me to do, she would have died within days. But I wonder what the difference would be, other than legal, between my authorizing the hospital to stop her dialysis and my strangling her in her ICU bed. In the latter case, I would be arrested and charged with murder. The former case is also murder, but it wouldn't be called that and no one would be arrested. I wonder if the hospital would have charged for removing the dialysis line, billed Medicare for executing her. I will save my discussions with Dr. Death for a later chapter.

Reva had many medical problems that had developed after S squeezed the trigger on her, the blanket pulling, on that fateful day in the dialysis center. Before then, she was a determined, vivacious, and relatively independent woman who was on the verge of being hired for a new part-time social-worker job.

What follows are excerpts from my journal for the period described above. The journal reflects my emotional responses at the time, rather than retrospectively.

7/17/19 Wed. What can I say? Another day. Lunch. Then back to Reva. She is still in ICU but more comfortable. The doctors do not communicate. We mill around in the dark and hit objects, stones, wagons. I can't tell what they are because of the dark.

7/18/19 Thurs, 9:40 p.m. Usual day. Visited Reva twice. She is in ICU still. If removing fluid from her chest can be done Fri. or Sat. the latest—Fri. better because non-dialysis day—then her BP may be under control.

7/21/19 Sun. 6 p.m. Reva is weak. But I spoke to nurse later in day. She has begun to use Forinef 0.1 mg every 12 hours. Took first dose this afternoon and nurse said her BP is higher. Very hot today, like a desert. Reva very weak. I pray that she survives.

7/22/19 Mon. 10:40 p.m. Reva got dialysis today. She is weaker. But she ate a whole dish of meatloaf which I fed her. Her brother says, hope for the best but be prepared for the worst. I would be insane and would not care that I was insane except that she is alive and every morning I wake and when I become awake feel the deep darkness but also the hope because she is alive and I start the day.

7/23/19 Tues. 11:30 p.m. Reva off the norepinephrine as of 6 pm. BP good when I left her. Rabbi came today, prayed, all three of us did. She seems stronger. Hope that the "event" is reversible with patience and care.

7/24/19 Wed. 10:56 p.m. Reva using less norepinephrine. They had to do one mcg during dialysis but were able to shut it off afterward. But she is very tired and had not slept well last night.

7/25/19 Thurs. To HNH where Reva is partially quarantined. You have to wear gown and gloves in room. Nothing airborne but amputation site infected. Culture came back showing vancomycin resistant enterococcus. Her BP is good, though, and she is off norepinephrine, at least for now, and I hope for good. Encountered Leland who was pushing me for hospice and end of life care for Reva. Said she would never return home. Would be in one hospital or another and would live only a few months. Said she has so many things wrong. Said they can't do dialysis without norepinephrine, she has weak right ventricle, pulmonary hypertension and now infected wound site. I was outraged. She is a fighter and will continue to fight. Dr. Singer examined her prior to dialysis tomorrow. Said not to worry. Said we can say no to hospice. He intends to give her dialysis tomorrow beginning with no norepinephrine and use norepinephrine only if it becomes necessary. Reva made me a birthday card but I had to leave it there because of her infection. Nothing airborne but bacteria in leg. Surgeon has to look at it. Found out tonight infectious disease doctor looked at it but did not prescribe. She will come home to me. It may take longer than I planned but she will come home. I was looking and am looking for around Oct. She has been accepted into SELECT hospital and if she goes there, she will go to rehab after. Leland is thinking in money terms, what Medicare will pay. How dare he ask Reva to accept to end her life! She is alert and cognizant although weak and not in any pain except from pressure sore, and her BP is much better and holding its own, perhaps because of the addition of Effexor. Reva and an aide sang happy birthday to me.

7/28/19 Sun. 7:15 p.m. Reva has been very weak the last few days, since Wed. She sleeps most of the day and night. Almost impossible to communicate with her but she did become alert this afternoon when she must have heard me discussing her mortality in the hallway with a nurse. Her BP then went up to 107 and she communicated better for a little while. I cannot touch her now or kiss her because she has an infection at surgical site. Everyone entering room has to wear disposable gown and gloves. It is vancomycin resistant enterococcus. It is not being treated. They plan, at least the nurse says, to transfer her to SELECT long term care hospital in Rochelle Park. They haven't used norepinephrine and Fri. they dialyzed her without it but then had to turn it on for a few hours afterwards, as her BP dropped to 80 and her heart rate dropped.

She is fighting. I am fighting. I pray that we have a few more years together. She is an angel from heaven. She had a heart bursting with love and she gave it to me, she gave all her love to me. Brave and optimistic words do not make salutary actions.

7/31/19 Wed. 10:10 p.m. Finally completed HR at Ramapo. Took Franklin Turnpike. This will be my route. Then to Reva. She had just come back from dialysis. She greeted me but almost immediately fell asleep. Her tray came but I could not wake her to feed her.

8/1/19 Thurs. 8:12 p.m. Reva does not eat when I feed her or try to. She will be transferred to SELECT. I hope that she has not lost the will to live. Her life is incredibly painful. Pressure sore. She needs to be shifted every two hours, day and night. I know now, as of today, that she will never return home to me again. The extremely soft and difficult to understand speech, (though intelligible) which I thought was temporary I know now is not. The pulmonary hypertension and right ventricle atrophy is causing heart failure. There are people I can blame and will blame but it makes no difference. I don't think she will live until winter. She may die in weeks or at best months. As I entered our building from the back parking lot, I realized Reva will never return here. There are people I can blame but that will not *extend her life. My happiness is over as is hers. I must now, starting tomorrow, buy two graves. I love her and always will. When my time comes, I will be buried next to her.*

CHAPTER SIXTY-ONE

RETURN AND RETURN

In early August, Reva's blood pressure was stable enough so that she no longer needed norepinephrine during dialysis, and she was moved from the ICU back to the intermediate floor. However, she was given a room at the end of the corridor without a roommate because of her infection. Dr. Leland said that the skin at the amputation site had turned black, and the blackness was moving up of what remained of her left leg. He said she had dry gangrene.

On my first day to visit her in her new room, I encountered Dr. Thaddus, the surgeon, in the hallway. He had just seen Reva. He said that the black area was dead skin that would slough off in a few weeks and that no surgery or debriding was needed. "I wouldn't touch it," he said, and hurried away.

I thought it was strange for him to say that he wouldn't touch it, by which he meant, I surmised, that he wouldn't treat it. I later read that the treatment for dry gangrene is antibiotics and debridement. But Dr. Thaddus never debrided the site, although, I think, Reva was started on antibiotics. I never saw the black skin. I had seen the stump before it became infected, but I would not look at it now.

The same precautions for entering her room were in place: wearing a disposable gown and disposable gloves.

Reva was awake and cognizant but was becoming increasingly lethargic. She was also hardly eating. I called this to Leland's attention. I noticed how thin her wrists had become. Leland ordered a chart to be posted in her room, which was to be filled in by everyone who fed her, including me, indicating what she ate and how much of it.

One afternoon, I arrived just as she returned from dialysis. Her food tray came at the same time. I pointed out that it included vanilla pudding. "My favorite," she said. I fed her one spoonful but that is all she would eat. "I'm full," she said. She also said to me then or at another time, "Something is wrong with my stomach."

I don't know if she ever communicated problems about her stomach to the doctors.

Because of her increasing lethargy, Leland ordered a neurological consultation. I was visiting her when the neurologist, a woman, came.

The neurologist asked Reva a few questions but did not perform a physical examination. The following is a reconstruction of the neurologist's questions and Reva's responses, as best I remember. Reva replied in a low, dispirited voice.

"What is your name?"

"Reva Prosnitz."

"Where do you live?"

"Hackensack."

"Who is this?" (Pointing at me.)

"My husband."

"Are you afraid of anything?"

"Dying."

This exam took less than five minutes. Then the neurologist got up to leave. I began to ask a question but she brushed past me out of the room without acknowledging me. I confess I lost my temper at her rudeness and shouted after her, "Bitch!"

I had questions to ask about my wife's health, but she wouldn't even give me the courtesy of acknowledging me. I was furious.

The neurologist recommended some medication to Leland, but he rejected it because, he said, it would further decrease Reva's appetite.

I felt a little vindicated when I read Reva's medical records from Holy Name after her death and came upon the neurologist's report. The vindication was not from what was in the report, that Reva was depressed, but the letters after the neurologist's name: D.O. She was an osteopath.

Reva's lethargy increased and she hardly ate. In my naivety, I associate good nutrition with healing, and I suggested to Leland that he might consider ordering a nasal gastric tube so Reva could be tube fed. She had an N/G tube while she was kept sedated before her amputation and was fed a liquid that contains nutrients and calories but minimal amounts of potassium and phosphorous, which are dangerous to patients with kidney disease.

Many years ago, I had an N/G tube for more than a week while I was fully conscious. I recall it as somewhat uncomfortable but not painful.

Leland agreed and a nurse practitioner came to Reva's room one afternoon while I was visiting and attempted to pass it but was unsuccessful.

That evening, after I had returned for my second visit of the day, a house doctor came with a thinner N/G tube and successfully passed it.

While he was passing the tube down one of Reva's nostrils, she kept saying "No. No. No. No." That was the last word I ever heard Reva speak.

Reva could have refused the tube. I made the suggestion to Leland. I could not order it. There is an alternative, which I did not know about at the time: intravenous feeding, which Reva also had the right to refuse. I acted on her behalf only when she was unconscious. Ironically, about a week after the N/G tube was passed, the *New York Times* ran the obituary of the physician who invented intravenous feeding after he noticed, as a young resident, that healthy patients were dying following routine surgeries. He determined that they had starved to death.

But I did not know about intravenous feeding when I suggested the N/G tube to Leland. I am sure that Leland did.

After the tube was passed, Reva calmed down, but she did not speak. An N/G tube does not prevent speech, as a breathing tube does. An N/G tube goes into the esophagus, not the trachea. But Reva had been speaking little before, as her lethargy had increased.

A portable X-ray machine was brought to the room, and an X-ray confirmed that the tube was in proper position. The nurse now put mittens on Reva's hands to prevent her from pulling it out, and then the nurse fed her from the tube.

I felt that Reva would be calmer if she heard my voice while the doctor inserted the tube, but the doctor would not allow me in the room during the procedure, so I stood outside. I read the 91st Psalm in a voice loud enough for Reva to hear. This was one of my favorite psalms with its soaring imagery of salvation. But now I can no longer read it or say it. The Psalter, today, for me has 149 psalms.

When I visited Reva the following day, she was half asleep. She did not speak, but before I left, she extended a mittened hand. The nurse informed me that once she could discontinue the heparin drip and resume the oral blood thinners that she had been taking before she was in the hospital, she could be transferred to Prospect Heights. But I wondered how she could do physical therapy with a skin infection and her hands mittened. My hope, of course, was that she would soon resume eating. I recalled that when I had had an N/G tube, I was able to eat with the tube in place. After I had eaten two meals, the tube was removed.

One morning, a few days after the tube was inserted, I visited Reva and was surprised to find Dr. Leland and several nurses in the room. Reva's heart monitor showed extreme fluctuations. At one point, her heart rate was forty but then went higher. Reva was sitting upright in bed. She did not speak; it seemed that she could not. There was a look of terror in her eyes that I had never seen before in her or anyone else. Even the horror movies I have seen cannot replicate it. I shall never forget that look as long as I live. "Your wife is dying," Leland said to me matter-of-factly.

He ordered transporters to return her to the ICU. While she was being transported, within Reva's earshot, as if she were an inert object, he urged me again to hospice her, to disconnect her from all tubes including dialysis. He said that he doubted that she would survive the day.

From the first day that she was in the Holy Name ICU in June, the doctors were pushing me to arrange for end-of-life care, to give up, to let Reva go. I refused now as I refused then. Leland was annoyed.

"I wouldn't do this to my wife," he said

I asked him if he would want to be in hospice if he were in Reva's condition.

His enigmatic reply was, "I would not allow myself to be in her condition."

Perhaps I misunderstood him. Did he mean that he, at the age of fourteen, would not have allowed his parents to force him to be treated by a doctor who prescribed lithium or some other toxin? Children have little say in these matters.

I went down to the ICU and was there when they brought Reva in. One of the nurses who had cared for her before began to cry. Reva's gentleness affected everyone. ICU nurses see many sick people and many deaths. But this nurse was crying.

CHAPTER SIXTY-TWO

DR. DEATH

On Aug. 9 at 1:40 a.m. my cell phone rang. It was the ICU at Holy Name. Reva had gone into another cardiac arrest. The nurse wanted to know if they should resuscitate her. I said yes. It took eleven minutes to restore Reva's heartbeat.

I don't know why they called me. I had never signed a DNR. I don't know how much time was lost before they began resuscitation. As there was no DNR, they were obligated to resuscitate her.

This, her second cardiac arrest, occurred a few days after she was transferred back to the ICU. On the morning of the transfer, when Leland told me, "I would never do this to my wife," he also predicted that Reva wouldn't live through the day. She lived for almost five more weeks. She was very sick, but she might have recovered. I could not abandon hope.

If I had consented to let Reva die, as Leland and other doctors at Holy Name wanted me to, I would be even more haunted than I am today. I would always feel that she might have lived and regained at least partial health.

I have had more than enough experience with doctors who mistake themselves for God. Reva's illness and death were ultimately caused by Dr. Nathan S. Kline and other psychiatrists who poisoned her with lithium for eighteen years.

After the second cardiac arrest, she was intubated and sedated. She could not speak because of the intubation, although she had stopped speaking several days earlier.

It was about this time that I bought a radio for Reva and set it up in her room. The radio was with her for the duration of her life. As she was sedated and could not easily watch television, I felt the radio would relieve boredom. Every morning when I visited her, I tuned it on to WQXR, New York City's only remaining classical music station. Reva and I both enjoyed classical music. Every evening at about 10:00 p.m., I called the ICU to remind the nurse to shut off the radio so Reva could sleep. I also made sure that the nurses put the eye drops for glaucoma in her eyes each morning and evening, and I continued to refill the eye drop prescription.

In retrospect, I think that this regular routine that mimicked a partial normality, and my twice daily visits, helped Reva survive through the summer almost into the fall.

After her second cardiac arrest, Holy Name's patient advocate suggested that I meet with a bereavement counselor who could refer me to a therapist.

I have only met two professional bereavement counselors in my life, but that is two too many. Few people I have known have been more offensive. They impressed me as ghouls who enjoy having power over people who are grieving and are at their most vulnerable.

After Reva's death, I entered a bereavement group for widows and widowers that met weekly for eight weeks in the rectory of a Roman Catholic Church. This was a helpful and compassionate group, and more than two years later I am still in contact with some of its members. It was sponsored by the church and was free. The group had three leaders who were all former members who had received training. They knew bereavement firsthand.

The bereavement counselor at Holy Name met with me in the hospital lobby. Her usual workplace was Holy Name's hospice, which was located in another town. She referred me to a social worker who did not have an office but visited people in their homes. I spoke on the phone to the social worker, an Orthodox Jewish woman, and decided to reject counseling.

I did, however, speak to the ICU nurses. As I mentioned earlier, I found that the best time to talk to an ICU nurse is after midnight when they have less to do. I asked one of the nurses taking care of Reva if she thought Reva might recover. She replied that she had seen patients sicker than Reva recover.

On another late night call, a nurse suggested that I make an appointment with the palliative care doctor, who shall be known in this memoir only as Dr. Death.

The following day, I telephoned Dr. Death and made an appointment with him.

Dr. Death was a tall, young doctor with a stethoscope dangling jauntily from his neck. We met in an office adjacent to the ICU that I didn't know existed. Until then, most of my conversations with Holy Name doctors had been on the fly. The doctors were always standing unless I caught them at their computer stations. No other doctor at Holy Name sat in a chair opposite me (although behind a desk) to conduct a conversation. This is in Dr. Death's favor.

Indeed, my first meeting with Dr. Death did not go badly. It became a three-way conversation, as I called Joe Brezin in California to join the discussion. He advised Dr. Death to discontinue some medicines that Reva was taking.

Subsequent meetings with Dr. Death, however, proved stressful. Like Leland, he attempted to persuade me to let Reva die. Dr. Death also asked me if I had firearms or knives at home. He advised me to cancel my teaching assignment for the fall at Ramapo College. Indeed, he generated so much anxiety in me that that I feared he would contact Ramapo and cancel the assignment himself. I called him and he said he would not do this.

Dr. Death said I could continue to have Reva treated aggressively, in which case she would live a few more months at the most, or I could agree to have her terminated, disconnected from all machines, including dialysis and, "She will die peacefully in a few days," said Dr. Death.

I would not allow Reva to die at the will of Dr. Death or any other doctor. I told Dr. Death that I knew Reva's treatment would take longer than I had anticipated, but I was hoping to have her home with home nursing care and an aide by October. However, I did give Dr. Death permission to order morphine and sedatives for Reva as needed, and, at his and Joe Brezin's urging, I signed a DNR.

My hope for an October homecoming notwithstanding, I was aware that Reva might not survive. After her second cardiac arrest, the pulmonologist told me that Reva would not leave the ICU alive. I contacted a Jewish funeral director, and I bought two adjacent graves in George Washington Memorial Park, a nonsectarian cemetery in Paramus. Long before Reva's final illness, before S pulled the blanket on her foot, Reva and I discussed where we would want our bodies buried and agreed on this cemetery. When I bought the graves, I still hoped that they would remain vacant for years to come.

CHAPTER SIXTY-THREE

TRANSFER

My mother died in August 2000 at the age of eighty-four. The funeral was in Rhode Island, where she had lived the last nineteen years of her life, but her body was transported to New Jersey for burial in the Prosnitz family plot in a cemetery in Kenilworth, a town south of Newark.

The burial was on a hot, sunny Sunday, and numerous family members and friends attended the cemetery service. A black butterfly flew over my mother's coffin as it was lowered into the grave.

The butterfly was the eastern black swallowtail, which has the distinction of being the official state butterfly of New Jersey, so designated by former Governor Chris Christie.

The black swallowtail isn't completely black but has a fringe of silver dots on the outer edge of its wings. But the dots aren't always visible when it is in flight.

The flight of the butterfly over my mother's coffin at that moment is a mystery written in a language that no human being can understand. The butterfly is a letter in an incomprehensible word.

On an August afternoon in 2019, I parked my car in the parking lot of our apartment building after visiting Reva. As I walked toward the rear door, I saw a black swallowtail butterfly on the parking lot pavement. The butterfly was disabled, struggling, occasionally flapping its wings in an effort to rise, which it could not. I watched it transfixed and took a picture with my phone. Then I went inside without disturbing it further.

The next day when I told Dr. Death the story, he said harshly, "So you left it for someone else to kill!"

But I didn't know if the butterfly would die or regain strength and fly off. It did not. When I returned home after speaking with Dr. Death and visiting Reva, I saw fragments of the butterfly on the pavement near where I had seen it struggle. I don't know if someone crushed it and it had later been ripped apart by cars or if a car ran over it. Some silver dots were visible on one fragment.

I considered what message there might be in the butterfly's destruction: that Reva would die? That her body's struggle to overcome disease was in vain? Or perhaps that I would die and my struggle was useless, for I was also flapping my wings on the ground. I hoped for the latter.

Dr. Death asked me if I thought there was a fate worse than death. I answered conventionally: intractable pain. But Reva's pain, if she experienced any, was controlled through drugs, and pain is usually not a component of septic shock, which was the primary cause of her death listed on her death certificate. Indeed, as previously mentioned, after Reva was transferred to SELECT Hospital on August 21, the doctor asked her if she was in pain, and she shook her head. I was in her room at the time.

Reva seemed cognizant, although she couldn't speak because of the breathing tube. But she followed commands, both in Holy Name and SELECT. The pulmonologist told me that while they were resuscitating her after her second cardiac arrest, they were pumping oxygen from bags into her lungs.

But I could have told Dr. Death, but didn't, that a fate worse than death is breaking a solemn promise, and I had promised Reva on September 2, 2018, before the surgery on her left leg, that I would authorize extraordinary measures to revive her and keep her alive if she went into cardiac arrest. During the period when she was awake and conscious in July, she did not revoke her decision, and I would not betray her.

Perhaps she would now have allowed herself to die, but I could not make that assumption. And she was not in pain and she showed signs of cognizance.

On August 17, a surgeon from Holy Name telephoned me. She said that a CT scan of Reva's stomach showed a small amount of "extra luminal air," which indicated that she might have a perforation in her small bowel. The normal course would be to operate, the surgeon said, but they could not because Reva was too weak to survive general anesthesia, so instead they were treating her with massive amounts of antibiotics and intravenous nutrition. The surgeon said they were now using the N/G tube for drainage, not for feeding. I called Joe Brezin, who said that the treatment might work. Reva had been running a low-grade fever and had an elevated white blood cell count but the white blood cell count had come down, which was a favorable sign.

Later that day, Leland's nurse practitioner called me and blandly asked if I wanted to put Reva in hospice. For, it seemed, the 200th time, I said NO and the answer remains NO as long as she is not suffering.

The following is an excerpt from my journal that I entered later that day:

Reva has shared my life for 35 years and we will be married 32 years in January. We have done everything together. She has always been there for me and, I hope, I for her, and she is still here, only a mile or two away, but very sick, but sick people can get better.

Reva had been intubated for more than a week, and Dr. Thaddus, the surgeon who amputated her leg, said it was necessary to perform a tracheotomy, to cut a small hole in her trachea and insert a tube connected to the respirator. He said that intubation was not for long-term use. He also said that the tracheotomy could be reversed and eventually removed if she recovered, and the hole would close by itself. He asked me to rescind the DNR before he operated the following day. I did so.

But Dr. Thaddus could not do the surgery because the next day Reva was again running a low-grade fever. She was still intubated when she was transferred to SELECT Hospital.

Reva's condition had stabilized and the treatment for her stomach seemed to have worked, at least temporarily, as a second CT scan did not show extra luminal air. On the evening of August 21, she was transferred to SELECT hospital. This was a Thursday, a regular dialysis day for Reva. Leland wanted her transferred in the morning, but I insisted that she have dialysis first and be transferred afterwards. I had not reauthorized the DNR, and Leland asked me if I wanted her transferred "with full code," that is, with no DNR. I said I did. She was transferred by ambulance in the early evening.

I was waiting for her at SELECT. I was shaky about the transfer and had asked Marjorie J., my friend from Christ Episcopal Church, to wait with me. As I wrote earlier, Marjorie's youngest daughter, Mary, who had been a social worker at HMHUMC, died from brain cancer at thirty-eight, leaving behind a husband and two young children.

The ambulance technicians wheeled Reva into the single-floor SELECT Hospital. Reva was off the propofal and her eyes were open. There was a puzzled expression on her face, as if she wanted to say "Where am I now?" But she couldn't speak because of the breathing tube.

CHAPTER SIXTY-FOUR

SELECT

When, in July, Dr. Leland first proposed transferring Reva to SELECT, and I went on a rainy day to inspect the hospital, the Holy Name social worker, who had informed Reva and me of Leland's decision, apparently did not invite a representative of SELECT, a one-floor, for-profit hospital that few people in Bergen County have ever heard of, to visit Holy Name to speak to us. Had the social worker done so at that time, when Reva's condition was more hopeful, we would have learned some facts that might have made a difference in our decision. That social worker was on vacation in late August, and the covering social worker had the acumen to ask a nurse from SELECT to come to Holy Name to introduce the hospital to me. Reva was by this time too sick to participate in the discussion or to sign transfer papers.

From the SELECT nurse, I learned that SELECT had free valet parking, so I would still be able to visit Reva every day, twice a day, and would not have to hunt for a parking space and, perhaps, be unable to find one. I also learned that Dr. Weizman's nephrology group, which had been Reva's nephrologists for almost twenty years, from the time before she was in dialysis, was among the nephrologists who supervised dialysis at SELECT. This made a huge difference to me. Reva would be in the hands of doctors who knew her, at least for dialysis. It leant credibility to SELECT.

I did not have those facts weeks earlier when Leland first proposed the transfer, a time when Reva was alert and not intubated. Perhaps she would be alive today if we had that knowledge then. But now, more than a month later, she was in SELECT.

SELECT did not have full-time doctors. The doctors came to the hospital after they had finished their regular office hours. Dr. Bakshi, a tall Indian pulmonologist, was the doctor assigned to Reva.

Dr. Bakshi was amazed at how sick she was. "She shouldn't be here," he said. "Then where should she be?" I asked. "Holy Name," he replied.

When doctors disagree.

Nevertheless, she was in SELECT, and I was in Reva's room while Dr. Bakshi examined her. Marjorie J. was with me.

It was a large private room. There was a second bed, but Reva was the only patient occupying the room. Dr. Bakshi asked Reva to raise her arm. At first there was no movement. He turned to me and said, "You see, she doesn't follow commands." But I said, "Look!" Reva had, indeed, raised her arm but her right arm. Her left arm was closest to the entrance to the room, and Bakshi seemed to be focusing on that arm. But Reva had had dialysis earlier in the day and the fistula was in her left arm, which was tired from the treatment. Dr. Bakshi then asked Reva if she was in pain. She shook her head. He seemed encouraged. When he had completed the examination, he turned to me and said, "My diagnosis is septic shock." He said that Reva would be dialyzed by Weizman's group and that the SELECT doctors would try to wean her from the breathing tube, for which Reva no longer required sedation. Dr. Bakshi said that after a while patients get used to a breathing tube.

Another doctor, Dr. Ali, told me that Holy Name had sent over incomplete records with Reva and an incomplete and contradictory list of her medications. When I left the hospital later in the evening with Marjorie, Dr. Ali was in his office on the phone with Holy Name. I went home feeling somewhat consoled, or perhaps I wanted to be consoled. Dr. Ali was at work, doing his job as a doctor.

The following is an excerpt from my journal for August 22, the day after Reva was admitted to SELECT:

Visited Reva. Her white blood cell count is down to 14 but she had 103 fever last night but it was 97 this afternoon. Dr. Bakshi examined her and said she is doing better. He will try to extubate her next week once she is off the norepinephrine. She was on a low dose today. She is alert and awake. She held my hand tightly. More pressure than a few days ago. I remain hopeful.

In another excerpt on August 23, I wrote that a nurse informed me that Reva's blood tests were good.

As in Holy Name, I set up the radio, tuned it to WQXR, and called the nurses' station every night at 10:00 to tell the staff to turn it off so Reva could sleep. I also brought the eye drops and instructed the nurses when to put them in Reva's eyes.

On August 26, I spoke to Dr. Ali, who said that Reva had been intubated so long that a tracheotomy would be necessary. But I noted in my journal my hope that Dr. Bakshi, a pulmonologist, would still be able to extubate her. While I was visiting Reva, an infectious disease doctor came into her room. I asked him what kind of infection she had. "That's a good question," he replied. He said that her blood cultures were coming back negative, but her temperature in the night was as high as 103, but it dropped back to normal by day. She is being treated with strong antibiotics, he said.

There were three potential sources for Reva's infection that I knew of. One was from the amputation site, which had failed to heal and which now showed signs of dry gangrene, a type of gangrene that does not suppurate but needs to be treated with antibiotics and debridement. Reva was receiving antibiotics, but the site was never debrided, neither at Holy Name, SELECT, nor later at St. Joseph's. I was also told that the pressure sore that had been Stage 1 for so long when she was home had opened in Holy Name. I never saw the open pressure sore, but the nurses had to turn Reva every two hours. The third potential source of infection was the return of her stomach perforation, which was diagnosed from a CT scan after she was transferred to St. Joseph's.

I noted in my journal for this period that my brother calls me almost every night and that Reva's brother never calls and speaks to me only when I call him. I spoke to friends, and clergy and parishioners from Christ Church.

CHAPTER SIXTY-FIVE

ST. JOSEPH'S

On August 25, Reva's hemoglobin dropped to seven and she required a transfusion. She last had a transfusion years earlier after she returned from the University of Pennsylvania following her failed transplant. On August 26, I visited Reva in the morning and then drove to Ramapo College for an orientation for faculty teaching freshman writing in the fall. I was scheduled to teach two sections of this course, each meeting two mornings a week for two hours, so I would be at Ramapo College four mornings a week. I was also scheduled to teach one course at William Paterson University on Wednesday afternoons.

I had not followed the advice of Dr. Death, the palliative care doctor at Holy Name, and had not canceled my fall teaching, but I never taught the Ramapo courses, and August 26, 2019, was the last day I was on the Ramapo campus. Reva's condition had worsened, and I canceled the first week of Ramapo classes and resigned from the college before the second week began. I sent an email to the department chair explaining my reasons. Fortunately, a replacement was available. I was surprised, however, a few weeks later to receive a check from Ramapo. I was paid for attending the orientation session.

I did, however, teach the full semester at William Paterson. The class met on Wednesday afternoons from 2:00–4:40. I canceled only the class following Reva's death. I emailed my students that there had been a death in my family. I returned the following week.

The SELECT physicians had attempted to titrate Reva from the breathing tube, that is, to gradually lower the amount of oxygen supplied by the respirator. Reva produced some of her own oxygen but not enough for the breathing tube to be removed. While I was visiting

Reva in the late afternoon of August 29, Dr. Bakshi informed me that Reva needed to be transferred to St. Joseph's Hospital in Paterson for about a week for a tracheotomy and tests and procedures. Then she would be returned to SELECT, he said. SELECT had no surgical facilities and no CT equipment. Several weeks earlier, Joe Brezin had told me that Reva should not go to an ER in her condition. Dr. Bakshi assured me that she would be transferred directly to the ICU "or a step-up floor," an intermediate floor.

I signed the transfer papers and waited in Reva's room for about two hours until the ambulance came. SELECT was served by a private ambulance company. It was about 8:00 p.m. before a single ambulance attendant arrived on the floor. Although there may have been a driver in the ambulance, I saw only one attendant. I watched as he strapped Reva on the gurney and wheeled her off. As she was expected to return to SELECT, I left her few belongings in the room, but I took the radio to bring to St. Joseph's the next day. Then I left SELECT and returned home. I took some Valium and went to bed.

At 3:00 a.m. the phone rang. It was St. Joseph's ICU. Reva had just been transferred there from the ER, where the ambulance brought her and where she spent five hours. The ICU nurse wanted my permission, which I granted, to put in an intravenous line. I took more Valium, turned off the phone, and fell back to sleep. I was exhausted and slept until 10:00. When I woke, I found that there had been six phone calls from St. Joseph's. I called the hospital. At 7:00 a.m. Reva had gone into cardiac arrest, her third cardiac arrest. It took twenty-five minutes to resuscitate her. The nurse told me that she was getting oxygen during the resuscitation and later was obeying some commands.

The third cardiac arrest broke Reva. She steadily declined and died eleven days later. Had she been transferred directly to the ICU, as Dr. Bakshi assured me she would be, she might not have gone into cardiac arrest. She might have progressed and made at least partial recovery. St. Joseph's Hospital is located in the heart of downtown Paterson, a city rife with crime, violence, and drugs. I can't imagine what the St. Joseph's emergency room is like. An ER, any ER, was no place for a patient as frail as Reva, a patient whose life was hanging by a thread. In the ER, she had to be seen by ER doctors. It is possible, even probable, considering that the ICU asked my permission to put in a line, that her intravenous medications, including the antibiotics that were combatting her infection, had been discontinued. I feel Bakshi had betrayed me. But I cannot sue. No lawyer would take the case. When Reva left Holy Name, her prognosis was "very grave." As I wrote earlier, after her death I consulted a malpractice lawyer whose medical consultant, a retired ER physician, reviewed Reva's Holy Name records, all four hundred pages of them. He said that it was unlikely any lawyer would take the case. Reva had too many ailments. Besides, no lawsuit would bring her back to life. But if I had known that Reva was going to the ER, I would not have signed the transfer papers, or I would have insisted that she be transferred in the morning after she had a night's sleep, and I would have come with her.

And if I had followed the ambulance instead of going home, how was I to stop the driver from bringing her to the ER? Bakshi had apparently not ordered her to be sent to the ICU. When I confronted him a few days later at St. Joseph's, he shrugged it off. He said that patients enter the hospital by way of the ER.

I went to St. Joseph's later the same day that she had the cardiac arrest. Reva was sedated. She was on norepinephrine and was scheduled for dialysis that evening.

The following are excerpts from my journal for this period.

Aug. 30. Fri. Drove to St. Joseph's with Fr. Jim Warnke and we had lunch later. Reva sedated and inert. Trach is scheduled for Tuesday. Nurse is pessimistic that she will ever return home. They are doing dialysis every day to reduce swelling throughout her body. I will have to buy cemetery plots, one for her and one for me, I hope under a tree. She will be buried with her wedding ring on, and I will never take mine off. I will be buried with it. As Fr. Jim said, she is the love of my life. She is in bad physical shape, yet I cannot give up hope. If I had put her on DNR, she would be dead now. There was no perforation in her stomach. At Holy Name they wanted me to put her in hospice because their CT scan showed a perf. She does not have sepsis, the nurse said, although she has an infection. How can I give up hope, no matter how slim the hope, of saving the love of my life as long as she is not in pain? And since she is sedated, she should not be in pain.

Aug. 31, Sat. Went with Erwin to visit Reva. She was getting dialysis. She is getting it every day. Her eyes were open and there was a terrible look of woe in them. She seemed to be trying to say something to me and her lips were faintly moving but she couldn't say it. She has a breathing tube which will come out Tuesday and be replaced by a trach. She is very sick and may not live, and if she does her mental state is uncertain. I was in anguish whether to put her on DNR, but after talking to the nurse decided to wait, at least until the trach procedure. I think she does not want any more procedures. She may just want to let go, but I can't tell what she is trying to communicate.

Sept. 2 Monday. Reva did not have a good night. Nurse said she did not go into cardiac arrest but her blood pressure dropped, so now they are using three different IV blood pressure medicines to raise her blood pressure. Spoke to doctor. He will draw a sample of fluid from her chest. Dialysis suspended for today and nutrition eliminated. Her WBC was over 30. Doctor does not know where the infection is coming from. Said it might be from pressure sore on her buttock or from amputation site, which is black. She has no fever. Doctor said she is in septic shock. Nurse said they are not even turning her because they are afraid of setting something off, producing a trauma. Trach scheduled for tomorrow called off because she is too sick. I authorized them to put her on DNR for CPR only, that is, to do everything else to treat her and not neglect or eliminate anything except chest compressions if she goes into another cardiac arrest. One silver beam: Doctor says she follows commands, so cognitive functioning might still be there. Tomorrow I must buy grave sites.

Sept. 4, Wed. This is the lowest period of my life. Resident Dr. Rachel Aboud called to say that CT scan showed that Reva has a bowel obstruction in small intestine and it is inoperable because she will not survive anesthesia. The nephrologist did not give her dialysis today but will try tomorrow. She is on three vasoconstrictors. She no longer follows commands. She is sedated and kept comfortable. She may not survive much longer, but she is a valiant fighter. All happiness, joy and love I have ever known, I know from her. Life without her is inconceivable. I taught first class at William Paterson today, Wednesday. Class is two hours and forty minutes once a week. I hope to continue this, but I canceled first two Ramapo classes due to family emergency. But I hope I can do these. Pray for Reva's recovery. I will be meeting with her medical team tomorrow at 3. She has been there for a week or longer and now they are first meeting with me. I think it is a palliative care team. I want Reva to survive and recover her health or at least a substantial part of it. Fr. Jim says we can ask God for anything except sin, so I ask God for Reva's recovery.

Sept. 5, Thursday. Went with Marge J. to St Joseph's. Met with intensivist and palliative care team. My instructions: Keep treating her aggressively but keep her out of pain. Keep her on DNR. Doctor said hope for best but be prepared for worst. I will call a lawyer or lawyers tomorrow about Dr. Bakshi sending a patient as frail as Reva to the ER. How can I live without Reva? A series of bad things happens: Dr. Bakshi sending her to the ER at St. Joseph's. Joe Brezin said months ago she should never go to the ER in her condition. S pulling the blanket, and all the other harm done to her. I gave up the teaching job at Ramapo, and I promise God another donation to charity if Reva pulls through.

Sept. 6. Fri. 12:45 a.m. Will spend as much time with Reva as I can today. Sat. morning I will buy graves. My time with Reva may be short. If Reva dies and I live another ten years, what will I do with them? I hope I don't live more than a year or two after her. Saw her today. She was sleeping. Her WBC is lower, 23.4 from over 30. Thy will be done. I tell her how much I love her and I kiss her on her forehead. I must buy her a new stuffed lion. This might never have happened if I had been with her at the angioplasty in June. It is just, justice, that I withdrew from Ramapo. Life closes in. The pendulum swings. I feel her arms holding me as I write this. She is here with me. I feel her in place next to me in bed. There is breath in her body. Companion. Friend. Beloved. Do not leave me.

Sept. 8. Sun. Reva on full life support. I pray she survives but hope is dimming. Reva's love makes the small cup of my heart run over. I never deserved such great love as hers. I never thought this would happen, yet I know it does. I wish we could have had a few more years.

CHAPTER SIXTY-SIX

LAST DAYS

For as long as I live, I will never forget the woeful expression in Reva's eyes that day, August 31, when I visited her and she was awake. This was an expression unlike the look of terror in her eyes in Holy Name the day before her second cardiac arrest.

I kissed her forehead when I arrived, as I always did. I couldn't kiss her lips because of the breathing tube, but her lips were faintly moving. She was trying to say something but no sound came forth. Even without the breathing tube, she may have been too weak to speak. I don't know what she was trying to say. Perhaps she will tell me when I am with her on the other side. In this life, I will never know.

The tracheotomy was done a day or two later and the breathing tube removed. According to the medical records, she tolerated the surgery well. It was performed in her ICU room. Only local anesthesia was needed. She now had bandages and a towel covering her neck. A tube was connected from her throat to the respirator, which made a soft regular gurgle. It was not Reva breathing but the air pumped in and out from the respirator. Her chest rose and fell with regularity, but most of the movement was mechanical.

She was sedated and slept most of the time. Her body was moist with fluids that were oozing from it, and she was getting dialysis every day to attempt to remove them.

Unlike at Holy Name, nobody at St. Joseph's or, for that matter, at SELECT, urged me to put her in hospice, to disconnect her from dialysis and the antibiotics and the respirator. The staff followed my wishes: to treat the disease aggressively but not to perform CPR if Reva went into cardiac arrest again. She was frail. I didn't want anyone or anything pounding on her chest. I don't think she would have survived a fourth cardiac arrest, anyway.

I had prayed aloud over Reva every time I visited her, sometimes with clergy of various faiths. I had *The Book of Common Prayer*, the Episcopal Prayer Book, in her room and I prayed prayers from it at her bedside, especially the prayers for the sick, but I omitted "In Jesus's name," which ends many prayers, or any reference to Jesus or the Trinity. Reva was Jewish, and I omitted the special Christian-faith content. Sometimes I went down on my knees and prayed at her bedside.

I also had a Jewish Psalter in her room containing the Psalms in Hebrew and English. It was a beautiful, hard-covered book from home with gold Hebrew lettering on the cover. I do not recall how we acquired it. The Lubavitch rabbi who visited her in Holy Name told me to recite the psalm numbered for what would be her next birthday. This was Psalm 67, which I would pray at her bedside.

On Saturday September 7, I was visiting Reva in the late afternoon when the dialysis nurse, a male Filipino, came to the room with the machine to begin dialysis.

I prepared to leave for the evening, but before leaving, I placed the Hebrew-English Psalter at the foot of Reva's bed, where her amputated left foot would have rested. The book was well out of the way of the dialysis equipment. I put it on her bed to comfort and protect her through the night. If she died in St. Joseph's, I intended to have the Psalter placed in the coffin and buried with her body.

When I returned to visit her Sunday morning, the Psalter was not on her bed. I searched the room, but couldn't find it. I informed the nurse, who also searched the room. She put on gloves and a gown and searched the dirty laundry basket and the dirty laundry bin outside the room. It wasn't there.

It was Sunday, and the person in charge of the hospital was an administrative nurse. The ICU nurse contacted him, and we met in the hospital lobby. He gave me the name and number of the hospital's head of security, Jim Miller. I spoke to Miller Monday, and he called me back Tuesday. He said security had questioned the staff that was on that night as well as the dialysis department and had reviewed the video of people entering and exiting Reva's room Saturday night and Sunday morning. (There is no video in the room, he told me.) All persons questioned denied knowledge of the book, and he said that no one was seen on video carrying it from the room.

Theft and even murder occur in hospitals. The people who work in hospitals aren't saints. Although Reva was born in Paterson, which at one time had a large Jewish population, few Jews live in Paterson today. The book, with its gold Hebrew lettering on the front cover, may have looked like it had some value and been stolen. Or it may have been thrown in the trash. A rabbi later advised me not to be overly concerned about the loss. He speculated that it may have been discarded inadvertently by the cleaning staff. But to take it from a patient's bed? Now it could not be buried with Reva, and from that Saturday evening her condition rapidly worsened.

It is difficult to recall how I spent the summer of 2019 when I was not visiting Reva twice a day. Most of my journal entries for this period are about my visits to Reva. It was a summer of hell and hope. I had procured teaching positions for the fall and spent time planning and preparing syllabi for both the William Paterson course and the Ramapo courses, although I did not teach the latter. I read the *New York Times* every day, but most of the books I read were religious books: parts of the Bible, a book about the psalms, and an anthology of Western and Eastern religious writings.

In the evenings, I would sit on the couch and make phone calls. The phone calls were my lifeline.

In August, I went to the Art Center of Northern New Jersey to remove the two pastels by Reva that had been on exhibit at the annual senior art show. The show was over and a notice had been sent to artists to remove their work. I went with J., a friend who lost his wife in 2012. Reva and I had dined several times with J. and his wife before her death. The pastels are now hanging in my apartment, which is in the same building as the one Reva and I shared. But I moved to a smaller apartment after her death.

Surprisingly, I slept well most nights that summer. That was partially because of exhaustion from the days of visits and dealings with doctors, but also because I began taking Valium almost every night.

The following are excerpts from my journal from that summer. Most of these were written when Reva was in Holy Name. Some are from the period of SELECT.

8/12/19 Mon. 11:01 p.m. Reva's temp this eve down to 97.4. They had her off norepinephrine when I went to visit her. Had meeting with Dr. Death, the palliative care doctor. Transition social worker at meeting. Dr. Death said I should cancel my employment at Ramapo or at least give them warning. Warning of what? I left two phone messages telling him how wrong he is about this. For a while this afternoon, I feared that he would contact Ramapo on his own. This, however, I think would be illegal. Reva sleeps under the propofol. In a little while, I will call the night nurse and see how Reva is doing. She will get dialysis tomorrow. Visited her twice but did preparatory work for Ramapo and hung her two pictures in living room. They are beautiful. She has created beauty from her beauty, and I pray that she will create more. She has vast potential, only a part of which she has been able to use, so far.

8/13/19 Tues. 11:32 p.m. When I wake in morning I do not want to get up to face another day of grieving and anxiety. But once out of bed, I try to follow from one step to another. It is like driving in a blizzard. I think of the next foot or two, not ten miles away.

Reva off propofal, but she is not responsive. She cannot speak because of the respirator, but makes little response. They had the mittens off her hands because she is too weak to fight the respirator. She just lies there in the bed. I asked her to squeeze my finger. There was the faintest movement, barely discerned pressure. Two or three weeks ago, when she was in the ICU the first time, she gave a firm squeeze. Before I left this evening, after praying over her, I smoothed her head over and over and told her over and over that I love her. She blinked. But I have no idea how much of her brain function will return. Dr. Moss, the pulmonologist, said she would never leave Holy Name. In other words, she will die in the ICU. Her brother is also pessimistic. All medical opinion seems to be pessimistic. It's her heart, weakened by end stage pulmonary hypertension and more than 50 days in bed. Dr. Leland said she has a large pressure sore on her buttock and the wound on her amputated leg, while not suppurating, is black. It has not grown in blackness, he said, according to nurse, but dry gangrene has crept up the leg because she is not getting sufficient circulation. They are going to try to wean her from respirator tomorrow. Stress and grief are enormous.

8/15/19 Thurs. 11:31 p.m. In 15 days classes resume. What can happen in 15 days? The unknown. Saw Reva twice today. When I came this morning, she squeezed my finger with mitten off and after dialysis. And she did not want to let go. Not a super-hard squeeze but not a velleity either. There was pressure. But she has more signs of multiple system collapse. They took her off heparin because of blood in her stomach. Not having heparin puts her at risk of stroke, Leland said. He said, in the room with Reva, whom he and the nurses seem to think is inert and unable to hear or comprehend what she hears, that he would not do it to his wife. He is again pushing me to put her in hospice, which I refuse. I asked Leland if he would want to be in hospice if he were in Reva's condition. His strange reply was that that he would not be in Reva's condition. Perhaps I misunderstood it. I signed for trach to be done Fri. They have to remove the breathing tube. Her WBC was up to 28. Low grade fever, 1.02. Later in day, 1.06. Earlier in day, 98. It varies.

8/17/19 Sat. 6:48 p.m. Frightened. Terrified. I texted this to Fr. Michael when I arrived home from Holy Name yesterday. Erwin came up for a while. Fr. Michael came this morning with Dunkin Donuts coffee and breakfast. First day since Reva was hospitalized that I didn't visit. Could not. On verge of breakdown. She is sedated and sleeps anyway. Surgeon called this morning and said CT scan shows she has hole somewhere in stomach. Normal course would be to operate but they can't because she is too weak to survive general anesthesia. So they are treating with massive antibiotics and intravenous nutrition. They are using N/G tube for drainage not feeding. Surgeon later spoke to Joe Brezin. Said there was a small perf in bowel. JB said WBC coming down. Treatment may work, but she is extremely sick. She had dialysis today. Am working on syllabi but do not know what fall will bring. Leland's NP called. Wanted me to put Reva in hospice. 200th time Leland, Feldman or some other schmuck of a doctor asked this. The answer remains NO. as long as she is not suffering. Fr. Michael said he was under propofol. He said you remember nothing. If she is in the grave, she can't recover. And she won't be suffering earthly pain. Now she may, perhaps have a medically remote chance to recover and sedation and narcotics control discomfort and pain. I know I may lose her. Everyone dies. But I will not precipitate her death as long as she is not suffering. I may not visit tomorrow either. Or I may go in evening. I don't know if she knows I am there. I will call nurse later. Plan to buy graves Monday. J. will accompany me. Hope we do not need them for a few years. I don't know what the fall or late summer will bring. Pray Pray Pray for Reva.

8/18/19 Sun. 9:25 p.m. wake up but do not get out of bed for half an hour or more. I do not want to start the day and am reluctant to do so. Too late for church. Worked on syllabi. Visited Reva with Fr. Jim. Want Reva transferred, if medically feasible. I don't know if I can teach the Ramapo courses. Teaching is much bound to Reva's progress. If there is progress and hope, I will be heartened.

8/19/19 Mon. 1:22 p.m. No Valium last night. One of only two nights in last 60 days that I did not take Valium. According to calls from Dr. and my conversation with nurse, Reva improved today. More alert. WBC 15.2. Temp normal. Leland wants her transferred to SELECT today. I asked him to wait until tomorrow after her dialysis. I don't know what they are going to do.

8/21/19 12:01 a.m. Visited Reva today in Holy Name. She was getting dialysis. This early evening she was transferred to SELECT. The doctors were surprised at how sick she is. But they had her off the propofol and she was awake and followed commands of a doctor to raise her arm and she shook her head when he asked her if she was in any pain. She could not speak because of breathing tube. Marjorie J. met me there. It was difficult to do alone. But I feel better that she is out of Holy Name.

8/22/19 Thurs. 10:06 p.m. Visited Reva. WBC down to 14 but she had 103 fever last night. But it was 97 this afternoon. Dr. Bakshi examined her.

Said she is doing better. Will try to extubate her next week once she is off the norepinephrine. She was on a low dose today. She is alert and awake. Held my hand tightly. More pressure than a couple of days ago. I remain hopeful. Worked on syllabi.

8/23/19 Fri. 11:44 p.m. Saw Reva twice today. She is awake and nurse said her blood tests were good. On low doses of norepinephrine. Hope they can stop it next week and wean her from respirator. Worked on syllabi.

8/25/19 Sun. 9:17 p.m. Fr. Jim visited Reva yesterday. I drove him. I visited Reva twice. In morning she seemed uncomfortable but calmer this evening. However, her hemoglobin is 7 and they are going to give or have already begun to give her a unit of blood tonight. Did not go to church. Always hard to get out of bed and start the day.

8/26/19 Mon. 9:40 p.m. Day proceeded orderly. Saw Reva before I went up to Ramapo for orientation. She grips my hand and squeezes it when I ask her to but she seems lethargic and often sleeping. She had dialysis today. Spoke on phone to Dr. Ali who said she has been on respirator so long a trach would be necessary. But hope Bakshi will still try to wean her. Infectious disease doctor came by. She is getting strong antibiotics and I asked him what kind of an infection she has. He replied, "That's a good question." Her blood cultures come back negative and her WBC is coming down. But her temp spikes in the night as high as 103 and then by day is normal. The last thing I want is for Dr. Death to be correct in is his assessment: That she will need trach, PEG and then live a short time in a nursing home and die. I will be meeting tomorrow with her team: pharmacist, case manager etc. but not Dr. Bakshi. I hope he can begin weaning her and that she can be weaned.

CHAPTER SIXTY-SEVEN

DEATH

On the morning of September 10, 2019, I drove to George Washington Memorial Park and paid for the grave. Over the years, Reva and I did not speak often about our deaths, and neither of us had a living will. However, several years before her final illnesses, we discussed arrangements for burial and decided on this cemetery. It is a fifteen-minute drive from Hackensack, so the surviving spouse can easily visit. It is nonsectarian, so it accommodates our religious choices, and it differs from most cemeteries because it has no headstones. Graves are marked by bronze markers with or without granite bases. There is an all-faiths chapel, which contains cremation urns on the second floor and another large building that contains urns. The absence of headstones gives the ninety-eight-acre grounds a parklike setting. A visitor (for who enters a cemetery of his or her own volition but a visitor) drives under an arch at the front entrance and immediately encounters an enormous statue of George Washington, sword resting in his hands, kneeling in prayer. The area is said to have been frequented by Washington and the Continental Army during the American Revolution.

I probably would have chosen cremation for myself, but Reva wanted burial. Cremation, she said, reminded her of the Holocaust. So I, too, will be buried.

Reva wanted our graves to be near a tree, and we were, for want of a better word when it comes to cemeteries, except alive, lucky. A couple had moved and sold the plots they purchased back to the cemetery. Two plots next to each other were available on a knoll near the far eastern edge. A huge pin oak tree is at the foot of the plots.

I wrote a check that day for the full amount for one plot. The other I reserved and arranged to pay off in twelve monthly installments. It has been paid in full.

I said to the cemetery employee who sold me the plots that I hoped they would not be occupied for some years. But I paid for one, acknowledging the gravity of Reva's condition.

Soon after I returned home, Dr. Matthews, an intensivist (the medical term for a doctor who works in ICUs) from St. Joseph's called. He wanted to know if I intended to visit that day.

"Of course," I said.

"You should come soon," he replied. "We've given her some medicine to keep her numbers up, but it doesn't look good."

Fr. Michael was on vacation. I called Fr. Jim Warnke, the legally blind Episcopal priest and LCSW, to whom months before Reva had confided her fears of losing her leg. Fr. Jim said he would take an Uber and meet me at the hospital.

In the ICU, the nurse said that Reva had taken a turn for the worse over the weekend. She was now lying in bed, her eyes closed, sedated and, I hope and pray, pain free. Her mouth was gaping wide open, as wide as possible. She was stiff and unmoving.

Fr. Jim arrived a short time later. We prayed. Fr. Jim sat next to Reva at the head of her bed and softly sang a lullaby. It may have been the same lullaby that he had sung to his own children many years ago. He had a fine voice. I had heard him sing in church.

I looked at Reva's heart rate monitor. I forget the number, but it was low, between 40–50. I said to Fr. Jim, "I think in another half hour it will reach zero." Five minutes later I looked again. It was zero. I looked at my watch. It was 3:12 in the afternoon.

I went into the corridor and spoke to the nurse. "I think she is dead. Her heart rate is zero."

The nurse entered the room without rushing. I had signed a DNR. What had come was expected.

The nurse put her hand on Reva's neck to find a pulse.

"I will get the doctor to confirm the death," she said.

I sat in a chair near the window and texted Joe Brezin in California, "Reva's gone."

I broke into tears.

While we waited, Reva's chest continued to gently rise and fall, propelled by the respirator, although her heart had stopped. It was a strange sight, now carved into my memory.

After about ten minutes, a nurse practitioner entered the room. She, too, put her hand on Reva's neck to find a pulse. She looked down Reva's throat with a small flashlight and listened for her heartbeat with a stethoscope. She may have done some other tests. I don't remember.

"The time of her death is 3:25," she said.

The nurse said they would wash Reva. Fr. Jim and I were allowed, according to hospital rules, one hour to gather her belongings and leave the room.

Joe Brezin had texted back that he had told Susan (his wife) and they both cried, and that he would say *Kaddish* (the Jewish prayer for the dead) in a synagogue that evening.

I discarded most of Reva's belongings that were in the room, including *The Book of Common Prayer* that had been with Reva in three hospitals. I reasoned it was contaminated with germs. I had a copy at home. I also discarded the radio for the same reason. In fact, I don't think I took anything away. There were too many germs. Gloves and a gown, although not a mask, were still required to enter Reva's room.

As I stood in the corridor with Fr. Jim, Dr. Matthews came by and expressed his condolences. We shook hands.

I offered to drive Fr. Jim to his home in Teaneck. I went to the hospital's multitiered garage, retrieved my car and picked him up at the hospital entrance.

I had cried when the Reva died, but now my eyes were dry. In retrospect, I think I was in emotional shock. The great grief, the grief that I will bear as long as I live, was waiting, readying itself. As we drove, I said to Fr. Jim, "I can almost hear Reva. She is in another place, and she is asking, 'Where's Howie?'"

"It is all new to her," he replied. "It will take her a while to get used to."

Fr. Jim was raised as a Roman Catholic. He would sometimes take out a set of rosary beads and pray silently with them. Being legally blind and unable to read, even large print, he didn't have access to causal reading or reading emails from a phone while waiting, although he had a mobile phone that operated audibly, even describing people and objects that were in front of him.

I left him at his house and waited, as I always did, until he was through the front door. Then I drove home.

I do not have a recollection of the rest of the day; only notes from my journal.

I have informed Harriet [Reva's friend], Frank [my brother], Rabbi Glustrom [a neighbor], Marla G. [Reva's therapist, and now mine], Jayson, and Erwin [two friends]. I have been grieving all summer. But this is a new chapter, a new book. I don't know what this is, but I am without Reva physically. Her spirit lives in me and we will, I pray and hope, be reunited in the next world. No man could hope for a better wife. She is all the joy, happiness and love I have ever known.

CHAPTER SIXTY-EIGHT

• • •

Sept. 11, 2019. Dream. I have just finished teaching a class and am leaving the empty classroom. A young boy or girl, with mermaid looking body, unable to walk or get up, is lying in hallway being bullied by two males who remind me of two male students I had at Montclair State who, on Fridays, wore white shirts and red ties. Both wanted to be cops. I dream there are two flat cookies on the floor, and the pair is trying to make the disabled person eat them, slide them into her or his mouth. I protest and I see a security guard, and I tell the guard what is going on. But the guard says the disabled person is a nuisance who is always hanging around and needs to be made to leave. Interpretation, added 11/4/19. The disabled person is Reva, now without ability to use either leg. I did not like those two kids at Montclair. They were frat boys. The one I disliked more wanted to be a state trooper. Their identical and formal clothes on Friday might have had something to do with their frat or a job but in the dream they represent, not overt thugs, but respectable destroyers, doctors, psychiatrists, who are trying to feed the disabled person something destructive (read lithium). The security guard reveals the medical thinking among the doctors: Get rid of her.

Perhaps mercifully, my memory is vague of the days immediately following Reva's death. My journal records day-to-day facts. There were mundane things I attended to. I had to transfer our joint investment account into a single account. (All our money was in joint accounts. The only separate accounts we had were for IRAs, in which we were each other's beneficiary.) Then there were funeral arrangements. A rabbi had given me the name of a Jewish undertaker while Reva was still in Holy Name. The undertaker, Burton Rosenstein, worked for a funeral home that arranged funerals for all faiths and had a separate Jewish division. A woman cantor worked with Robert

Alexander, the funeral home's director, and was available to officiate at Reva's funeral. I had spoken to the cantor on the phone when Reva was in Holy Name. She was also the cantor at a large Bergen County Reform synagogue.

Reva was Jewish and, although she had friends at Christ Church, especially Fr. Michael Gerhardt, and although approximately a third of the people who attended her funeral were from the church, she would have a Jewish funeral, as she would have wished.

Under strict Jewish law, Jewish funerals are conducted within a day or two of death. But strict Jewish law was not a concern now. I had never arranged a funeral before. Among other issues, I had to wait until the transfer of money was finalized so I could pay Robert Alexander, the undertaker. Because of the delay of the funeral, Burton Rosenstein suggested embalming Reva's body, ordinarily not something Jews do to their dead. I rejected this. Her body remained in the morgue at St. Joseph's. Robert Alexander, who supervised the funeral, suggested leaving her body there until the day before the funeral. There was no charge to keep the body at St. Joseph's, while Alexander charged per day to refrigerate a body in his funeral home. I kept her body in the St. Joseph's morgue until the Sunday before her funeral on Monday Sept. 23, when it was transferred to the funeral home.

I met with Alexander and the cantor in Alexander's office. But when I arrived home, I called Rabbi Simon Glustrom, the ninety-five-year-old retired rabbi who lived in our building. Although elderly, Glustrom was still physically active and mentally sharp. He had written a number of books about Judaism and was working on a new one. As I mentioned earlier, before his retirement he was the rabbi at Fair Lawn Jewish Center, the Conservative synagogue a few blocks from where Reva's parents lived and where Reva grew up. Her parents had been members of his congregation.

Had Reva and I not decided on a civil marriage in Fair Lawn Municipal Court and, later, on an Orthodox Jewish wedding, Rabbi Glustrom would have probably officiated at our wedding. Reva and I met him again and his wife, Helen, after we moved to the Prospect Avenue apartment.

Once during an emotional crisis, which fortunately did not result

. . .

in Reva's hospitalization, Rabbi Glustrom and Helen came to our apartment (Reva had phoned them) while Fr. Michael was there. So we were all friends.

I had asked Fr. Michael to preach a nonsectarian sermon at Reva's funeral. He knew Reva and had visited her in Prospect Heights and HMHUMC after the burns to her right foot and also at Holy Name in the last months of her life. Reva had met privately with Fr. Michael before my baptism. I never asked her what they spoke about, although I asked Fr. Michael after her death. He said that she supported me in my choice but was clear that it was not a choice she would make for herself because of her parents' experience in the Holocaust. I wish that Reva had not thought so much about that unfortunate subject. As I wrote earlier in this memoir, Reva participated in my baptism, reading the passage from the New Testament that we chose, 1 Corinthians 13.

At her funeral, Fr. Michael spoke about Reva's courage and determination, of her indefatigable spirit, and he gave an example of it that he had observed. However, he did not conduct the service. Rabbi Glustrom did.

With two clergymen of two different faiths speaking, Reva's funeral was unusual. I was the only other speaker, delivering the eulogy.

I chose a coffin, a wooden box without metal, as Jewish law forbids metal in a coffin. The idea is that the body should return to the earth as rapidly as possible. Metal would delay this physical transition. The coffin had the Star of David carved on the lid. I could not bear to see the coffin above the ground, as I had seen my mother's before it was lowered into the grave, so I arranged with Alexander to have the coffin lowered into the grave, although uncovered with dirt, while the funeral service was conducted in the all-faiths chapel at the cemetery. There was no funeral home or synagogue service. I paid for the funeral, the coffin, and the cemetery charge for opening the grave, but I asked Joe Brezin if he would pay for a buffet luncheon afterwards in the private room of a local restaurant. He agreed to.

It was very important to me for Reva to be buried wearing her wedding ring. I first put that ring on her finger on Friday afternoon January 29, 1988, before Judge Jonathan Harris in Fair Lawn Municipal Court.

But because Jewish law prohibits metal in the coffin, I chose, at first, not to have her body prepared in a traditional Jewish *tahara* service, where devout, specially trained Jews of the same sex as the deceased wash and enshroud the body while reciting prayers and psalms. I was afraid that the ring would not be buried with Reva, that it might even be discarded.

A few days before the funeral, Robert Alexander asked me to bring the wedding ring and some clothes that Reva would be buried in to the funeral home. At that time, he introduced me to a young man, a funeral director (undertaker), who worked for him and would be preparing Reva's body for burial. I was concerned about a male preparing her body. Alexander assured me that utmost respect was observed. "It's like going to the doctor," he said.

But when I got home, I phoned Rabbi Glustrom, who said that women should prepare a woman. I called Alexander and explained that my reluctance to the tahara service was because Reva would not be buried with her wedding ring. Alexander promised me that he would open the coffin the morning of the funeral and put the ring on Reva's finger and text me a photo. I then authorized the tahara service, and Sunday night before the funeral, Reva was ritually prepared by women of the local tahara society.

Reva's left ring finger was so swollen that Alexander could not slide the ring over the joint. He phoned me. I suggested using KY jelly, but he was reluctant to do this. So the ring was placed below the joint on her left ring finger, and Alexander texted me a photo confirming this. It was all right—as long as the ring was on her finger, where it had been in life.

These details of daily life, which include preparations after it ends, kept my life going.

There are biologists who say that the body does not die all at once, that there is no absolute line of demarcation between life and death, but that the body dies gradually over days and weeks.

On September 19, four days before Reva's funeral, I had a strange experience. I woke in the middle of the night and got out of bed to urinate. As I walked to the bathroom, I thought, "How can this be? How can I be walking? I'm dead." It took a few moments for me to realize

. . .

that Reva was dead, not I. Then on waking a day later, on the morning of Sept. 20, when I opened my eyes to the sunlight coming through the window, I thought, "How can this be? How can I be seeing? I'm dead." Once again, the realization came that I was not dead—that Reva was.

I cannot explain this phenomenon. It happened only twice, although, as I write these words, more than a year after Reva's death, I dream of her almost every night. Some dreams seem like visitations.

I have no answer.

CHAPTER SIXTY-NINE

WORK

About thirty people attended Reva's funeral, and most came to the luncheon afterwards. No one had reserved the all-faiths chapel that day, and the cemetery allowed us to use it. Otherwise, the entire funeral would have been a graveside service. After the chapel service, we walked up the knoll to the grave site.

The coffin had already been lowered into the grave; the earth that had been removed was piled next to the grave, and a shovel thrust in the earth. Joe Brezin and I, as Reva's closest kin, recited the Mourners Kaddish, and Rabbi Glustrom chanted another prayer. Then, as is the Jewish custom, mourners who wished to took turns shoveling the earth into the grave and covering the coffin.

My family was represented by my brother, Frank, and his wife, Beverly, who drove down from Rhode Island; my sister, Linda, who drove from Massachusetts; and my cousin Danny from Manhattan.

Reva's family was represented by her brother, Joe Brezin, who flew in alone: his wife, Susan, had a dental emergency. Rosalind, the minister, Joe Brezin's sister-in-law, was also present. Other mourners included friends of Reva's, former classmates from Fair Lawn High School, mutual friends and acquaintances, and parishioners from Christ Church. The only obituaries appeared on the funeral home's website and in the *Jewish Standard*, a weekly published in Teaneck. I wrote the obituary for the website, which the *Jewish Standard* adapted. But I had called people and informed them of Reva's death and the time and place of the funeral. After the luncheon, I returned alone to my apartment.

The William Paterson semester had begun. I taught only one course in the fall 2019, having resigned from Ramapo College when

Reva's death became imminent. The William Paterson course was a required course in public speaking, a subject I had taught often at William Paterson and other universities. It met on Wednesday afternoons from 2:00–4:40. I had taught the first class of the semester but cancelled the second, emailing my students only that there had been a death in my family. But I resumed on the third week and continued to teach until the end of the semester.

The regular rhythm of work gave my life some purpose and structure. Although I was at the university only one afternoon a week and most of the assignments were oral, there was still written homework to grade, so I had some work to occupy me during the week.

William Paterson is located in Wayne, just over the Haledon border. Driving there, I would take Haledon Avenue, which passes through the small working-class towns of Haledon and Prospect Park. Haledon Avenue is about a half mile uphill from the Passaic River.

The river seems to create a geographic boundary between Paterson and adjacent towns, but the boundary is illusory. As one nears William Paterson University, the east side of Haledon Avenue is in the town of Prospect Park, but the west side of the street is part of Paterson. So returning home each Wednesday afternoon, I passed through a far edge of Paterson, the city where Reva was born, spent her childhood, and died.

Although the class officially ended at 4:40, I would usually dismiss the students at about 4:15. I was focused on the teaching and had rapport with the students. But at about 3:30 every Wednesday afternoon, as I knew the class would soon end, a depression fell over me like a shadow. I concealed this from the students, but when I left the classroom and walked out of the modern classroom building, which had a full-length glass wall comprising one side of the lobby, I felt profound sadness. In a few minutes I would be driving home, and there would be no Reva to greet me. For thirty-five years, thirty-two of them as husband and wife, we shared our lives. Now I would arrive home to an empty apartment. She was gone.

One afternoon, as I walked through the lobby after class, a large man in street clothes in his late thirties or early forties who had just entered the building, hailed me. "Hey, how are you doing?"

I didn't know him. I had never seen him before, but we began to talk—he, taking the lead in the conversation. He said he was a student and a recently retired cop from North Bergen, a town in Hudson County. I told him I was a professor and added that I had been a newspaper reporter, but I mentioned nothing about the death of my wife. He wished me a good day and we parted.

The only explanation I can think of for this sudden burst of bonhomie and questioning from a total stranger was the despondency written on my face that must have alerted his trained policeman's eye. I was dressed as a professor, wearing a tie and carrying a briefcase. I was sad. Ahead of me was the drive home, perhaps with a stop at a Dunkin Donuts, and emptiness. Returning from William Paterson on Wednesdays was one of the saddest hours of my week.

In the evenings, the round of phone calls was still important to me. I needed to have a sustained conversation with at least one or two people every evening. I heard from some cousins with whom I hadn't spoken in years. I frequently spoke with my brother and some friends, as well as friends of Reva's.

The Covid-19 pandemic was still five months in the future, and I dined with friends in local restaurants and went to a performance of Shaw's *Pygmalion* by a local theater group, and I explored with a friend, also a recent widower, several nature preserves in Bergen County. Although densely populated, Bergen County has some natural habitats which environmentalists have fiercely and successfully defended from development. My preference is for wetlands. Because of this, one of Reva's many pet names for me, especially before she became disabled and we were more involved in outdoor activities, was "Swampy." I think my attraction to wetlands—marginal places that are neither solid land nor water—is, in part, because of the marginality of my life. Reva's life, too, had been marginalized.

I attended Christ Church a few times before houses of worship were closed because of the pandemic, but could no longer feel the closeness without Reva. I was, and still am at this writing, a member of the vestry, the church's governing body, and attended some of the monthly vestry meetings. On All Saints' Day, the Sunday following Halloween, I participated in the annual memorial for the dead and lit a candle for Reva. She would not have objected. She was Jewish but had an open mind and a relationship with Christ Church, its parishioners, and its clergy. In the absence of most other social life because of her disability and dialysis schedule, Christ Church and the coffee hour after Sunday services and the occasional luncheons, served as a social outlet for her. In fact, she was listed in the parish directory as a parishioner. She did not object. The only requirement for being a parishioner was to come to the church and identify oneself as one. There were no dues. People pledged and contributed what they could when the plate was passed on Sundays.

But Reva had also been a member of the Kiddush Club at the Temple Beth El in Hackensack, a group of women who organized and paid for the *Kiddush*, a small meal following the Saturday morning services. But she did not join the temple as a member, which required annual dues. I pointed out to her that there was no reason for her to join, as she could attend anytime. However, she contributed to the fund for a new roof for the temple building.

The temple had a few steps to enter the front door, but as the staff knew she came when she could, a metal ramp was put out for her. However, there was no wheelchair-accessible bathroom.

I regret today never having accompanied her to a service, as she so often accompanied me to church, but after her death I attended some services to say the Mourners Kaddish. My Uncle Milton, my father's brother and a co-owner of the family business, had been vice president of this temple in the 1980s. The longtime rabbi, Michael Schumeister, went to medical school in New York City while officiating at services on Friday nights and Saturdays. He became a psychiatrist but continued to officiate as a rabbi on the Sabbath as late as 2019. The building has since been sold to the Lubavitch Hasidim and has become one of its Chabad houses.

Reva once asked Rabbi Schumeister if he provided pastoral counseling as a rabbi. He did not. Reva and I first met him before we were married, and we had considered marriage at Temple Beth El with him officiating. As a reporter years later, I phoned him. I thought his dual life as a rabbi and psychiatrist would make an interesting feature story. What, for example, would he say about medicating people today who hear voices, yet on the Sabbath extolling them as holy men? He declined to be interviewed. "My patients do not know I am a rabbi," he told me.

CHAPTER SEVENTY

CARDINALS

A rhythm, a sense of regularity, was important to me after Reva's death. But I did not have an abundance of activities. On Wednesdays, I taught. While Reva was still in Holy Name, I had begun therapy with the LCSW who had been Reva's therapist, and after Reva's death I went from once-weekly to twice-weekly sessions. I thought that if I went into therapy because of the loss of Reva, it was better to have a therapist who had known her. The therapist, Marla G., had her office in her condo on Prospect Avenue just four blocks from our building. Reva had been able to ride there in her motorized wheelchair, although in bad weather I would drive her or she would drive herself in the van. But I had never met Marla until I began therapy with her. After Reva's death, walking to the twice-weekly sessions on Tuesday and Friday formed another part of the rhythm. Marla, an observant Reform Jew, inquired about bereavement groups for me and referred me to one sponsored by the Church of the Presentation, a Roman Catholic Church in Upper Saddle River. The group met for eight weeks on Monday mornings. I had missed the first session but joined on the second week.

The group consisted of about twelve recently bereaved widows and widowers, except for one woman who had lost her longtime boyfriend. The three group leaders were former members who had received training.

It was a good group, and I am still in touch with some of the members. Most lived in the Saddle River/Upper Saddle River area near the New York State border, one of the most affluent sections of Bergen County. Until the Covid-19 pandemic, we would gather informally for lunch in a diner or at a member's home, usually once a month.

The group met in the church rectory in a living room setting with a separate entrance. The Monday bereavement group and the lunches after the group sessions had ended formed another part of the rhythm. In addition to the sessions, members telephoned each other, as part of the bereavement program and on their own.

I was one of three widowers and, to my surprise, one of the youngest members.

I remained in contact with Fr. Michael and Fr. Jim and some church members, but went to church less often. After the pandemic struck in March 2020, and the churches closed for in-person worship, I attended some of the Zoom services but not often. I also attended some of the Zoom vestry meetings.

In December 2019, the Church of the Presentation held a Christmas party for all past and current members of its bereavement groups. I drove up with a fellow widower from my group who lived in Hackensack. I was surprised at how many people were at the party, which was held in a gymnasium-sized room in the church, and that a few were considerably younger than I.

Marla told me that I rationalized Reva's death by saying that death comes to all. But it does. Reva had sixty-six years of life. She had much physical and emotional pain in those years but also creativeness, productivity, happiness—and always, unfailing love.

Reading continued to be my main source of recreation, as it has been since I was fifteen. One book I read during this period was *A Grief Observed* by C. S. Lewis, a short book that Lewis initially published anonymously. It consists of excerpts from a journal he kept following the death of his wife.

Lewis married late in his life and his marriage lasted only five years before his wife died. Yet I found Lewis's grief similar to my own, although I had married younger and had been married longer. Like death, grief is universal.

How could I go on living without Reva? At times, I thought of suicide but not in the immediate future. I told one of my doctors that I did not want to live past the age of eighty but that I could hold on until then. I am still holding on and will make a decision at that time.

One way I try to console myself is to acknowledge the universality of death and the awareness that my time will come in the not-too-distant future—perhaps in the next hour (who can say?)—and that I will be buried next to Reva. The other consolation I have is the intrinsic sense that Reva is with me in spirit, the unexplainable mystery of love. It is like a man or woman living in a horrible, dark, chaotic place full of pain and torment but who has a key that he or she believes will ultimately unlock a door to a place of bliss. One difference between this key and all others is that it cannot be lost. Perhaps the key is ourselves, our own bodies that will, in good time, unlock the door.

Soon after Reva died, I asked God for a sign that her spirit continues and that she and I will be reunited in the next world. I asked for a specific sign.

The cardinal is a monogamous bird, and although the brilliant red male stands out, the smaller brownish female is almost always near her mate. When I see a male cardinal, I look around and usually find the female.

After Reva's death, I asked God to let me see a male and a female cardinal together in the next six months. I would take this as a sign that Reva and I will be reunited.

But from October 2019, to this writing in December 2021, I have not seen a female cardinal.

Of course, in the colder months I spent less time outdoors, especially since Reva's death and the coming of the pandemic.

Walking in Hackensack, I have twice seen a male cardinal, but although I searched for the female, I did not find her.

The second occasion was in the late summer of 2020. As I was returning from a walk, I saw a male cardinal perched on a tree near the parking lot of the building where I live. There is some wooded property nearby that belongs to the railroad.

I looked diligently for the female—on the trees near the parking lot, in the bushes, in the wooded property. I spent almost half an hour quietly searching for her. But I was unsuccessful. The male ultimately flew away.

I was disappointed. Had I found the female, I would have felt that God had given me a sign. But upon reflecting about the incident, I feel that perhaps God had given me a sign. I know the male and female cardinal are almost always together. But I could not see the female. So I cannot see Reva, but she is with me.

www.ingramcontent.com/pod-product-compliance
Lightning Source LLC
Chambersburg PA
CBHW020351170426
43200CB00005B/129